PRAISE FOR *CHIEF EXECUTIVE TEAM*

"The author says, 'impossible is a tag we put on things we don't understand yet.' Then he builds the entire book around helping you to understand better. Suddenly, lots of things become possible! This book has depth and breadth, but more importantly, it has practicality. It's a book for doers. It's designed to be used and applied. Get the executive team right and results show up throughout the entire organization. Read and apply this book, then call the author."

– Jim Cathcart | High Achievement Mentor, Author of The Acorn Principle and The Power Minute | Austin, Texas.

"Executive Team dynamics is the detail people forget about and hope will happen. Chief Executive Team brings tried and tested strategies to make it happen and drive grand ambition and vision."

– Rob Small | Miniclip | President & Co-Founder

"What makes for great leadership? Being able to adapt quickly and efficiently to unpredictable circumstances. Being nimble, malleable, and having the ability to solve complex problems that ensure the success of a business. Ricardo's book provides key, actionable steps to effectively transform leadership teams into well-oiled machines. If you're not adapting and changing, you're dying."

– Jeffrey Hayzlett | Primetime TV & Podcast Host, Speaker, Author and Part-Time Cowboy

"Ricardo Vargas' book, *Chief Executive Team*, really could not have come at a better time. In today's world of extraordinary disruption, the last thing companies need is a macho, "know it all" CEO who simply doesn't know what to do! Transformational change requires a new type of strong leadership at the top; one which draws less from personality, but much more from diverse and inclusive contributions, and this book shows us how to achieve it."

– Andrew M. Vine | The Insight Bureau | Founder & CEO

"*Chief Executive Team* is like 'Good to Great' for executive teams. Only more practical."

– Sandra Jossien | Vorwerk Switzerland | General Manager

"*Chief Executive Team* throws light upon the REAL job of a CEO. It gives a clear framework to improve performance on all dimensions of that job. If you are a leader who cares for results, read it."

– Inês Lima | McDonalds | Marketing Lead
International Operated Markets B.U.

"You read *Chief Executive Team* and you see differently. It provokes a paradigm shift for top leadership."

– Nuno Pargana Brás | LEO Pharma | Vice-president
Cluster France, Canada and BeNeLux

"This is a wakeup call for CEOs. It shows how dysfunctional executive teams can get without the leader noticing. Any CEO's mission is to create a *Chief Executive Team*. Ricardo will guide you through."

– Helena Bento | CEO JMDB | Board Member and General
Manager Fundação Francisco Manuel dos Santos

"New rules for the game of leadership. A must read for CEOs."

– Daniel Araújo | Asseco PST | CEO

"*Chief Executive Team* creates a radically new space in management literature. It bridges the gap between books on leadership and books on company culture by answering the question: how does CEO behavior create company culture?"

– Hugo Contente | Laureate Australia & New Zealand | Vice-President People and Culture

"Reading this book is like taking a deep look in the mirror of our own leadership and analyse the way we see the effectiveness of executive teams. It provides a clear understanding on how the structure of a team contributes to reach the best possible dynamics and the highest possible level of results."

– Ricardo Parreira | PHC Software |CEO

"Only collective intelligence can turn the potential of your company into performance. You need a Chief Executive Team to ignite that genius. Access here."

– David Azevedo Lopes | AEON Topvalu Co. | President & CEO

"Reading this book will feel like Ricardo attended your executive team meetings to help you reconnect the dots and solve leadership paradoxes."

– Moussa Zaghdoud | Alcatel-Lucent Enterprise | Executive Vice-President Cloud Business Division

"Leadership is a quest to transform people and companies with authenticity and humility. We need to conceive together what we don't know that we don't know; what to do when we don't know what to do. This book sets you well on that journey."

– Antonio Mariani | GB Foods Italy | General Manager

"The challenge of an executive team is to navigate the company through a VUCA world to get to the ultimate goal: growth. There are many ways to get there. This book gives you a novel approach to find yours."

– Hillary Roche | Vorwerk International |
Senior Vice President Marketing

CHIEF EXECUTIVE TEAM

THE TRANSFORMATION OF LEADERSHIP

RICARDO J. VARGAS

IGNITE PRESS
Fresno, CA

Published in the United States by Ignite Press.
ignitepress.us

ISBN: 978-1-953655-53-0 (Amazon Print)
ISBN: 978-1-953655-54-7 (IngramSpark) PAPERBACK
ISBN: 978-1-953655-55-4 (IngramSpark) HARDCOVER
ISBN: 978-1-953655-56-1 (E-book)

For bulk purchase and for booking, please contact Chief Executive Team:
info@chief-executive.team

Library of Congress Control Number: 2021901179

Cover design by Divya Balu
Editorial support by Pat Iyer
Interior design by Jetlaunch Layout Services

1st Edition February 2021

BRIEF CONTENTS

CONTENTS

CHAPTER 6 – P FOR PURPOSE

CHAPTER 7 – P FOR PROCESSES

CHAPTER 8 – P FOR PEOPLE

CHAPTER 9 – P FOR PROBLEMS

CHAPTER 10 – P FOR POSSIBILITIES

INTRODUCTION

A TRANSFORMATION OF LEADERSHIP

I have a good executive team and that's not great

I HEADED TO the concrete and glass building of the multinational pharma company to meet Frank, the Human Resources Director. We had a routine meeting scheduled to update the impact of our development project on sales growth. I had been training the sales reps team for one year. I observed and diagnosed their meetings with doctors in private practice, hospitals, and care centers. I learned everything about their products, attended their internal team meetings, and memorized all their processes, to design the sales approach and the competency development workshops that would increase their sales. I knew that the results were coming in as planned. This was going to be a short and sweet meeting.

When Frank quickly dismissed speaking about the project, I knew something else was on his mind. In contrast to how slowly he moved his big body around the meeting room, he was a quick thinker.

"We have a problem," he said. "And it seems unsolvable because I cannot address it from where I am."

Since I was a systemic family therapist, if you want to engage me fully, just start with the words, "We have a problem." You will get my six senses focused on the following words. I love problems, especially the ones that people deem unsolvable because from a systems thinking perspective, *impossible* is a tag we put on things we don't understand yet. When we successfully map the why, the how, and the what of event patterns, we also see the world with eyes that allow for the "impossible" to happen.

Nevertheless, I was not ready for what followed.

When we successfully map the why, the how, and the what of event patterns, we also see the world with eyes that allow for the "impossible" to happen.

Frank rambled about the dynamics of his executive team. Company sales, marketing, and financial results were good, but he felt that the team could achieve so much more. He was not sure what prevented it. He said, "It's like we are a team but not really a team. We function as a group of people who are supposedly a team but fail to perform as one in subtle yet critical ways. We have some dynamics that are not functional, but we are also not overtly fighting each other.

"I can't pinpoint it. I already addressed this with the General Manager, and he feels the same way. We did several team building workshops in the past, but they don't seem to help. It seems that the problem is the team dynamics, but when we do team building activities, everything is fine, and people perform greatly in that space."

You must time travel to March 1997 to understand Frank's perplexity. This meeting happened before Google, Euro currency, the millennium bug, 9/11, Facebook, Twitter, the Great Recession, and Covid-19. This was the end of the twentieth century, as close as it gets to the dark ages of information. Coaching was not a profession; experts in executive team development were not common, and neuro-something fads did not exist.

Teambuilding experiential workshops were a staple of the 1990s. We did high ropes, low ropes, outdoor, indoor, LEGO, raft building and rescue, kart building and racing, construction-destruction-reconstruction of "civilizations" in the woods, rock climbing, and rappel, night orientation with strategy-based riddle solving, Broadway-type shows illustrating company values… You name it; we did it.

We now know all about the importance of guaranteeing "learning transfer" from training and simulations to the real situation. Still, back then, consultants thought putting together people to do things out of their routine would help them develop the skills and relationships required to solve their daily life problems. I thought so, too.

"We know what to do in all teambuilding exercises to be a successful team; we just don't do it in real life," Frank explained. "When we are making decisions, designing and executing strategy, solving pressing problems, working hard to achieve company goals, we instantly forget what we know is right and revert to business-as-usual individual focus."

On that chilly March afternoon, this combination of words electrified me: "We have a problem… it's the team dynamics… seems unsolvable… I can't address it from where I am…" The words shook me out of the lethargy I had been feeling for the previous three years.

From solving family problems to improving company performance

Three years earlier, on a sweltering June 1994 afternoon in Sevilla, Spain, my life took an unexpected turn. This shift occurred at the *Virgen de Macarena* Hospital Psychiatric Ambulatory Service, where I was doing the practice for my

Masters in Systemic Family Therapy. With a previous degree in Work, Organizational, and Personnel Psychology, I decided to pursue a career as a family therapist. I went back to study and performed over 1500 hours of supervised work at the unit, but none of that helped me during that June afternoon.

I was facing failure, a big one. One of my patients, a seven-year-old boy, was being victimized by his family with several covert methods. None of these were crimes; none of them could be proved; none of them could become the legal basis for social intervention, according to the law. None of them could even be called out because there was plausible deniability for all of them. None of them were even consciously chosen by the family.

The boy showed psychological symptoms in response to a specific family dynamic of instigation and triangulation between generations of the family clan. This last sentence is long-form for "his mind was seriously messed up by his family" with a pathological dynamic that we were unable to disrupt.

I say "we" because we worked in multidisciplinary therapist teams in the psychiatric department. Usually, in systems family therapy, a team of two to four therapists works together with the family. I was doing individual work with this boy, and as an individual, I felt "I" was unable to disrupt the patterns and improve his life. That was keeping me awake at night. And it seemed there was no reason for it. We had much worse cases.

This public health service was the last hope for severely psychologically disturbed people. People came in from different areas of Andalusia, often having been unsuccessfully treated by other medical teams. We had anorexic girls coming in with nasogastric feeding, transported on a stretcher or wheelchair. They were so weak that they were unable to move by themselves. We had teenagers with early signs of schizophrenia and all types of addiction. We had very depressed adults, suicidal. We treated trauma and abuse survivors.

Why was that boy's story touching me so much? That afternoon, during a discussion with my supervisor, I figured it out. It was very close to my own story.

I am a survivor of physical and emotional abuse. My upbringing included several years of a constant stream of violence, neglect, and emotional aggression. This occurred during and after a war experience. No wonder this affected my psychological health in ways I had not yet fully perceived at the time. It would take years of therapy for me to be able to even speak or write about this.

Due to the civil war we were going through in Mozambique, where I was born, when I was around the age of that boy, I was sent by my parents to live with distant relatives in a different country. Cut off from my family, feeling abandoned, I had to become an adult overnight to face a hostile environment. And all was coming back at me on that hot afternoon.

"You have to let go of this case," my supervisor said after we spoke about my difficulties. "You got emotionally involved, and you can't think objectively."

For almost a year, I had made my contribution to this boy's developmental process. Letting go felt like a betrayal, but I knew my supervisor was right. It was in the best interest of my client that I quit the case and prepare a colleague to take over.

The fact that I had not yet tidied my past and made peace with it prevented me from being a good therapist. I understood that I would not be any good at working with children until I solved my issues. And often, in family therapy, you must deal with them.

That conversation with my supervisor shattered my dreams. I wanted to become a systemic family therapist. I pursued a degree for it. I learned and practiced hard. Now, it seemed that I had to move on to the next thing and forget everything about it. I didn't realize how often smaller dreams are shattered to use their pieces to build bigger ones. That unexpected result would still take time to mature and emerge.

Finding the right leverage point

After leaving the field of family therapy, I worked as a consultant for an international management consulting company for the following three years. I underwent different types of training and leadership development. I sold, managed, and delivered thousands of hours of change management, leadership development, team building, and personal development projects. Those hectic years as international consultant, were so successful that I became a partner in the firm in record time.

During this period, I put aside my dream of becoming a family therapist. It was not something I could do for a living. Coming to terms with it required me to suppress the competences and skills I'd developed during my training. Then Frank called me for that apparently aimless conversation about the problems in the executive team.

Frank did not expect a solution. Later he told me he just wanted to listen to himself speaking the problem out loud. He did not think I could develop a solution from his story. After all, they had an excellent executive team. They were achievers by any standard. They just had some difficulties in becoming a great team.

When Frank said, "I can't address it from where I am," I had an epiphany. We used to say a similar sentence back at the hospital team: "We need a different leverage point to crack this one."

All the systems thinking training, skills, analysis tools, and intervention techniques that I had diligently learned during my years working with families suddenly came out of the box where I had locked them. My insights mixed harmoniously with all the leadership development and change management competencies I had built as an international consultant. A new vision of who I was and the purpose of my life emerged instantly. A new way to use everything I had learned to improve lives became crystal clear.

I was born to be a catalyst for other people's development. I used to think of therapy as the noblest way to do it. But there is no noble way. An infinite number of possibilities exists to support people in their development processes. And any combination of competences I could use to achieve my purpose was noble.

Yes, Frank needed a different leverage point to get his executive team from good to great. And I could provide that. I jumped forward in my chair, excited, and said, "I can help with that."

An infinite number of possibilities exists to support people in their development processes.

He asked, "How can you help with that? This is not classic leadership development. This is not the usual training. We tried team building of all sorts, and it did not make a difference."

Has anyone done this before?

At the time, coaching was just an idea in the head of ten people worldwide, and I was not one of them. I explained, "This is the area for which I trained before becoming a consultant. I am not only a work and organizational psychologist, but I'm also a certified systemic family and group therapist. I can work with your executive group to help you overcome challenges and help you to implement more effective, productive, and satisfactory patterns of relationship."

Frank's facial expression moved from shocked to curious in half a second as he protested, "We are not mentally disturbed people!"

I laughed. "No, you are not. But you and your CEO think that the team has difficulties in actualizing its potential due to relationship dynamics. I have the competencies to support you in solving those difficulties. By chance, I developed these competencies in a clinical setting. I am not judging, not applying any clinical diagnosis. I can use systems models and processes to help you generate the change you desire."

He wanted to understand what systems thinking was and what I could do. I explained the difference in problem definition and problem-solving by using linear versus systems thinking – I will describe that later in this book. I designed a couple of charts to explain what the process could look like, how we would identify and tackle the issues, where we would start, and what my role would be. That drawing became the basis for my first methodology for the development of a Chief Executive Team.

Frank was both excited and appalled. "Conceptually, this looks great, but it's high-risk. It doesn't look like you will be in control of what happens in the sessions. Did you ever do this before?"

"Many times, with groups and with families of patients. I know the methodologies, the facilitation techniques, the bumps and holes on the road. I know all the ropes. I just never did it with an executive team," I told him in complete honesty.

He paused for one minute, something very unusual for him. I could see his eyes focusing alternatively on different points of the space around us as he played scenarios in his mind. When he finished, he looked back at me as if coming back from a faraway place and said, "I know you. I trust you. Let's start with the diagnosis and a pilot, a one-day workshop. We'll see how it goes and take it from there."

That's exactly how it all started. That one-day workshop became a one-year engagement during which I prototyped *The 6 P's of Executive Teams®* methodology, and Frank's executive team went from good to great.

Twenty-three years to develop and three months to write

During the following twenty-three years I got my credentials as Professional Certified Coach®, Certified Management

Consultant®, Certified Speaking Professional®, Work and Organizational Psychology Expert, Psychological Coaching Expert. I started and managed consulting companies on two continents, implemented consulting projects in eighteen countries, and lectured at different universities. During these two decades, I studied management research on the effectiveness of executive teams, developed an assessment tool to diagnose the specific needs of each executive team compared to that benchmark, designed several services to support executive teams of many business sectors around the world, and refined *The 6 P's of Executive Teams®* methodology.

Meanwhile, Frank retired. Last year I met him again by chance at an event. We exchanged a few words, and he challenged me. "Where's the book on that P's methodology of yours? You should share it with the world."

His words echoed in my mind for days. It did make sense, but it didn't seem possible to fit another book writing process in my calendar. I'd already published three books in three countries on leadership, personal development, and company culture management, with traditional publishers, plus had self-published one book, and contributed chapters to two others. I knew how cumbersome the process was. So, I parked the project for better days.

Instead of better days, Covid-19 arrived. During the lockdown, I stopped traveling, all in-person commitments, projects, speaking engagements, and presentations. Because I was staying at home, I decided to have a go at it.

This book is the result of my two decades of practice in developing Chief Executive Teams. I don't see myself as a coach, consultant, speaker, trainer, psychologist, or therapist anymore. I am all of that and none of that. My work over the years mixed competencies, viewpoints, models, and techniques from all those areas. It morphed into an agile way of delivering my methodology for developing effective executive teams: *The 6 P's of Executive Teams®*.

Although all interventions I do with executive teams use the methodology as a reference point for diagnosis and design, I never perform two interventions the same way. Each team is unique. Each company is unique. Each person has their perspectives about how things should evolve. I adapt to all that and support ineffective teams to become good and good teams to become great.

Your executive team is leaving money on the table

If you could change the way one team interacts to make the most impact on the company, which would you choose?

- The agile team?
- The research and development team?
- The sales team?
- The marketing team?
- A special project team?
- A functional team?

The Executive Team has the power to maximize or destroy the work of any other team in the company, including itself. But top executives don't consider themselves a team, because usually they don't function as one.

The Executive Team has the power to maximize or destroy the work of any other team in the company, including itself.

Executive teams tend to be the worst team in the company, exactly where you need the best one.

Research from the last twenty years with thousands of companies of all business sectors around the world shows that when you improve the dynamics of the executive team, you impact these key performance indicators of the company:

Return on

- Assets,
- Sales,
- Equity,
- Stock performance,
- Profitability,
- Productivity,
- Sales growth,
- Market share,
- Operating result,
- Budget compliance,
- Innovation performance, and
- Employee engagement.

The list goes on and on.

The results of improving teamwork at the top are too good to miss. But how many companies put their leadership team through a program that improves their effectiveness and efficiency? Very few. It all boils down to one thing: Right now, most executive teams leave a lot of money on the table. This book shows how to reverse that.

Right now, most executive teams leave a lot of money on the table.

Crises intensify the need for Chief Executive Teams

Improvement is even more critical during a crisis like the one we are facing now. Crisis means you have less time and fewer resources to recover from bad decisions. During a crisis, you must make better decisions faster. You are in a zero-tolerance zone. You have no margin for error. A Chief Executive Team allows you to make faster and better decisions. This translates into better strategy and more effective execution, producing more results.

Especially in crises, having a team's thinking power to figure out the best way forward, instead of only one individual, can make a big difference. A team can process more information, consider more viewpoints, evaluate more options, and solve more problems effectively.

A transformation of leadership

The most damaging myth for leadership effectiveness is "The good CEO knows it all and does it all." This myth disengages people all over the company, from the executive level down to the individual contributor. It gets the CEO interfering with everything, either because they think they know better or because they must hide the fact that they don't know better.

The most damaging myth for leadership effectiveness is "The good CEO knows it all and does it all."

Fixed mindset describes a situation where people believe that theirs and others' qualities, such as intelligence, talents, or competences, are rigid attributes that can't be changed. If you have a fixed mindset, you will spend more time trying to prove you know something than learning more about it. You will focus more on what you can already do than on what you cannot do.

Growth mindset is the opposite.

- You build on your abilities with a pure desire for learning.
- You embrace challenges and accept criticism as ways to improve your skills.
- You find inspiration in others' success and believe you must strive to grow.

- You team up with others who can add perspective and knowledge to the process of achieving ambitious goals.

The myth the CEO can know everything required for the success of a company is 100% fixed mindset. It assumes everything stays the same, and no one learns or develops better ways to move forward. It also embeds the assumption that market changes are predictable; therefore, it just takes one informed person to figure the right way of dealing with them. This notion can trigger some good laughs in 2020.

Teams entered the corporate world many decades ago. When we needed something vital done fast, we created project teams. The implementation of self-organized teams in manufacturing has improved the quality of products continuously since the 1950's. Fast forward to today, and teams are ubiquitous in corporate life. They contribute to many of our results, our joy at work, and professional identity.

The myth the CEO can know everything required for the success of a company is 100% fixed mindset.

The importance of executive team leadership

The notion that company leadership is better performed by a chief executive team instead of a chief executive officer can feel very threatening. People experience the fear of dilution of accountability, loss of effectiveness, and loss of power through "democracy."

Allow me to be straightforward. We don't think of the loss of accountability and effectiveness in any other team in the company. Every day, everywhere, companies are made, developed, and changed by teams. But when it comes to manage them, we tend to forget

Companies are made, developed, and changed by teams.

the benefits of collaboration. Companies are usually not managed by an effective and efficient executive team.

In fact, as I will prove in this book, executive teams can increase collective and individual effectiveness and accountability. The fact that top management teams are unique in the way they are built and operate, makes it more difficult to design processes to increase effectiveness and efficiency. However, we must not shy away from that challenge. When we solve it, we reap outstanding benefits.

And no, companies are not democracies and should not become that. You will not read anything like that in this book. Developing and managing an executive team does not weaken the formal power of the CEO. Instead, it creates a more prominent type of power the CEO can use to transform the company: team leadership.

For too long, we have been thinking of leadership as an individual characteristic. We crave so much for heroes to save the day that leadership face value is all about the CEO's personality. But the real value of leadership is about Chief Executive Teams transforming companies and leaving a legacy of personal and business growth.

We have the wrong CEO job description. "Know it all" and "do it all" are not success factors. Quite the opposite. It's time for a transformation of leadership.

A step-by-step process to transform executive teams

On these pages, you will find a concept, a methodology, ideas, implementation stories, and anecdotes that will allow you to understand step-by-step how executive groups can become Chief Executive Teams.

In the book, I use the term "executive team" to name teams responsible for creating any organization, designing its strategy, managing its execution, and determining its future according to their Vision. In different business contexts, different names are given to these teams: leadership team, senior leadership team, management team, project management team, top management team, executive team, the board of directors, c-suite, executive suite, among others.

We have the wrong CEO job description. "Know it all" and "do it all" are not success factors. Quite the opposite. It's time for a transformation of leadership.

I understand the differences in the different names. I am not concerned about distinguishing them because *The 6 P's of Executive Teams®* methodology can be adapted to function with all of them.

A global marketing and product development team used my methodology to create a unique organization, disrupt their current business model, and beat their competition with innovative approaches.

Many formal top management teams, composed of CEOs and their direct reports, used *The 6 P's of Executive Teams®* to

- revamp dormant businesses,
- transform their companies to reach a bold Vision,
- recover the company's credibility in the market after management mistakes,
- consolidate mergers and acquisitions,
- increase company efficiency and productivity,
- increase market share, and achieve market leadership, among other achievements.

Extended leadership teams, including different hierarchical levels, increased their management and leadership effectiveness and efficiency by using my method.

C-suite teams used it to redesign the vision, mission, and strategy of their companies and get everyone engaged with them.

Functional teams of regional clusters worked as well with *The 6 P's of Executive Teams*®. The Chief Financial Officers of local operating companies in the Western Europe Region of one pharma company used it to improve their region's resource management efficiency. The marketing directors of a consumer electronics corporation's operating companies used it to redefine the global company strategy and positioning.

According to the definition I use in this book, they all are executive teams because they generate a Vision, design a strategy, create and manage the organization, and lead their people to execute it.

Chief Executive Teams deliver extraordinary results by engaging people with their strategy. It's all about leadership, but of a different kind.

What applying *The 6 P's of Executive Teams*® can do for your company

Chief Executive Teams deliver extraordinary results by engaging people with their strategy. It's all about leadership, but of a different kind.

Extraordinary results are an expected outcome of Chief Executive Teams. This is what you can learn with *The 6 P's of Executive Teams*®. This book can be different things to different readers.

If you are a CEO, you will get inspiration, a process, tools and tips to increase your executive team's efficiency and effectiveness. You will understand which behavior mode you tend to fall into and its advantages/disadvantages. You will know the benefits of developing an executive team, and the costs of not doing so. You will get insight on the unproductive dynamics of executive teams and why they happen and what you can do to improve them.

Suppose you are the president or board member of a multinational company. In that case, you will have a clear vision of what can be done to improve the quality of management (read results) in all your local operating companies. When you have an ambitious or disruptive strategy, this methodology can harmonize local leadership practices under a global company strategy.

Suppose you are a Chief People Officer responsible for managing company culture, employee engagement, leadership practices, and adherence to values, talent, and potential. You will understand why and how different voices in the executive group can turn into a leadership babel that will drain your people's souls. You will appreciate the external constraints to develop executive teams and get practical tools to manage them. You will diagnose the gaps and know what your executive team needs to do to become better, faster, and more ambitious.

If you are an aspiring CEO, you will get a clear picture of the behavior modes you can fall into once you are in the position. You will understand how the same logic you apply on your way up the career ladder can be detrimental to the results you produce when you are at the top. Right from day one, you can get the process of developing a Chief Executive Team. As the CEO, you will get ideas, tips, and practices to make that happen. You can reap benefits from this book for longer than any other type of reader. Just come back to it at different phases of your executive team's evolution and implement a bit more of what I share.

If you are a member of any type of executive team, you will gain insight into how you can contribute to the development of a Chief Executive Team, the usual hurdles, and how to counter them. You can influence your peers and your manager about the benefits of going in that direction. You can develop critical thinking about how individual and collective behavior influence each other to produce better results. You can have a bigger impact.

Overview of the book

Good news: you don't need to read the full book at once. This book is divided into three parts, each answering a specific question.

1. "Why do we need chief executive teams?"

This is answered in Chapter 1, "The elephant in the room" where I share a summary of the available research on how the effectiveness of executive teams impacts the company's results and why you can't afford missing it.

2. "What gets executive teams in the pit?"

This is answered in Chapters 2 to 4. There you will learn to understand three types of constraints that prevent the CEO from developing a chief executive team:

i. Their own mental model and behavior modes, together with the costs generated by them – in Chapter 2, "It's Happening on Your Shift", and Chapter 3, "And you will pay the price".
ii. The structural causes common to most executive groups that ruin their effectiveness as a team and
iii. The business-as-usual generic approaches to solve the problem and why they fail – both in Chapter 4, "Been there, done that and have the scars to prove it".

3. "How do I develop a Chief Executive Team?"

Chapters 5 to 11 address this goal. Chapter 5 is an outline of *The 6 P's of Executive Teams®* methodology. By reading this chapter you will get a high-level understanding of my model for developing executive teams' effectiveness and efficiency.

Each of the subsequent chapters is a detailed explanation of each P of the model: P for Purpose, P for Processes, P for People, P for Problems, P for Possibilities, and P for Potential. Each P is one dimension of team effectiveness that impacts company performance. Any of these chapters can be read as a stand-alone solution to specific team challenges.

The epilogue is not a section. It addresses one last question "Do I need an external advisor for this?" by explaining what the role of an external advisor is on such projects.

The value of research

Disclaimer: I am a research practitioner. This means that my practice is based on peer-reviewed published evidence. It also means that my practice contributes to research advancement by designing experiments, collecting information to feed research, and writing the occasional scientific paper.

The use of the word research can provoke adverse reactions. People tend to think of research and science as things that happen in labs and are talked about by crazy-looking university professors without any connection to the real world. Research became short for "theoretical and useless stuff that academics speak about."

Yes, there are models and theories, but most importantly, research and its models are about understanding how things work to predict the outcomes of different decisions. Work, Organizational and Personnel Psychology research collects data from thousands of companies, operating in real markets, in the real world, managed by real executives like you and me. This collection of information analysed with the right statistical methods used to extract meaning from it, framed in ever-evolving models, gives us the most accurate understanding of how the world works at any given moment.

Science evolves, and what was once established can be determined incomplete or even false later. But I believe that the strong peer-reviewing process of scientific journals, accompanied by the best expert judgment, implemented with self-criticism and constant feedback, provide a better know-how foundation for a management consulting process.

I believe in authentic development experiences for CEOs and executive teams. That is my commitment.

Sometimes my clients ask me why I don't follow the latest management fad or don't apply the flavor of the week tool. Most of the time, the answer is simple: Those tools and ideas are not supported or are even contradicted by peer-reviewed published research.

I don't believe in buzzwords. I believe in authentic development experiences for CEOs and executive teams. That is my commitment.

1

THE ELEPHANT IN THE ROOM

"I keep bringing Ricardo to work with my teams for over 10 years because he is one of the best facilitators. He doesn't tell you what to do. He just brings the "Beauty" and the "Beast" out of the team, helping us to deal with both. The beauty is the Vision. The beast is the way to get there."

– Kai Schaeffner | Thermomix North America | President

Executive team effectiveness is the elephant in the room

I AM ABOUT to start the workshop. Around the room are seated ten top executives of a multinational company. They look awkwardly at me because I took the tables away. They search around to find a place to hold their laptops for some emailing during the day. Or so they thought they would. We all know each other. We all know why we are here. We don't need introductions and small talk. We will dive headfirst into hard work.

I have individually interviewed each of them. I have surveyed the effectiveness of the top executive's group dynamics with a comprehensive 130 item questionnaire. The CEO, executive team, and their direct reports answered it. I went through their strategic plan and know where they are lagging. I know their *desired* company culture and values and their *real* company culture and values, and what they are supposed to do themselves and get others to do to close the gap. I went through all available climate and engagement surveys. I know what their clients, employees, suppliers complain about, and what they have been doing and not doing about it.

I analysed a massive amount of qualitative and quantitative data; I have a clear-cut idea of why, how, what, and precisely where things need to change to increase effectiveness and efficiency. I know which of their behaviors are promoting a performance culture in the company and which are not.

I smile, look around at all the faces, and know that these very people will behave and perform in a completely different way in a couple of months. They will become a much more effective and efficient team. The progress is predictable and familiar to me; I have seen it happen so often in companies of all business sectors around the world. I take a deep breath and soak it in, savoring these moments when we see something for the last time. Their world is going to disappear forever. I cannot help it; I love change, especially when I am the one bringing it.

There is an elephant in the room that everyone has been avoiding. It stinks; it blocks the way; it heats the air; it consumes the oxygen. Over 99% of the people in the company see it but pretend they don't.

I ask the group, "Please write the name of your team members on these moderation cards." And they do. I pin all moderation cards on the board and ask, "Why did most of you not put the names of your colleagues in the room on the list?" They look puzzled. The overwhelming majority of times, only the CEO puts the names of their executives on the list. All other executives just name the members of the functional teams they manage, or the names of some other project teams they belong to, or in some cases, the names of one or more people in the room who work closely with them on an assignment or process. But in most cases, executives do not list colleagues around the room on the moderation cards.

It is so compelling that most people do not consider the executive team they belong to as their natural number one team. There are reasons, because these are the people who

- they fight with for the CEO position.
- they must divide the budget with.
- take resources from them.
- slow down their projects with "idiotic" regulations and processes from their departments.
- they did not choose to work with.
- align with different interest groups inside the company to promote opposing policies.
- belong to the "wrong" generation, gender, ethnicity, nationality, university education, among many other characteristics.
- underperformed in critical projects, or who did not excuse their unjustified underperformance in significant projects.
- prevent them from being in the spotlight all the time because they also occupy the stage.

Why should they consider them as their team?

Enter the elephant. Executive team effectiveness is the elephant in the room. It disturbs everyone in the company, but it's so big no one dares to do something about it.

If you can change the way one team interacts, to make the most impact on the company, which would you choose? The Agile team? The R&D team? The sales team? Any other special project team? A functional team? The executive team can maximize or destroy the work of any other team in the company, including itself. But top executives don't consider themselves a team, because usually, they don't function as one.

Executive teams tend to be the worst team in the company, exactly when they should be the best.

My work is about changing that.

A transformation of leadership needs to occur at the top of companies. Don't take my word for it; I am only the catalyst. Just listen to the market speaking.

Compounded innovation effects

The world is changing. Gordon Moore's law states that computing capacity doubles roughly every two years. This held true since he pronounced it in 1995.[1] In the beginning, it might not have made any difference. Doubling a small amount of something is not much. But consider how computing capacity is compounded over the years, fuelled by the increasing interconnectedness of the globalized world.

First was the internet, then the internet of things, the cloud, augmented reality, virtual reality, artificial intelligence, robotics, self-driving cars, DNA sequencing, genome editing, biocomputing, 3D printing, blockchain, 5G, serverless computing, drones, biometrics, pandemics, work at home, industries disappearing… It's hard to keep up even with the names of innovations that pop up every year with the potential to disrupt our lives.

Let us take one of these inventions and map some of its impacts. What do you think will change when self-driven cars become widely available as the standard option? Car ownership will decline because car rental, car manufacturing, car dealing companies, and any other company that owns a car fleet can monetize its cars 24/7, making pay-per-use cheaper than car ownership.

The architecture will change as we will not need as many parking spaces where we live and work. City planning will alter as well: there will be fewer cars on the streets and no need for parking spaces. Professions will disappear – drivers for hire, driving instructors, and traffic police. Lifestyles will adapt to a decrease in commuting burden as you don't need to go to work anymore. Transportation and distribution companies will adjust their business model. But insurance, navigation, travel, public transports, leisure, and hospitality sectors will also change or go bust. I am sure you can think of many more business sectors disrupted by one single innovation than the ones I put in this paragraph.

Do the same exercise for the top fifty tech inventions of the last five years and combine each of them with the effects of the others to amplify the result. You will realize one simple thing: we are about to experience more change in the next thirty years than humanity faced in the previous 5,000 years.

Yet, most executive teams believe they can continue managing their businesses as they did in the last century.

Management paradoxes

We live in a world where something and its opposite are valid at the same time. As our businesses are going digital, you would expect people to be less necessary. But talent was never so scarce. A recent study identified a lack of one million workers with different levels of IT skills in Europe. We have an excess of competencies for the old business world and not enough people with the technical competencies required to build up businesses in the new world.

We are required to be efficient and innovative at the same time. And innovation is, most of the time, an inefficient process. Its trial and error modeling, testing, and pivoting tend to burn resources in the search for new products, processes and business models. This leaves shareholders nervous and asking for "low-risk innovation." We all know that doesn't exist.

We are haunted by sustainability in every business decision we make, but short-term results were never so necessary. Sustainability requires playing a long-term game.

These paradoxes exist because market complexity is growing exponentially. Therefore, for any business, many alternative strategies can be successful. Several market approaches are profitable. Executives may endorse varied growth philosophies in their pursuit of targets. Choose one business sector, and you will find companies being successful today with entirely different business models. Which of them will still be around in twenty years?

At any moment, for any business decision, you can identify many paradoxes that have to be adequately managed for the company not to run into worse future problems by solving the current ones. From the management point of view, this has a clear consequence: Companies need to find a balance between being excellent at what they do and becoming good at something else at the same time.

And this is not management as usual. Executive teams need to step up their game to meet the complexity and paradoxes of the Twenty-first Century. And CEOs are struggling.

Gartner's *CEO and Senior Business Executive Survey* released in 2019 detailed the top three goals for CEOs in 2019-2020: growth, digital transformation, and structural development. Drawing from 473 business leaders from 32 countries, it identified their strategic business priorities for 2019 and 2020. This study (done in the pre-Covid era) shows that risk management and cost control were not top-of-mind for CEOs.[2]

Companies need to find a balance between being excellent at what they do and becoming good at something else at the same time.

The focus on cost control and risk management for sure has become critical after Covid-19. But they will not replace the previous strategic goals. They will operate as another dimension of requirements for the business strategy to fit the current market. Focusing on growth, digital transformation, and structural development while controlling costs and managing risk is an excellent source of the decision-making paradoxes I mentioned before.

No more is there either/or decision making for executive teams. Teams must design and execute both/and strategies:

- Short *and* long term
- Efficient *and* innovative
- Bold *and* risk-free

Anything and its contrary are the new normal in decision making. How can that be done?

The critical skills gap

The *Conference Board Report of 2020* shows that the most significant internal roadblocks for company growth, digital transformation, and structural development were attracting and retaining talent, developing innovative products and cultures, and creating the next generation of leaders.[3]

PwC's annual *CEO survey of 2019* reported that 79% of CEOs worry about the availability of critical skills to build their companies. In other words, there's a significant skills gap in the market, a gap companies need to fill to be able to succeed. The immediate consequences of the gap are rising people costs, lower quality customer service, inability to innovate, passing market opportunities, and missing growth targets and strategic initiatives.[4]

Upskilling the workforce is so far producing mixed results. Depending on how advanced their upskilling programs are, only 15% - 37% of CEOs reported their impact on business growth as quite useful, on the same survey. With a sharp increase in pessimism about the global economic factors, in the 2020 edition, 53% of CEOs expected a slower world GDP growth rate.[5] This prediction has an impact on the level of uncertainty for their decision-making.

It seems that CEOs have a pretty good image of the challenges ahead, a clear idea of the direction to take to tackle them but are worried their people are not following them. And for a good reason.

Trouble at the top

Neal Kissel and Patrick Foley interviewed 20 current and former CEOs of large public companies and published their findings in *Harvard Business Review* online in January 2019.[6] They found out almost 50% of CEOs said the role was not what they expected beforehand. They identified three *underestimated* challenges:

1. Newly appointed CEOs stagger under the demands of direct reports. They state they are spending too much energy and time managing their direct reports.
2. Relationship management across the company, moderating or solving conflicts, and making decisions around conflicts pose a challenge. There are too many silos in the company; teams are fragmented; people don't think systemically, and a lot of that is about relationship management.
3. The third challenge that a new CEO faces on the job is information flow. They wonder, "Am I getting from my people the information I need? Is the information I'm giving, the strategy, or the vision, getting to the lower levels of the organization?" This top-down and bottom-up flow of information taxes them.

These are the issues: energy drain, relationship management, and information flow management. CEOs join the position, thinking they are going to focus on managing the business. They end up spending most of their energy with executives, direct reports, and their teams and wasting time with the fragmentation of the top team, internal politics, relationship repairing, and information management. They spend less time than they need and want on managing the whole company, business, and overall strategy.

Usually, when I share these insights with CEOs, they highlight one of the things I just said and object by saying, "Yeah, yeah, but those are CEO rookies, recently appointed to the role, so of course, they are inexperienced. They don't know how things work."

They usually think, "This doesn't apply to me, a seasoned CEO." However, in 2010, researcher Fred Adair found out that usually CEOs believe their teams are better than the teams themselves think they are. Adair asked CEOs to use criteria to rate the performance of their teams. When the CEOs rated the team performance as a team, they gave a higher rating than when the team answered the same questions. The CEO might say, "On a scale from 0 to 5, with 5 being highest, I'd say my team is a 4.6". But the team members would say, "No, we are a lousy team. We are a 3.5 at best or more realistically a 3.2."

Using my proprietary *The 6P's of Executive Teams® Assessment Survey*, I rate executive teams on 23 dimensions of effectiveness. I complete this assessment before each executive team development intervention. Each of these dimensions has several factors. I usually find that the executive team gives itself a different rating than the CEO. But if you look at their direct reports, the middle managers who report to the executive team even rate the team with lower performance than all the executives, including the CEO.

Usually, the CEO is the last one to know about the problems in his or her team. And this is unrelated to how seasoned the CEO is on the job. When you are the alpha animal, others carefully manage the information they give you. After all, they want to influence your decisions to favor their projects, people, and interests. It's only human to do that. They will not tell you about the realities of conflicts, politics, incompetence, or problems. It's for the CEO to find out when issues become so bad that results suffer. By then, it is, of course, a bit late.

CEOs tend to live in an information bubble that creates a distorted view of who they are, what they can achieve, and how much their teams back them up. They think that they lead a team, whereas most often, they manage a loose group of individuals.

The Difference Between a working group and a team

Before explaining what we need executive teams for and how to develop them, it is essential to clarify what a team is and is not.

Most people think that just by bringing a group of people together, having them meeting each other, sharing information, and making some decisions, they become a team. If they implement actions side by side, in projects or processes, it's even better. But people can do all those things and still not be a team.

We need to distinguish a *working group* from a *team*. A working group is a group of people who interact to share information, points of view, and knowledge to make decisions that will impact individual responsibility areas.

Let's say I am an executive who is part of a working group. We might come together to a specific meeting to make decisions or share information. But in the end, we leave this meeting room, and it's going to be my responsibility to carry out the decisions. If I follow what we agreed, if I take the information as valid for my decisions, in the end, it's about me. I own alone my areas of responsibility. No one else will have a sense of failure or responsibility if I miss my targets. It was my job to get there.

A working group is focused primarily on delivering individual work products; the formal boss must make all coordination efforts. In a working group, CEOs exert their power through personal accountability. It doesn't matter how efficient the meetings are or how much information is shared; only the boss authorizes discussion, decision, and delegation.

The working group does not need to have a specific purpose of its own. They usually assume the broader organizational mission as their purpose. Without a specific purpose there is no basis for a shared team identity. I will develop this idea further in Chapter 6 – P for Purpose.

When I ask CEOs if their team has a purpose to inspire and guide the joint effort, most of the time, I get "yes" as an answer. When I ask about the purpose, over 90% of the time, I get the response, "It's the company's Mission and Vision." In that case, I know I am about to work with an executive working group.

A team is a group of people with complementary competences, equally committed with common purpose, goals, and processes, for which they hold themselves mutually accountable.

Unlike the working group, a team is focused on delivering collective work products. Chief Executive Team members openly exchange information and make decisions together; they also work together to provide outputs that demand collaborative effort. This requires a specific team purpose, translated into performance goals that build on one another to maximize impact.

Team accountability is both mutual and individual. A high-performance team does not dilute personal accountability – quite the opposite. It creates the conditions for personal responsibility to be enhanced by mutual accountability.

People participate in each other's decision-making process because they are committed to joint purposes, goals, and processes. Therefore, any of us can act as guardians of the effectiveness and efficiency of the team. We all own the processes and are supposed to act on them while we share and defend the same goals. We can individually determine if the decisions we are making are aligned with the common purpose.

In a capable team, each member is accountable for increasing the effectiveness and efficiency of themselves, the team, and each other. A good team is apt to identify if and when each type of work organization mode is required: an individual or team. Being a team does not mean everybody is doing everything together. That is mindless. The team brings additional critical thinking to know when teamwork is relevant and when it's not.

Chief Executive Team members engage in collaborative efforts, projects, and tasks that go beyond individual job objectives and even company mission. This is required if the team has the vision to transform the organization they are leading to create a much better future.

The most crucial output that an executive team must deliver is leadership. Chief Executive Teams share the task of leading the company through a transformation.

The right of positive interference

One fundamental principle separates a working group from an effective team. I call it *the right of positive interference.*

In a team, you have the right of positive interference. That means that whatever you are doing, whatever decisions you are making, or executing, however you are managing your people, another team member has the right to interfere with that in a positive way. That is, in a way that looks for the best interests of the whole company–a proxy for the greater good.

What does this mean in practical terms? It means that team members always consider they are accountable if they, others, or the whole team do something wrong. Accountability is mutual – I am responsible for you and the team; you and the others are accountable for me. I have your back, and you have mine. You will let me know if I am doing something substandard; you will expect I step up my game; you will support me in getting there. I will do the same. We are in this together. And "this" is the transformation of the company.

Consider what occurs in the operating room. The surgeon wants to begin the operation and skip the safety checklist. The operating room nurse must speak up and insist that the team go through the steps to ensure they have the right patient in the right room for the right surgery on the right part of the body.

If I am the surgeon, I should recognize this questioning is done for the greater good of the patient, to fulfill our purpose as healthcare providers. As the operating room nurse, you have the right to positively intervene in my areas of responsibility. I will give you feedback. I will welcome feedback. I will have and assume good intentions. It means that the common good, purpose, or vision guides our actions.

By adhering to the right of positive interference, we focus on the effectiveness of the whole instead of the individual.

By adhering to the right of positive interference, we focus on the effectiveness of the whole instead of the individual.

The right of positive interference does not exist in a working group. Instead of promoting continuous improvement and company transformation, interference in those groups can become a weapon of massive disappointment, resentment, and conflict. If implemented too early in a development process, it can become counterproductive and spark a downward spiral in team dynamics. When executed by an executive team who agreed on a common purpose, vision, and strategy, it can speed up creating a Chief Executive Team and boost the company's transformation through its actions.

Do companies need executive teams?

Any intelligent and efficiency-mindful CEO might ask right now, "I get it; executive teams can be a beautiful thing to have, but do I *need* to develop one? Can't I get the same results if I just bring together a group of competent people to get the job done and get on with it? Is it worth the investment of energy, time, resources, mine, and everybody else to go that way? As you said, 'CEOs already spend more time and energy to manage relationships than expected.' Isn't this going to drain me even more? What if the conditions are not right? We are under tremendous pressure of time and results; there is a crisis going on if you haven't been around for the last year. How can we afford to do this?

"What about the risks? What if some team members boycott the initiative and I lose face? What if I lose control of the group because I empower them? What if the Board disagrees with this movement? I would lose my credibility just by trying.

"This is micromanagement. I don't want to go into the team's areas of responsibility to tell them what to do and not. This action will dilute individual responsibility and get everybody frustrated by my interference. How will I hold the individuals accountable then?

"We don't need to be friends; we just need to be productive together. Teams are unnecessary at this level; my people are too competent to need them. This is not the way we do things in this company. You will need to convince me to go this way."

As an organizational consultant, I have heard it all. I could write one full chapter about objections to executive teams and the specific answers to them all. Some of the next chapters go into more detail on how the CEO's beliefs and behavior modes sometimes prevent the executive group from becoming an effective team and the impact these beliefs and behaviors have on the CEO's leadership, credibility, and influence. I will also explain in the last chapter why some of the objections of CEOs are groundless.

A Chief Executive Team is not about being friends or diluting responsibility. Nor it is about filling gaps of competence or weakening the CEO position. It's about getting the company to a different level. It's a transformation of leadership.

CEOs know this instinctively; they've been implementing teams all over the organizational structure for decades.

- Self-managed teams are the basis for continuous improvement in manufacturing.
- Project teams are the building block of technical execution.
- Research and development teams are pushing innovation forward.
- Process teams are streamlining the functioning of our companies.
- Customer service teams are redesigning our organizational charts putting clients at the center.
- Agile teams are making enormous changes.

Do CEOs think they can continue to do business with executive teams organized in silos? They know this is not going to work. Results are weak compared with what can be obtained with a fully functioning executive team. Having a working group at the top sets the worst possible example for a performance-enhancing company culture. Everybody can see it except the executives. It's the invisible elephant, remember?

Very often, in crises, when risk, resources, and individual competence don't add up to a solution, CEOs get their direct reports to work as a team to find a way out of the pit. But as soon as the sun shines again, they revert to the standard approach of silo management. It's a pity that so much potential to produce outstanding results is wasted in everyday business situations. Chief Executive Teams hold the key to business excellence because they allow the time and resources to maximize efficiency while preparing meaningful transformation.

Becoming a team only to help the company out of a crisis is better than nothing. But it leaves most of the money and happiness on the table.

You need to establish a chief executive team because you can't afford not to do it. Business as usual is draining money, ideas, engagement, and creating the company's wrong performance culture. To understand this, we just need to look at how the executive team dynamics impact business results.

What's on a CEO's mind?

Earlier in the chapter, you learned that, according to Gartner's *CEO and Senior Business Executive Survey* of 2019, there are three main concerns in the minds of top executives: growth, digital transformation, and structural development of companies.

You need to establish a chief executive team because you can't afford not to do it. Business as usual is draining money, ideas, engagement, and creating the company's wrong performance culture.

To foster growth, you need cash. Investment is essential. You require innovation skills and processes to be able to transform the business digitally. You can't keep the same business model and expect results to increase or remain the same, under the significant market transformation we are going through. Your company must engage people to develop and redesign the company structure and prepare the next generation of leaders. You also need engaged people to execute your strategy and produce the right results.

What is the impact of having a real executive team instead of a working group? How does the team affect the company's financial results, innovation, and engagement (the critical dimensions of strategy by CEOs)? The next three sections dive into each of those dimensions.

I don't want to transform this book into a Ph.D. dissertation, so I will cite only a handful of studies that show the breadth of research done on each topic. You can find a list of references at the end of the book.

Chief Executive Teams are good for business

To cut a long story short, having a chief executive team is good for business. If you want to cut to the chase, you only need to read this paragraph. Having a capable executive team improves the financial KPIs of organizations. These factors are impacted: return on assets, return on sales, return on equity, stock performance, profitability, productivity, sales growth, market share, operating result, budget compliance, net charge-offs to average loans, net worth to total assets, and delinquent loans on total loans, among others. If you do not take my word for it, then read the rest of this section.

It is common to understand that the executive team's good strategic decision is related to better financial outcomes for a company. If we prove that some characteristics of the team's functioning improve the quality of strategic decisions, we should measure their positive impact on the money. That was what Tony Simons, of Cornell University, set out to find with a group of colleagues. Analyzing data from 57 manufacturing companies, they established the quality of debate in the executive team (open discussions of task-related differences and the advocacy of different approaches to strategic decision making by the team members) was positively related to profitability and sales growth of the company.[7]

If you work in a credit company, financial health can be measured by a combination of key performance indicators: net charge-offs to average loans, net worth to total assets, delinquent loans on total loans, and return on assets. Together with a team of researchers, Murray Barrick of Texas A&M University analyzed data from 94 top management teams of finance companies, provided by the National Credit Union Administration. They found top management teams (characterized by high interdependence) had better performance and generated better company performance than top management groups, measured by the financial KPIs above. These results occurred when team communication and team cohesion were better.[8]

Using a sample of 115 Japanese firms, researchers Tanikawa and Jung discovered that CEO power could impair the benefits of executive team tenure diversity on the company's return on assets when *past* results of the company were good. In simple words, the more CEOs stifled participation of team members and aligned individual behavior with their expectations, the lesser return on assets the company had.[9]

Niels Opstrup and Anders Villadsen analyzed data from the Danish public administration about gender diversity and its impact on the financial performance of 91 municipalities.[10] They concluded that management teams' ability to create structures that facilitate behavior integration and cross-gender work is positively related to operating results and budget compliance of the municipality. Diverse genders working productively together and having processes to align individual behavior with team purpose are good for the budget.

Hyuntak Roh and a team of researchers published a meta-analysis of five studies done in ten countries in 2019. The study, covering hundreds of companies in multiple industries, reached several conclusions. The team determined return on assets, return on equity, return on sales, market share gains, productivity, and stock performance are influenced by the executive team's cohesion, team communication/information exchange, comprehensive information search, strategic consensus, and behavior integration.[11]

A Chief Executive Team can create a system of checks and balances that effectively mitigates risk.

A research published by Paul Gompers and colleagues, in 2020, uncovered a hidden liability of executive teams. They surveyed 885 investors, representing 681 Venture Capital firms, each of these screening on average 200 companies to make four investments per year. The management team was identified as an important factor in startup failures by 95% of the firms. More important for success than business related characteristics of the company, such as product and technology.[12] Having all the vital decisions for the company's future depending on the CEO's competence and personality is risky. A low performing executive team is also a liability. A Chief Executive Team can create a system of checks and balances that effectively mitigates risk.

These are only some of the hundreds of studies available about the impact of specific executive team dynamics on the company's financial performance. It does not matter where in the world you operate, what line of business you are in, or if yours is a private or state-owned company, big or small. Having a Chief Executive Team is good for business. It is not difficult to conceive that. Maximizing the return of your investment depends on having a deep understanding of the market, generating successful strategies, and leading the company to execute them. And all these are all about having a capable team at the top of your company.

Chief Executive Teams are good for innovation

Chief executive teams also foster innovation performance. Teamwork at the top impacts a company's ability to explore new business opportunities and exploit the ones that promise return. Effective teams improve the company's international diversification and entrepreneurial orientation, maximize return on R & D investment, and create a proactive culture of learning and risk-taking in the company. In short, this is what this section covers.

Digital transformation, new business models, crisis resolution, and CEOs' current headaches are dependent on companies being able to generate new ideas to monetize their core competences and reorganize themselves to execute them. Chief Executive Teams are instrumental in that.

New ideas are born from different ways of thinking. But to be acknowledged, discussed, tested, evaluated, adjusted, validated, implemented, and accepted, we must listen to and respect the person who puts them forward. In other words, if we kill the messenger, the idea will never arrive.

Killing the messenger is a popular game with CEOs and other executives. In general terms, it means that the inner circle of power does not accept you or value your opinions. And you can be out of the inner circle for many reasons: your age, gender, skin color, education, family name, nationality, tenure, among other characteristics that define you as uniquely you.

These individual diversity dimensions are vital as they equip us with skills, experiences, and viewpoints that make different (therefore creative) ideas more likely. If well-integrated, the executive team will reap the benefits of individual diversity. If they become the basis for prejudice and stereotyping between team members, they will destroy the team's effectiveness.

Company ambidexterity is the ability to explore new business opportunities and to exploit the ones that promise return. This is an essential concept in the study of innovation as it can be considered a precursor to it.

Ana García-Granero of the University of Valencia, along with a team of researchers, studied the level of CEOs' trust in their team and the executive team's ability to share decision-making and accountability. Both play an instrumental role in supporting the executive team to integrate diversity, engage in critical debate in positive ways, reconcile paradoxical demand, and foster exploration and exploitation. These factors facilitate company adaptation to changes in the market over time.[13]

Peng-Yu Li and Kuo-Feng Huang worked with a sample of 283 Taiwanese manufacturing firms in the information technology industry.[14] They analyzed the impact of integrating two types of executive team diversity on innovation: education and tenure diversity. Their study concluded that there was a stronger relationship between R & D investment and innovation performance in management teams with more significant tenure diversity. As for executive team educational diversity, it enhanced the relationship between international diversification and innovation performance. To simplify, having diversity in the executive team improves innovation only if we also use it.

Social stratification resulting from power and status differences between team members can trigger others' social categorization in the team. This, in turn creates the psychology of subgroups in the team, with the members of one subgroup evaluating themselves as better than the other. The person who thinks he or she is more qualified to make decisions "because I've been here longer" is focused on *tenure*. Another team member focused on *age* thinks, "These kids just joined the executive team. They are 20 years younger than us. What can they know?" Varying levels of education, gender, nationality, or skin color can also affect social stratification.

Christophe Boone of the University of Antwerp, Belgium, and colleagues analyzed data of 165 large publicly-listed manufacturing companies in 20 countries, over 10 years. They defined corporate entrepreneurship as "The process through which firms innovate, create new businesses, and transform themselves by changing the business domain or key strategic processes." A lack of social stratification and categorization in the executive team increases corporate entrepreneurship and subsequent innovation performance.[15]

Social stratification and categorization create an *us-versus-them* culture in executive teams and preclude innovation in the company. Seeing everyone in the team eye-to-eye fosters innovation.

Entrepreneurial orientation describes the extent to which an organization's top managers emphasize risk-taking, proactivity, and innovativeness in firm strategy. It is an essential predictor of the extent to which entrepreneurial behavior in the firm is encouraged, undertaken, and rewarded. Research suggests more entrepreneurially oriented firms tend to perform better, especially in dynamic environments, due to enhanced innovation capacity.

Sebastiaan van Doorn and two other researchers studied a randomly identified sample of 9,000 firms within the Netherlands operating in different industries. Interestingly, they concluded that the management team seeking external advice *by itself* does not support the team in devising entrepreneurial strategies for the company.[16] When executive teams combine this seeking for external advice with making sense and integrating the judgments of people who think differently from them, they achieve higher entrepreneurial orientation. They can support the innovation efforts of the company.

The company personnel's ability to learn and innovate either exists at the top or not at all. Innovation performance is boosted by Chief Executive Teams and undermined by executive silos. You must listen to people who think differently from you and then make sense of what they are saying to improve your company's innovation capacity.

Chief Executive Teams are good for engagement

Disclaimer: the following numbers can shock sensitive people. Reader discretion is advised.

The 2019 Global Study of Engagement, done by ADP Research Institute, found that 84% of employees only "go to" work. The percentage of committed people in the workforce is 16%.[17] These numbers were collected *before* the pandemic. When lockdown hit the market, many people stopped actually "going to" work. In a remote working-based reality, where being away from the company can also provoke emotional distance and disconnect from its people, culture, and goals, did these numbers get worse? And what is the impact of this when companies are already fighting for survival?

Employee engagement is the most potent lever for your company's results. Being in the top-quartile of engagement, instead of in the bottom-quartile:

- Increases shareholder return five times.[18]
- Increases sales productivity by 18%.[19]
- Increases wellbeing by 66%.[19]

- Reduces absenteeism by 81%.[19] (Absenteeism cost US companies over $84 Billion in 2013.[20])
- Increases operational efficiency, reducing 75% of quality defects.[21]
- Increases the total shareholder return by 100%.[21]

Companies with lower employee engagement have 12 times more turnover than their counterparts, with consequent financial, operational, quality, and performance costs.[22]

This small list of impacts on company results (among hundreds of conclusions generated by research around the world every year) prove that employee engagement is essential.

Employee engagement is the critical factor in how well you are leading your people, your company's sustainability and resilience, and the effectiveness of strategy implementation. It determines how much your people believe in you, buy into your strategy, commit to its execution, persist against adversity, and identify with and defend the company. As Walt Disney put it, "You can dream, create, design, and build the most wonderful place in the world, but it requires people to make the dream a reality."

Unless you have a fully digital company designed, operated, and maintained by AI and robots, you need people to make your company work. You're in business; therefore, you need people engaged with your company at all levels of the hierarchy.

Chief Executive Teams are instrumental in keeping them engaged. To use a military metaphor, executives are the generals who decide the war strategy. Middle managers are the captains, lieutenants, and sergeants who adapt the strategy to the terrain and unforeseen events, lead the troops on the ground, and keep them motivated to win.

As an executive "general", keeping the chain of command in their ranks is mandatory for your operations' success. If they desert their duty, your mission is in jeopardy. Operations can be compromised; intelligence is lost and can even be offered to the enemy. You have a shorter pool of talent for your higher ranks, thus decreasing your chain of command's quality, and troop's morale goes down, increasing soldiers' desertion. The same issues affect the business world.

Middle managers are critical to the company's competitive advantage. They link strategy *talk* and strategy *walk*, keep people focused on the game, and invite them to be better at what they do.

How can executive teams improve middle management engagement?

Rose is the CEO of the local operating company of an IT multinational in Spain. She is an incredibly smart, fast thinker used to comprehending everything about any business subject light years ahead of everyone else. She tends to get impatient about the slow speed of people around her. They take forever to find solutions and produce results. She has excellent self-esteem, is confident about her skills, and does not ask for help, support, or feedback. Instead, she precisely dispatches instructions, solutions, and orders. Rose's precision is admirable, and she is usually the smartest person in the room.

Because she interferes with everything the executive team does, Rose feels that all outcomes are, to a significant extent, dependent on her. Therefore, she sees no reason to compliment her team, and they report feeling she does not appreciate their efforts.

Luc is the CEO of the local operating company of the same IT multinational in Belgium. He has a bright mind and is an extremely competent professional; he knows a lot about the industry. Nevertheless, priding himself on being a fast learner, Luc enjoys being challenged. Luc keeps an open mind to the possibility of new ways of doing things, plays with scenarios all the time, and requires that everyone around him develop their skills. Being confident about his abilities and at the same time invested in his personal development, Luc actively asks how people feel about the way he leads the company. Luc regularly introduces changes in his management practice and does not follow a rigid structure. As learning is so essential for him, he gives people around him the challenges and time to learn. Luc follows the Agile Manifesto principle of "Individuals and interactions over processes and tools."

Who would you prefer to work with, Rose or Luc?

If you are like most people, you'll say Luc, because you have opportunities to develop, say what you think, be appreciated, and feel that you contribute to shaping operations. With Luc, you can make a difference. With Rose, you just carry out her directives.

It turns out that several research papers identify Luc's behaviors as increasing job satisfaction and decreasing turnover both in employees and middle managers.[23,24] This is even more true for women than for men. It seems that an arrogant CEO behavior creates more negative emotions in women than in their male colleagues.

But you can have the "Luc behavior," and yet your example might not produce the expected results throughout the company because your executive "team" obliterates it with their behaviors. If the executive group is fragmented and does not act as a team, if it is not perceived as trustworthy by the rest of the company, employee commitment will be low, job satisfaction will plunge, and turnover intentions will be high.

Most importantly, the way the CEO coordinates the team, supports them in developing a shared identity, communication accuracy, and making decisions by consensus, impacts middle managers' job satisfaction and turnover.[25,26]

The most damaging myth for leadership effectiveness

We go about our work-life surrounded by myths. The most damaging myth for leadership effectiveness is, "The good CEO knows it all and does it all." This old type of behavior by the CEO (I can hardly call it leadership style) disengages people all over the company, from the executive down to the individual contributor level. It facilitates CEOs interfering with everything either because they think they know better or think they must hide the fact they don't know better.

People's knowledge is based on their personal history, with their specific restrictions and limitations. This narrows down what we can process and understand. I know we can all accept that processing and making sense of more information results in better decision making, which produces better results.

If you only apply what you learned from your experience, you will not maximize the return on your team's capacity. Only when CEOs can humbly learn about different ways to think and act can they spark a fire to create the best company possible, starting with the current one. That's what I call the transformation of leadership. Chapter 10 – *P for Possibilities* – goes into detail on how that learning can occur.

> **Leadership face value is all about the CEO's personality. Leadership's real value, is about chief executive teams transforming companies.**

We've got the wrong CEO job description. "Know it all" and "do it all" are not requirements of success, quite the opposite. This myth should be replaced by the results proven Twenty-First Century alternative: "The good CEO develops a chief executive team to learn-it-all and transform the business."

How we function together in the executive team is directly connected with company results. Research data collected in thousands of companies worldwide shows that a capable executive team impacts the company's financial, strategic, innovation, and leadership parameters. Yet the business world seems to be oblivious to this.

We crave heroes to save the day. Leadership face value is all about the CEO's personality. Leadership's real value, however, is about chief executive teams transforming companies. Once we understand that, we can lead the elephant out of the room.

2

IT'S HAPPENING ON YOUR SHIFT

> "Being coached by Ricardo was transformational. I realized how everything we are is not definitive. Everything in us can be worked to progress."
>
> – Luís Prata | Red Stripe Jamaica | Managing Director

I STARTED COACHING Viktor individually when he was at the end of his assignment as CEO of the Italian operations of an industrial company. The previous years had been a rough ride. The company came out fat from a series of acquisitions of industrial facilities and needed to trim down costs. He had to adjust people and processes to meet headquarters' profit requirements.

Because they bought different companies, Viktor's company had different identities in its brands and workforce. They needed to create a common culture according to the new ownership structure. This required a full restructuring of the value chain, from the client back to the suppliers. This involved redefining and implementing brand strategy and equalizing conditions for employees of different original companies. An endless list of strategic, structural, operational, and sales problems had to be tackled.

Being an expat in Italy, Viktor did not know much about the local culture. His Human Resources and Communications Director had coached him on it at the beginning, and a culture change process was designed and implemented.

Viktor's executive team had ups and downs throughout the process. He appointed four of the nine directors during his tenure. With different levels of understanding and experience in leading change management processes, at some critical moments they had been stressed and irrational and made some wrong moves.

Some decisions and actions made the executive group come across as fractured into subgroups. Viktor acted on it when his team members or middle managers brought this to his attention. He spoke with his direct reports, made relevant decisions, and went on to the next pressing issue on the list. For him, the matter was settled.

He approached me when his term was finishing in the Italian market. It all had been so crazy that he wanted a safe space of executive coaching to reflect on his experience and structure his learning. He wanted to be better equipped to catch the next assignment that headquarters would offer at any moment.

Viktor is a natural-born learner. He thrives on information and is genuinely interested in his personal development. He strives to constantly become better at what he does.

Together we structured a process to transform his tacit learning into explicit learning. Through a series of coaching and self-learning exercises, he captured a lot of the subtleties of his internal cognitive processes and belief system that might otherwise have gone unnoticed. This was a good starting point, and he consolidated many learning points with it.

As a systems thinker, though, I am interested in how context and community can feed the individual learning process. This is usually a bigger pool to drink from.

We know that even small animals without significant cognitive processing capacity can join to create collective actions that are more complex than the individuals could achieve alone. The term "swarm intelligence" or "collective intelligence" doesn't only apply to bees and ants. We humans can also benefit from the wisdom of others, but more importantly, we can learn how differently from us they think about the same things. Equipped with that information, we can improve our information processing skills and become better thinkers and learners. The outcomes of this process are always more information, more alternatives to choose from, and more effectiveness.

Context and community can feed the individual learning process.

Learning increases personal freedom by providing better options to be ourselves and achieve beyond our restrictions.

Based on learning science, we structured a process for Viktor to capture what the collective intelligence of the company thought about his leadership effectiveness. Any human system will develop a set of beliefs, assumptions, and norms of how to deal with external and internal events. The actions of a prominent group member, an "alpha animal," determine how to originate and direct internal and external events.

A set of beliefs, assumptions, and norms about the CEO will emerge in the company as they perform their job. Consciously or unconsciously, people make a collective sense of the why, the how, and the what of the CEO's behavior, and

Learning increases personal freedom by providing better options to be ourselves and achieve beyond our restrictions.

create tacit rules of how to deal with it. We wanted to uncover all of that.

One of the actions Viktor implemented was to conduct exit interviews. Most of us are familiar with them. When someone we would like to keep in the team decides to leave the company, we conduct an interview to understand the process by which they arrived at that decision.

People make a collective sense of the why, the how, and the what of the CEO's behavior.

Exit interviews are important because when people have nothing to lose anymore, they are more willing to say the truth about their bosses, colleagues, and company. As they cannot be punished by saying negative things, they are free to be objective, and usually they are.

CEOs should conduct exit interviews at the end of their tenure. Focused on their exit, not on others'. You need quality information to learn before moving on to the next assignment. This is one of the best ways to understand what people felt, thought, and did based on your behavior. This provides a baseline to measure your professional growth as a leader.

As soon as he was informed about the next assignment and the date of leaving the country, Viktor conducted a series of exit interviews with executive team members, middle managers, and some individual contributors. And he got a shock.

CEOs should conduct exit interviews at the end of their tenure.

Piercing the CEO's information bubble

He started bottom up, speaking first with several millennial generation employees that he became close to during a high-potential development program. They told him how surprised they were at the fact that he allowed so much misaligned behavior in the executive team. He was unaware of the worst of it.

Executive team members were openly speaking negative things about the restructuring done, the decisions made, the leadership guidelines they were trying to establish, and each other. Outright hypocrisy was going on during his tenure there, Viktor realized. People were saying one thing and doing its opposite. His decisions were considered the source of it because he allowed all this behavior to go on. "Surely, he must have been aware of it," they noted.

Viktor thought, as most of us in his situation would, that young individual contributors tend to imagine that companies can and should be perfect. Therefore, they will tend to take a harsher look at what is going on and emphasize negative things. He embarked on conversations with a sample of middle managers that he hoped would counter that initial information. "These people will have a less idealistic notion of business and will show a better understanding of what we tried to do and finally achieved," he thought.

Middle managers, in their more realistic way, told him that his executive team members were lying to each other. Executive bosses instructed their middle managers to protect the resources of each department even when sharing them would benefit the whole company. They instructed their managers to "change narratives" about projects, mistakes, costs, to make decisions more palatable for other executive team members and for Viktor.

The level of "white lying" going on was not so "white" anymore. What started as "I will protect you from harmless truth" became "I will protect me from harmful truth." The omissions and distortions were changing the story so much that the characters could not even recognize it themselves. Middle managers were surprised that Viktor allowed so much of that. Surely, he must have been aware of it.

It is important to understand that his purpose with this information collection was not to confront everyone and squeeze the truth out of them. This was not a reckoning. He did not want to change who those people were anymore. He did not want to influence any decision after he went to another country. He was intentionally focused on becoming a better leader. That was the goal he defined in the coaching with me. We set up an interviewing process for that which allowed for his neutrality in conducting the information search.

Finally, Viktor spoke with some of his direct reports. A lot of blaming was going on and a lot of resentment, including grudges stemming from collective decisions where each team member thought they "lost" against someone else. Unresolved problems and unfinished business lingered in people's minds, generating a loop of negative emotions that prevented trust and functional relationships.

One of his direct reports told him, "This is the most dysfunctional team I ever worked on. Sure, we reached business goals, but only by luck did we not destroy each other in the process." As Viktor discovered, his executive team members also thought that he had allowed all of that on purpose. Surely, he must have been aware of it.

There's a technique in group therapy called confrontation. Through it, someone gets information that forces them to recognize their shortcomings and their possible consequences. We did not design Viktor's self-exit interviews deliberately for that. But the quality and amount of information that Viktor got was confrontational. It forced him to see a reality that had existed all along and that he had preferred not to see.

When Viktor saw the light, he saw the elephant. He thought that by making daily business decisions the team was coming together as a team and that by addressing tough relational issues in a by-the-way manner he was solving them. He had believed that by giving individual feedback he was aligning behavior and that because his executives seemed to behave well in his presence and said the "right things," they were doing a good enough leadership job. Because negative team dynamics were invisible to him, he didn't see them affecting the company.

CEO behavior maintains the problem

Living in a coherent universe of information means we don't get discrepant information. Most opinions and evidence we get come from sources that are so close to us they think like us. As you go up in the hierarchy of an organization, your information universe shrinks to give you what you expect to receive. Basing your decisions on that information becomes a liability. CEOs are at constant risk of making wrong decisions because they don't vary their sources of information.

As you go up in the hierarchy of an organization, your information universe shrinks to give you what you expect to receive.

His information universe was coherent enough to victimize Viktor. He did not get enough discrepant information during his tenure. He got it all at the end of it. That was a bigger and harder pill to swallow. As a fast learner, Viktor dedicated his best effort to it. He could not recover the impact of the previous years of blindness, but he could prevent all of that from ever happening again.

In Chapter 1 – *The Elephant in The Room* – I described the elephant. Lack of collaboration at executive team level prevents the company from achieving its highest potential. It is so big a problem and so prevalent that no one dares to do anything about it. But there is another possible reading for this. No one dares to do anything about lack of teamwork at the top because everyone considers it the job of the CEO. If the CEO is not addressing it, certainly it must be on purpose.

CEOs are at constant risk of making wrong decisions because they don't vary their sources of information.

The role that the CEO's behavior plays in maintaining the lack of performance of executive teams is rarely addressed. This is the focus of this chapter.

No one dares to do anything about lack of teamwork at the top because everyone considers it the job of the CEO.

To better understand it, we will use two dimensions to plot different CEO behavior modes in a graph: influence and impact. *Influence* is about how much CEOs can motivate their management team to do the right thing. *Impact* is about how much their actions affect the company's results.

Considering these two dimensions, five CEO behavior modes affect team dynamics. Four of them keep the problem going. The last one solves it.

Avoidance mode

Girija is an American-born and educated Indian woman who received a job offer as the general manager of a manufacturing plant in the southern part of the United States. During the first month in the new position, Girija scheduled a series of individual meetings with key managers. She explained the issues she observed with the managers' behavior directly to them.

The CEO (John) began hearing complaints: "Who does she think she is?" "I'm not going to take guff from a woman." "Why doesn't she go back to where she came from?"

When John called Girija into his office, he said, "You're doing this wrong and are not being sensitive to the culture of this company and to your position as an Indian woman in the South. Instead of sounding critical, you need to be less direct." After her initial reaction of defensiveness, Girija realized she needed to rethink her strategy, avoid making any clear-cut changes in the team, and change the way she gave feedback.

She decided to sit back and make more observations about the operation of the team and company culture before acting. She went into Avoidance Mode. At this point, she brought me in as advisor to help her understand the company dynamics and how to restructure her leadership behavior.

The Avoidance Mode is often a deliberate decision to avoid committing to a single leadership style to deal with your management team.

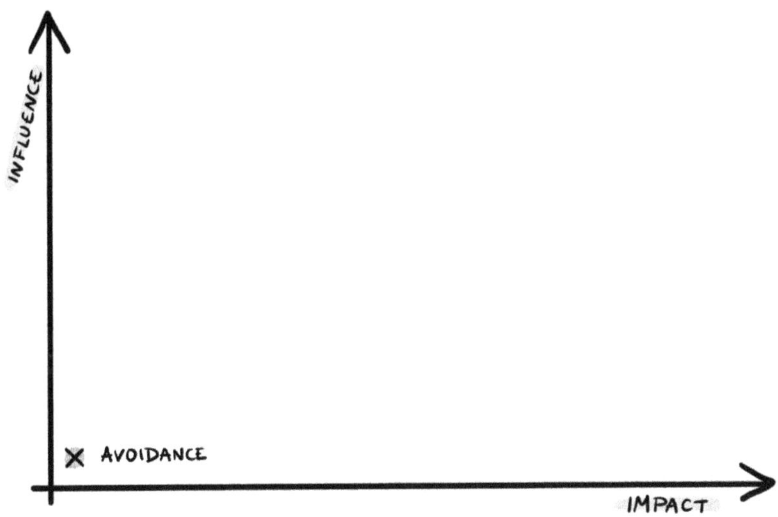

Figure 1 – CEO Avoidance behavior mode

As shown in Figure 1, the Avoidance Mode has *low influence* on team members and *low impact* on company results. In its benign manifestation, Avoidance Mode is a temporary leadership behavior typical of recently appointed top leaders, like Girija. It is usually justified by the need to understand a pre-existing team or a country's culture that's different from your own. Leaders who adopt Avoidance Mode assess the

In its malignant manifestation, Avoidance Mode leadership behavior tolerates dysfunctional employee behavior.

team before changing some of its members or deciding on the best leadership style and management processes to maximize results.

In its malignant manifestation, Avoidance Mode leadership behavior tolerates dysfunctional employee behavior.

Due to an exclusive focus on financial results, the leader may turn a blind eye to bullying, sexual harassment, absenteeism, or employee theft, if the money keeps coming in. Consequently, the situation can quickly spiral out of control with burnout, excessive use of sick leave, dissipation of company resources, resignations, litigation, and low morale.

When there is an effective leader above the Avoidance Mode manager, this leader needs to see the critical consequences of the inability to confront negative behavior and step in to limit the company's risks created by tolerating dysfunctional employee behavior.

The Avoidance Mode usually does not happen when leaders have a clear task pre-defined before their appointment that requires changing the nature of relationships in the top team, such as to restructure, downsize, or manage a merger or acquisition. As avoidance does not deliver under those circumstances, they usually go directly to other modes.

You know you are in avoidance mode when:

1. You feel (and the team feels) you still do not get a grip on some of the team members.
2. There's persistent misaligned behavior. You might have tried to deal with it. The problematic behavior seems to improve temporarily and then slides back to unacceptable business as usual.
3. You are pondering different options for intervening. You are taking your time to study the team, and you weigh the possible outcomes of being more directive.
4. You might have already tried another leadership behavior that did not work as you expected.

5. You know that your team members have different strategies to maximize their performance. Some want to focus short term and show results to get their bonuses. They react well to being told what to do. Other team members want to show their creativity. They are in the position for the long run; they think about vision and sustainability and not only short-term goals. They want mental space, not control.
6. You understand you cannot be directive and non-directive at the same time with different people, although they ask for that. You need to display a minimum of equality in decision making and people management to the team, for the sake of fairness.
7. You begin to realize the drawbacks of Avoidance Mode. Who trusts someone who changes allowed behavior depending on the person they speak to?
8. You want to make sure you get it right. For the time being you withhold your judgment and postpone action.
9. Management team members are not giving each other feedback. Things that seem obvious to you are not being taken into consideration because no one dares to give feedback to colleagues or to you. The feedback given to each other is not honest; people are just sugarcoating it.

You value:

When you are in Avoidance Mode you place a lot of value on the current reality of the team. That is what you need to assess before intervening.

The usual consequences of the avoidance mode are:

1. **Fragmentation**
   The executive team under a leader in Avoidance Mode becomes fragmented into subgroups, around clusters

of interest, informal leaders or identity signs. The subgroups might be the "old timers" versus the "newcomers," the "locals" versus the "out-of-town new managers," the "boomers" versus the "millennials," or "men" versus "women." Any kind of "us" versus "them" works to further fracture the executive team.

2. **Dysfunctionality**
   Middle level managers become less functional. Aware of the Avoidance Mode of their leader, they become watchful as they look for guidance. If there is no clear direction, they wisely don't commit to the CEO's ill-defined strategies. They say one thing and do something different just to keep an escape route available. For example, management team members say one thing in meetings and another in the corridor. They say one thing to their CEO and a different one to their colleagues.

3. **Information blindness**
   As a CEO in Avoidance Mode, you feel you are not getting all the information needed to make decisions. A lot of qualitative information is hidden. Executive team members are not openly honest to each other, and all other employees know that. Therefore, they assume that you "must know" and don't want to act on the dishonesty. Most of the time CEOs are the last to be informed of what is going on in the company.

4. **Complacency**
   There's complacency about inefficiencies at management team level. "Things have always been like this." "This is the way we do things around here." "We were successful in the last four years working this way; why change now?" "It's just a temporary phase; things will get back to normal."

5. **Inefficiency**
   Projects are stalled at executive team level and it's not clear why.

6. **Value destruction**
   Even a temporary Avoidance Mode phase can destroy your management team and damage the company. When the company is profitable, money buys you some time. But if you don't have a clear leadership behavior, the window of opportunity to maximize your influence on the management team closes. Your impact on strategy design and execution is compromised, and your credibility as a leader for the whole organization is gone.

7. **Urgency**
   Staying in this mode can be acceptable for a short period after taking office. Everyone in the company will accept that. But if you don't quickly move out of Avoidance Mode, you'll be back looking for a new job.

Command mode

Andrew holds the CEO position in a multinational FMCG company. His periods of work range from two to three years managing the operating company of said multinational in a country, followed by phases of one to three months without work until he is appointed to another country and the process restarts.

Meanwhile his company diligently pays him the salary even when he is not working, because Andrew has a unique skill; he is a fixer. He gets the local operating companies in trouble back into shape. He restructures, repositions, reorganizes, and repurposes companies to get them back on track to profit. He knows what and how to cut to make the surgery successful.

He is very clear on his leadership style. After a brief period of analyzing numbers and processes to get a clear picture of where the company is, usually before landing on site, he gathers three or four levels of managers in a town hall meeting to announce what he's going to do.

He has a kind of "canned speech" that he adapts to each company, according to the financial situation. But his main metaphor remains the same on all occasions. It goes like this:

"This company is a ship. A big ship. And its hull is leaking. I will tell you exactly what needs to be done to fix it. And as any captain, I expect my crew to do it. One thing I can tell you: We will have to cross stormy seas. Some of you will not be with the crew when we arrive at the next harbor. You might decide that the ride got too tough for you and you want out. That is normal. I also expect that some of you are not fit for the job ahead. If that is the case, I will make the consequent decisions about it, after a fair warning. But one thing I can tell you: Do not do things that make me throw you overboard. Because I will do it immediately."

This is the pep talk he gives to the top levels of managers in the organization, with small variations to accommodate to local flavor.

This is the mode I call Command Mode. The leader using Command Mode centralizes decision making to guarantee results.

Andrew never hired my services to support him in developing an effective executive team. I usually get to know his effects when his successor comes in and needs to clean the air of his negative impact on team morale and initiative.

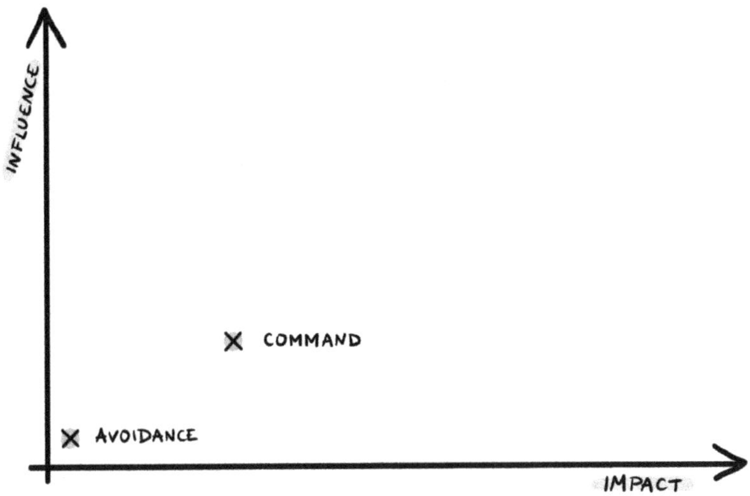

Figure 2 – CEO Command behavior mode

As seen in Figure 2, Command Mode has some impact on company results. When you centralize decisions, give orders and control execution, things usually get done. But the level of *impact is relatively low* due to the effects of Command Mode on the team's morale. People will contribute when and how you require but not with their best efforts whenever needed. Doing that would be too risky for them under centralized decision making. There you need to please the boss and that does not always come out of your best effort.

The Command Mode leader's *influence level is lower* than the impact level. Command Mode is not centered on influencing people; it's all about dispatching orders and guaranteeing that they execute them.

You know you are in command mode when:

1. You feel you must do everything yourself in the company for it to be successful.
2. *You* make most decisions concerning strategy, operations, routine problems, and extraordinary crisis situations. Everything lands on your desk because

you have trained your employees to rely on you and not take initiative to make decisions. "Just do as I say" echoes in your head as you give directions.

3. You validate and control the work of your direct reports. You regularly talk to people down the organization to get relevant information to evaluate the quality of what is reported to you. You micromanage your direct reports and incentivize them to mimic this style with the people they supervise.
4. You feel you are on a mission to get the most out of everyone in the company, to get them to deliver according to their maximum level of competence. Rather than wanting to develop them, you only want to get the most out of their current level of competence.
5. You feel you must directly control how your sales reps spend the company's allowances. You comb through expense reports looking for padding or any other example of such level of centralized micromanagement.
6. You are very explicit about who is in charge, who calls the shots, who is the rainmaker.
7. You are explicit about your power to terminate any contract in the company. You let your executive team know that probation is not a temporary phase. They are always on probation. If they fail or show that they are vulnerable, they are immediately out. You purposely don't make clear what is sufficient to fire them. You believe this will keep them on their toes and alert.
8. You believe that things must go your way to go anywhere at all. You have all the answers.
9. You confront, you are not afraid of raising your voice in required situations, nor of being perceived as harsh by your team or individual contributors. You believe being tough comes with the territory. The soft ones don't make it.
10. You limit the level of creativity of people down the organization. After all, they are there to execute a

strategy that you are expected to define. You are paid to think and decide. They are paid to execute. If everyone does their job, all runs smoothly. Usually, their ideas are just pipe dreams, anyway.

11. You don't tolerate mistakes. Any mistake is wrong, and people get punished for making them. You are quick to execute on this because you value the example it provides others.
12. Teams and team building are not your priority. You might accept that teams are important in some areas of the organization, to reach specific goals. But you don't believe this applies to a management committee or to the company in general. You believe cross-functional projects tend to be a waste of resources, because they blur roles and dilute responsibilities.
13. You divide to rule. Power struggles happen in the executive team because of your behavior mode. Executive team members compete for importance, favors, budget, resources, access to the board, your attention, and so on. You know how to get the most out of this competition.

You value:

When you are in Command Mode, you place a lot of value on your know-how. You rely on your previous experience in this type of industry, job, or company, or on getting a specific strategy executed.

The usual consequences of the command mode are:

1. **Low initiative**
   People reduce the risk of making mistakes by decreasing the number of new things they try. Tried and proven techniques are good; new and uncertain are not. Change is very risky; business as usual is safe and not likely to bring on the wrath of the leader.

2. **Fear culture**
   The culture of fear takes its toll. The first victim is innovation. Then job satisfaction, engagement, talent attraction and retention follow. Climate and culture surveys will eventually show it.

3. **Silo mentality**
   Departments stick to their silos and say things like, "This is my part, that is your part. Let's not step on anyone's toes." You can almost see the fault lines between departments, people, resources, and processes. Sometimes they are manifested by departments separated by different floors, buildings, offices, equipment, and dress codes. Functional processes within departments might run smoothly, but processes that involve two or more departments tend to stall.

4. **Blame game**
   There is a blame game between departments about who is not doing their job. Management team members also play the blame game with each other. If they have a good excuse, they believe they can get away with any failure. Most of the time a good enough excuse involves putting the blame on someone else.

5. **Things get personal**
   Interactions might sometimes get too personal, resulting in defensiveness and paranoia. Management team members think and say to each other, "You are doing this to *me*. You are preventing *me* from reaching *my* goals and implementing *my* projects. You are causing *me* to fail."

6. **Rough Communication**
   Communication styles get rough. Some executive team members might resort to bullying and raising their

voice (literally or metaphorically) to get their way. They are just mimicking you, the Command Mode leader.

7. **Disrespect**
   Rude behavior can turn into outright disrespectful behavior. When there is no witness, one-to-one interactions might overstep boundaries. Discussions in the executive team become disrespectful.

8. **Deception**
   Executive team members don't openly discuss issues. Whenever the CEO puts forth a topic that needs thorough examination, it doesn't happen. Discussions are superficial because managers seek the solution that will please their boss or the evidence that proves someone else is to blame.

9. **Lies**
   Executive team members lie to each other about numbers, deliverables, and KPIs. They make up the numbers to look good. Middle managers know everybody is lying to everybody else in the executive team. They get requests to prepare made-up numbers to present to the executive level. They hear, "This information is for our department only." Or they get involved in actively falsifying their activities, projects, and results, when they present them to other departments or to the CEO.

10. **Boycott**
    Management team members openly invite others to boycott other departments' processes, projects, and ideas. They tell their teams something like, "Those guys from [insert other department] are saying that we are [insert negative comment]. Let's show them that they cannot work without us."

11. **Sabotage**
    Management team members don't bother to tell each other what they can do better. When they see others are going to make a mistake, they wait for their colleagues' mistakes to profit from them.

12. **Credibility loss**
    Executive level leadership loses credibility by the day. You don't know about it, because you don't ask. You just say what needs to get done.

Involvement mode

Anne was given the job of revamping a fifty-year-old brand management company representing over thirty brands in the modern trade channel, for both import and export. Its results had been slowing down for some time, and the last three years had been stagnant.

When she joined, she had several actions on her to-do list. In her first initiative, she spoke individually with all sixty people managers of the company. She interviewed three levels of reporting to get input on their view of what the company had been so far, what was good enough to continue, and what needed urgent repair. She also took the chance to learn about current processes, decision making criteria, and business priorities. She asked a lot of probing questions.

Equipped with all this information, she understood what to delegate to whom. She personally explained to each director what she expected of them and how her view of the company's future connected with what they had just told her. She then gave them room to decide the best course of action on the way to reach the Vision. Setting up clear checkpoints, she would interfere minimally with the process.

She went on to create workshops for departmental teams to reflect on how they could improve ways of working and continuously change the company. Anne used the outcomes of these workshops to provide feedback for the top directors on how much their actions were meeting the targets.

This is the mode I call Involvement. You involve people in your decisions to engage them.

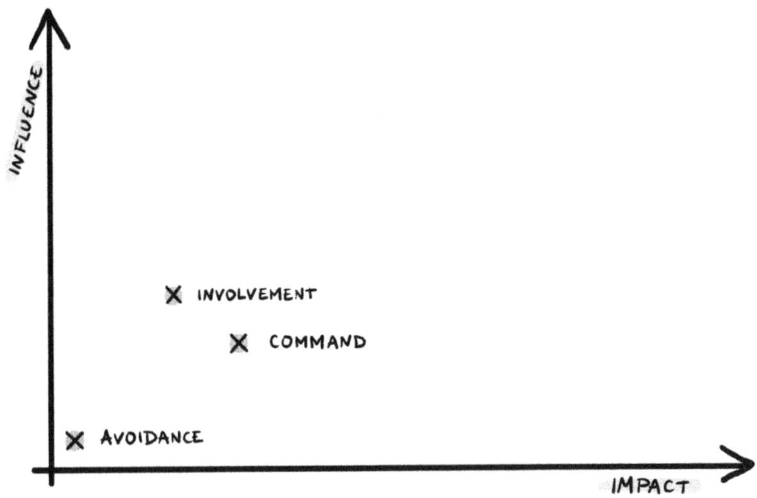

Figure 3 – CEO Involvement behavior mode

Involvement is the opposite of Command Mode. In Command Mode, the leader's impact is higher than the influence, as shown in Figure 3. The Involvement Mode behavior is *higher in influence* and *lower in impact.* When you involve team members in decision making, you are influencing their perception and behavior. However, allowing them to decide the how of execution, as this mode implies, leads to lower impact levels when the team is not structured around a common purpose.

You know you are in involvement mode when:

1. You believe that people must participate to buy into the decisions.
2. You empower people individually to make decisions at their level. You involve your executive team members in defining the "what" and the "how" of strategy. You

encourage them to do the same with their direct reports. You trust that better strategies will emerge from this.

3. You believe your executive team members can deal with most of the business issues, so you give them a considerable degree of freedom to act. They tend to use it within the functional space defined by their job, not so much trying things outside of those borders.
4. You delegate to motivate people to perform their jobs well. You believe that empowerment is intrinsically good, and that most if not all people will appreciate it and grow.
5. You work mostly on a one-to-one basis with your executive team members. You feel they are easy to manage as individuals, but not so much as a team. Communication, commitment, and cohesion in management team meetings are not as productive and efficient as you wish.
6. You want people to understand your ideas and concepts. You educate them by sharing your experience and information about the company, industry, and the market.
7. You focus on getting the relationship with each of them right so that they can motivate themselves to do the job.

You value:

When you are in Involvement Mode you place a lot of value on the motivation of your executive team members and other leadership levels. You believe that this is required for them to give their best.

The usual consequences of the involvement mode are:

1. **Personal agendas**
   Personal agendas are driving one-to-one relationships. No clear, pre-defined team agenda shapes the common

experience of personal relationships. Therefore, power plays exist, although your executive team members are less outspoken and confrontational than in the Command Mode. They tend to be more manipulative and create alliances behind the scenes.

2. **Domination/Withdrawal**
   You might get very different levels of participation because you leave a lot of room for individual motivation, competence, intelligence, influence, and power. The levels of those things vary in the team. This is evident in team meetings when you ask for clear input into decisions. You get mostly one of two answers: *domination* or *withdrawal*. Domination happens when one of the team members puts an idea forward and no one dares to confront it, even when there are some aspects obviously impracticable or false. When this person ranks higher on those dimensions of domination, a dispute might end badly for the challenger. Withdrawal can happen for many reasons as a consequence of Involvement Mode. It usually exists because you as general manager or CEO don't provide a safe context for the team members perceived as having lower ranking to contribute.

3. **Inefficiency**
   Executive team meetings become inefficient because of the lack of a clear team agenda for what needs to get done and how. Involvement Mode has a negative impact on clarity of roles and deliverables.

4. **Reduced delivery**
   Business commitments don't get delivered. Projects, tasks, and activities decided in management team meetings require a strict follow-up by the CEO to be delivered.

5. **Only you see the future**
   As Involvement Mode is focused on one-to-one relationships, only *you* are expected to see the global picture of the company, the maximum benefit for all. It is still your job to connect the dots and draw an image of where you are headed and what needs to get done to make it happen.

Operating mode

James is a high-potential General Manager of a multinational operating in 60 countries. He managed regional operations of big countries, then national operations of small countries, and when I met him, he had been appointed General Manager of the company's operations in a very profitable mid-sized country of his multinational.

Coming from the UK, James knew he faced a business and social culture quite different from his own. He also knew that he was going to manage a highly productive team, already established through three years of working together, and accustomed to getting praise for their business results.

Nevertheless, the company's strategy had to change to adapt fast to unexpected market changes of the previous year, and he knew that a culture change needed to follow in order to deliver what was expected from the executive team under the new strategy.

The question was how to go about it without losing the good things already in place in the company. How could he change the required processes without breaking the team spirit? How could he convince an already self-convinced team that they need to do things differently?

James decided to focus on the team processes to get there. By addressing the coordination, communication, decision making, conflict management, and other processes of the team's functioning, he expected them to realize that they needed to make changes in the team's functioning to generate the required changes in the company's functioning.

This is the mode I call Operating. You focus on getting team processes right, either to standardize results or to change them.

Operating Mode is on the *middle* of the graph. It is a combination of average levels of influence and impact to reach team goals, as seen in Figure 4.

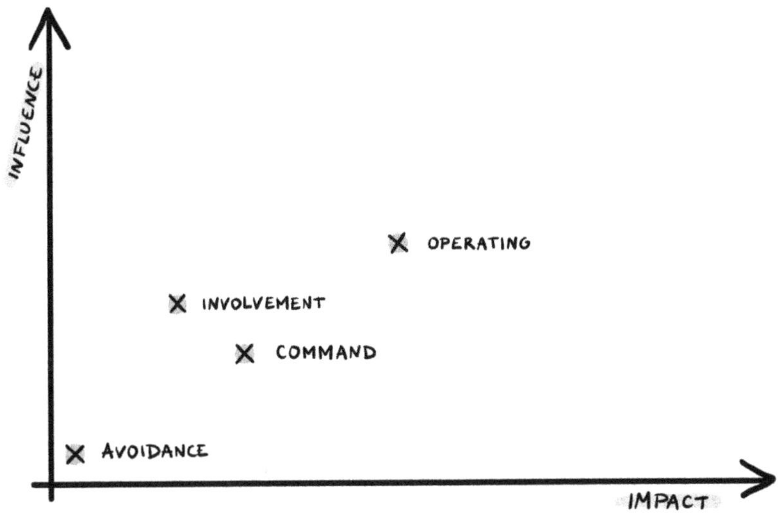

Figure 4 – CEO Operating behavior mode

You know you are in operating mode when:

1. You focus on team processes and operating principles to get your management team to perform. You make individual roles as clear as possible; together you establish rules of engagement.
2. You do your best to keep team meetings efficient. Time and process management are your focus.
3. You invest your personal time in mediating conflicts in the team. You try to keep the team from falling apart by keeping conflict manageable.

4. You bring the team to outdoor activities, bootcamps, and team-building experiences so the team members learn more about each other and how they overcome difficulties. You expect that this will translate into a better team experience and performance.
5. You hone your communication skills; you understand that communication is paramount to engagement. You encourage your management team members to do the same.
6. Relationships are cordial. People in the management team can productively speak to each other.
7. You give the team members feedback and they can give each other feedback within the scope of what needs to be delivered, but less on what needs to be created or on personal relationships level.
8. As a CEO you hear mostly positive things about your actions, decisions, and ideas. But somehow things don't move in the right direction fast enough.

You value:

When you are in Operating Mode, you place a lot of value on creating a common experience for your management team. You believe that a common experience (based in common rules and procedures) is the basis for a good team performance.

The usual consequences of operating mode are:

1. **Performance focus**
   The team is good at problem solving at the current level of performance and system maintenance. They are not so good at solving problems that require end-to-end systemic thinking and cross-functional collaboration.

2. **Functional trust**
   There is trust between team members, but trust is functional, not personal. They trust other team members'

functional expertise and capability, but not necessarily that the team will support their individual needs.

3. **Effectiveness plateau**
   Team effectiveness is good but tends to stay on a plateau. There are no major improvements in team effectiveness for a while; the team does not see the need for them. The level of satisfaction with current team results seems difficult to overcome. You see signs of complacency in the attitude of several team members.

4. **Resistance to change**
   Change triggers a considerable level of resistance. When you need to change existing processes or technology cross-functionally, you hear that people are happy with current levels of performance. They define a lot of "impossibilities" to change. They just don't want to jeopardize the current levels of performance of "their" departments.

5. **Task focused improvement**
   You take team time to reflect together about team performance. Most post-event discussions and action plans focus on what needs to get done and improved (tasks, activities, processes), not on how to create a more effective executive team dynamic to generate better outcomes.

6. **Individual excellence**
   Individuals are competency benchmarked in their fields of expertise, but the team is not a benchmark of a world class team in their industry or beyond. Somehow the team underperforms when compared to the individual competencies. You would expect bigger team power from such individually competent players.

7. **Lack of benchmark**
   Although performance is ok, your management team is not aware of how much it could still improve. They are unaware of the gap because there is no clear benchmark to compare against. You still did not convince them that an excellent team is achievable and that you have not gotten there yet.

Achievement mode

Kathy is the Regional VP of Operations of a pharmaceutical company in Switzerland. She supervises a cluster of nine countries, whose General Managers report to her. To create a team with individuals in this type of situation might be considered too big a challenge for most.

When Kathy joined the company directly to this position, she started out by listening to all of them. She then went on to define a common Purpose and Vision for what they would aim to achieve in the following three years in their cluster of countries. She discussed and worked through the coordination, communication and decision-making processes of the team to make it happen.

As the first signs of conflict between team members surfaced in operations, she managed to deal with them in a way that the team could learn how to avoid the same or similar type of problems in the future. She kept her general managers focused on how they could reach the individual results *and* support the team to achieve the common Vision and live the Purpose.

She always pushed forward an agenda for people development. First, the development of her team, then the individual development of the General Managers, and ultimately the whole region through them. This continuous development agenda started paying off and gradually she needed to intervene less and less.

Results of her cluster followed. Product launches were best in class and the company moved up in market share of its specialties in all the countries she managed.

All of this was done with minimal external support by me. I had worked with Kathy for over six years before that. It all started when she was the General Manager of another company in an European country. We did extensive work together to structure the team she managed then to boost company results under a difficult market situation.

When she was promoted to the current position she kept in mind the process we had followed before and adapted it to her current situation, only requiring sporadic inputs from me at critical points.

This is the mode I call Achievement. You know how to create an effective Chief Executive Team and you are delivering on it (see Figure 5).

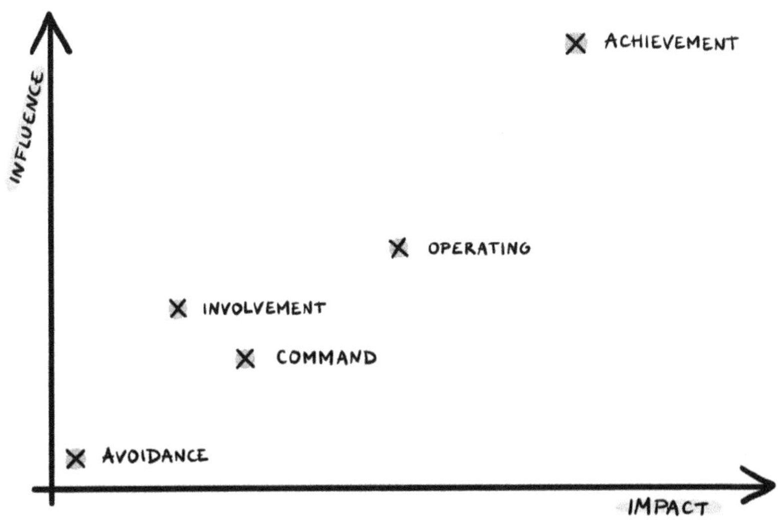

Figure 5 – CEO Achievement behavior mode

The best possible results, combining influence and impact, come from Achievement Mode. It is both high on influence and impact.

You know you are in achievement mode when:

1. Team members trust each other's competencies and intentions. They trust your capability to drive the company and that you will appropriately support them in performing their job and evolving to the next level of their career. You trust your team members individually and the team.
2. The team outperforms in difficult circumstances. This happens especially when no one knows how to deal with a market constraint or unpredictable event. Team members can learn from unstructured information and co-create the knowledge required to achieve success against the odds. They cooperate as a team to achieve it.
3. People in the team feel safe by being who they are. They know they are appreciated with all their rough edges. All their skills are useful on the management team. There is candid sharing ideas and confronting options because no one will take it personally.
4. Discussions can be emotion-based but don't get emotional. Executive team members know how other people will be affected by their decisions. Because they know we are all humans and feel things, they recognize emotions are just another source of information to take into consideration, not the drivers of their behavior.
5. What happens in the executive team meetings stays with the executive team. The team can fiercely discuss differences and data in meetings, but once a decision is reached, everyone will vouch for it. Out of the meeting there is only one voice: the team's voice.
6. People execute what they committed they would do. They deliver on their individual, group, or team's commitments. If needed, they go out of their function, job, department, and expertise to do it.
7. Your executive team is highly regarded in the company (and sometimes even outside) as a benchmark for how

a management team should look. You are respected not only for your team's technical competencies but also for team dynamics, efficiency, effectiveness, and delivery above and beyond their duty. Middle managers and individual contributors feel privileged to report to these leaders because they are inspired to grow personally and professionally.

8. Your executive team members (you included) walk the talk. They focus on their behaviors before asking anyone to act.
9. End-to-end systemic solutions are the default way of thinking in the executive team. When making decisions, it is only natural to think from the client perspective how all processes need to be designed and performed. No one has problems in contributing, challenging, listening to, and integrating ideas from other team members in their own departments.
10. Executive team members do not feel that they "own" the department they manage. They do not feel they have to protect "their people" from other executives' actions.
11. You are honest in communicating with your team. You openly share information about the status of the company. People find you inspiring. And you find it inspiring to work with your team members. You feel you learn with them as you go.
12. Your team feels capable of taking on any challenge and winning. The level of satisfaction and engagement in the team is very high. Everyone is proud to belong.
13. Your level of achievement is unrivalled in the company. There is a notion that you are writing a chapter of the company's history together.

You value:

When you are in Achievement Mode, you place most value on creating a new reality for your company with your executive team. You believe that a common vision for the future is key for higher performance of the team. You have defined and are creating a legacy. You know how to structure and motivate the team to achieve it.

The usual consequences of achievement mode are:

This one is easy. When you are in achievement mode, you should be collecting all the benefits that research demonstrates come with a fully effective Chief Executive Team. Everything I described in Chapter 1, as the positive financial, innovation, engagement, etc., results in the company should be happening to you because of Achievement Mode.

Crossing the line, from the push zone to the pull zone

This chapter describes CEO behavior modes in a sequence increasing in influence and impact. They are not stages or phases in the actions taken by the top leader. Rather, they are discrete modus operandi that anyone can choose to use.

Some CEOs stick to one mode all their lives. This mode is comfortable because they are good at that leadership behavior. Also, they stay in the position within the company if that leadership behavior works. When the behavior stops producing the desired results, they move to another company that can best profit from their favorite modus operandi and reward them accordingly.

Other leaders move back and forth between two or three styles depending on the company, circumstances, and team members' profiles. They adjust to the situation and can balance between modes, although they might have a preferred one. Typically, they move between Command, Involvement, and Operating Modes.

Few CEOs manifest all the modes during their professional lives. After all, belief systems underly these action modes, and we all tend to reject what we don't believe in.

My experience as an advisor shows that once CEOs lead a team in Achievement Mode and get the full return on their time and effort, they don't want to go back to any other mode. They might have to, in some circumstances. They can, if needed. But they will try to revert to Achievement Mode whenever possible.

The reason is simple.

Evidence shows that the impact on the organization of competence and leadership style of the CEO can be neutralized or enhanced by the executive team's functioning. Some forms of influence are more effective than others in creating the desired impact.

When you are in Avoidance Mode, you have no influence on how the whole organization perceives and integrates your individual competence and style. You deliberately avoid influencing your management team members. The consequence of this is low impact on the team's performance and zero influence on the image of you that gets amplified to the rest of the organization.

When you are in Command Mode, your impact is higher, but you are not driving people through influence. You command them. And they usually don't give their best efforts when you are not controlling. The image of you that the rest of the organization gets is of a harsh manager, hardly a leader.

Involvement Mode, on the other hand, increases influence. You focus on getting people to understand your view of the situation. But your impact tends to decrease compared to Command Mode. As you centralize less and manage through each individual management team member, you less directly control the impact on the company. Employees might get an image of you as a good not very competent person.

There is a line that separates *average* impact and influence from *high* impact and influence.

When you adopt Operating Mode by focusing on getting the basic team processes right, you already cross this line. Operating Mode marks the threshold of high influence/high impact zone (see Figure 6).

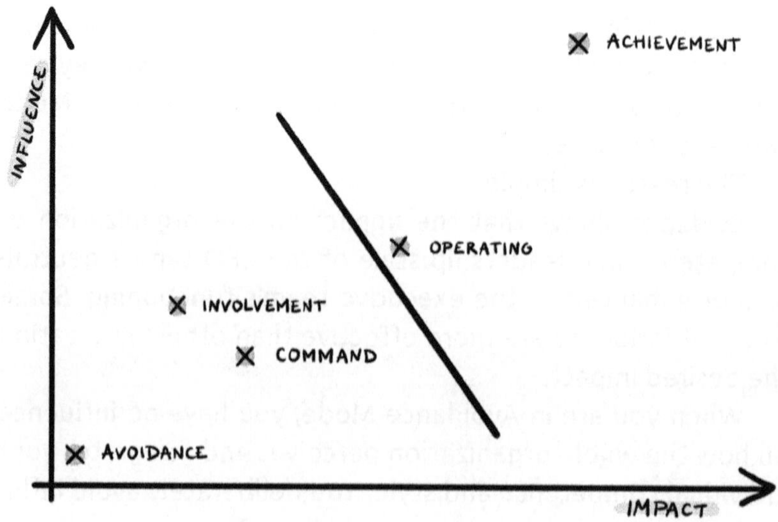

Figure 6 – The line between average and high impact and influence

When you are on the left side of the line, all strategies you might use as a CEO have two characteristics:

1. You do them.
2. Your management team can easily neutralize them.

You command, you involve, you choose to avoid and not be clear. It is all about you, you, you. Nothing gets done unless you do something. Your individual style drives the leadership style of the company, either permissive or directive.

I call this the *push zone*. You do the work. The executive team follows. Some people think this is what leadership is about, but they are selling themselves short. You can get much more out of your team's capabilities by being on the right side of this line.

In the *pull zone* you set the direction and create the circumstances for success. The team creates the reality, delivers on the strategy, manages the culture, honestly reports the numbers, and creates a legacy of true leadership (see Figure 7).

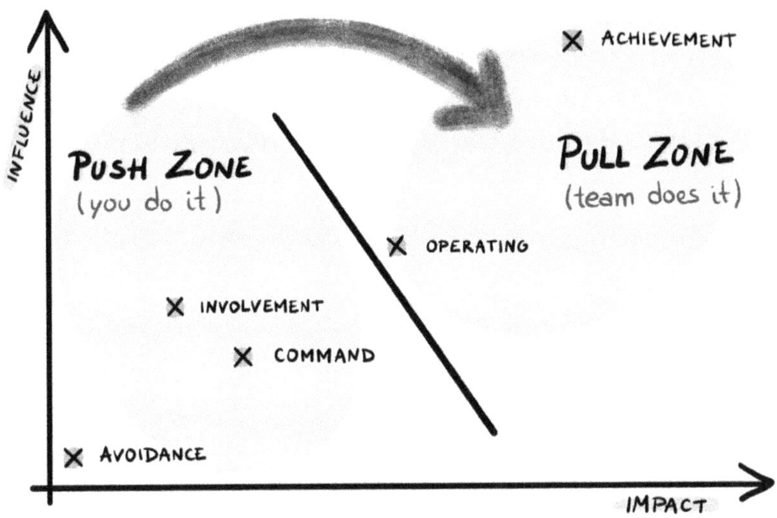

Figure 7 – Moving from the push zone to the pull zone

Bridging the gap from Operating Mode to Achievement Mode is easiest with structured help from an outside advisor skilled in understanding and supporting the necessary behavior changes.

As a leader, you want to cross the line and experience the initial level of release that you get in Operating Mode, but you really want to be in Achievement Mode. That is where world class teams produce results that other executive teams are unable to achieve. That is where you as a leader can expand the horizons of what you and everyone around you think is possible.

This book is about showing you the way to get there. But first let's look at how much it costs you to be on the push zone, the low influence/impact side of the line that divides the behavior modes.

3

YOU WILL PAY THE PRICE

"Coaching with Ricardo was instrumental in getting an external view on several topics for me as a manager and leader. The coaching was methodical, non-emotional, and helped me to put things in perspective to figure out the best approach. Not only to see the options but also to practice them. Insights from the coaching sessions come alive in the relevant situations and change happens."

– Sylvia Lin | Sanofi-Pasteur Portugal | Managing Director

I AM WRITING this chapter right in the middle of the Covid-19 pandemic. As pharma companies and government-funded institutes worldwide look for a vaccine to stop the virus, or at least an effective drug to fight it, we see the world going crazy.

Political and health authorities in many countries make and reverse decisions concerning what their citizens should be doing. Wear masks; don't wear masks. Keep social distancing to stop spreading; aim for herd immunity, and get everyone infected as fast as possible. The virus is harmless; the virus is dangerous. Lockdown kills the economy; lockdown saves the economy.

A lot of information is missing, distorted, and omitted. Many of us don't know where to get reliable references to guide our behavior. Fear and uncertainty set in as we witness disorganization, confusion, random decisions, mindless political fights, and social unrest. This is chaos.

To deal with the chaos we look for leaders—people who can tell us what to do, who will reassure us that all will be fine if we do the right things, and explain to us what we should do.

The antidote to chaos is leadership. Leadership protects us from chaos. But it needs to be effective.

Effective leaders make sense of a chaotic world, produce and support the right decisions, learn to adjust their actions, keep the organization focused and productive, protect their people, and ensure that all will become better human beings in the process.

The antidote to chaos is leadership. Leadership protects us from chaos.

The difficulty in complex, crisis or chaotic situations is one person can't figure out all those things in isolation. To deal with the world in the state it exists today, we need to have collective leadership at the top of companies and organizations. The collective intelligence of our best minds helps us win in dire times and thrive in easier moments.

In Chapter 1 – *The Elephant in the Room* – I addressed the gains companies can achieve by implementing effective executive teams. Although management research pinpoints more dimensions of impact than the ones I mentioned, I focused on the three main areas that CEOs are most concerned with: financial, innovation, and engagement key performance indicators (KPIs).

All variables referred to in these company performance areas are correlated to one or several dimensions of executive team performance. Some are even causally connected, meaning that research connected variations in executive teams' dynamics with subsequent variations in the company's KPIs.

If we increase the effectiveness of the executive team, we increase the return on sales. If we increase trustworthiness of the management team, we increase middle managers' job satisfaction.

CEOs and other executives managing top management teams may minimize the importance of effective team leadership for several reasons. The most important is they are unaware of how much money is squandered by leading solo and centralizing processes. This is understandable. They are not up to date with the research that counts lost money, as I addressed in Chapter 1 – *The Elephant in the Room*.

But apart from team inefficiencies that drain value from the company, CEOs are usually unaware of their personal costs. Each of the behavior modes I described in Chapter 2 – *It's Happening on Your Shift* – has a different impact on how the rest of the organization sees the top leader. These costs might be hidden, often ignored, but are always present.

We look at them in this chapter.

What executives value

Why are you a top manager? What do you most enjoy about it? You honed your management skills on the way up, taking the pain, and enjoying the good times. But there was always something about managing people, departments, companies that was intrinsically good. Even when times were tough, you considered being a manager as a bonus, an opportunity, the good side of the deal, the best part of your job. What was it?

Most of the CEOs I coach answer this question with a combination of specific motivations.

Impact

Top executives

- like to make decisions and find it meaningful to determine others' direction, of circumstances, projects, and organizations.
- enjoy action, easily assuming responsibility for decisions that make them and their companies grow.
- tend to work more than most around them.
- like to make their contribution and leave a personal mark in whatever they do.
- mostly try to avoid feeling helpless in the face of circumstances, which would negate their values.
- want to make a difference.

Competitiveness runs through their blood. Top executives want to be the best in their trade, job, or company. Whatever they get into, they want to beat everyone else to the finish line. They enjoy putting out the effort and taking the pain when they see they can get ahead. Some of them are overachievers who compete with a worse version of themselves. Triumph is the prize and they don't shy away from conflict. Discussion, argument, and dispute are part of the responsibilities and even enjoyable. Top CEOs see company results as the evidence they are winners.

Top executives want to drive how others work and live. They are all about impact. As Steve Jobs put it: "I want to make a ding in the Universe." Pure impact is the power to change others and circumstances, globally.

Pure impact is the power to change others and circumstances, globally.

Oprah Winfrey influences millions through her role as a billionaire media mogul. She completed a multimillion-dollar deal with Apple to create original programming. Her

Leadership Academy in South Africa lifts 1,000 girls out of extreme poverty. Oprah donates millions to charitable causes ranging from hurricane relief to UNICEF.[27]

Another example of a person with a huge impact is Muhammad Yunus, who was born in Bangladesh. He founded the Grameen Bank to grant poor people small loans on easy terms (micro-credit). From Dr. Yunus' personal loan of small amounts of money to destitute basket weavers in Bangladesh in the mid-70s, the Grameen Bank has advanced to the forefront of a burgeoning world movement toward eradicating poverty through microlending. Replicas of the Grameen Bank model operate in more than 100 countries worldwide. Along with Grameen Bank, Yunus received the 2006 Nobel Peace Prize for his work to create "economic and social development from below."[28] This is a huge impact.

Outstanding leaders are all about impact. The world will be different because of their actions.

Consider Elon Musk, the South African-born billionaire who became a millionaire at age 27 when he sold his first company to Compaq for $305 million. Since then, he has created businesses in online banking and financial services (ultimately named PayPal), space travel, automotive, and underground transportation[29]. Do you think he cares for the impact he makes in the world?

Outstanding leaders are all about impact. The world will be different because of their actions. This difference is not by chance; it is the outcome of clear intention and drive. Their chosen areas for impact and the specific goals they pursue may be defined in many ways: social, organizational, technological, entrepreneurial or any other. But in any case, the impact is the name of the game.

Leadership

Tyler Perry, the founder of Madea films, has earned more than $500 million and produces TV shows. He fulfilled his dreams by opening the 330-acre Tyler Perry Studios in Atlanta. After working on Hollywood movies where he was the only black person on set, he hires diverse crews. They include people who previously have not had a shot in this business. Many of his staffers at his studio are former inmates and drug addicts. He supports causes such as education and women's rights through his Tyler Perry Foundation, and plans to build a compound for battered women, trafficked children, and LGBTQ youth whose parents ejected them from home. He is leading the way to include those communities in society[30].

It is essential to a CEO to positively influence others and be perceived as an influencer of the largest number of people possible. This does not mean that you must be a blatant extrovert, or that you must impose your voice and style above everything else. Instead, it is about being recognized as someone who brings meaning and transformation to the organization, market, or society at large, as Perry is doing.

Effective leaders organize the action of their teams and galvanize their motivation by structuring the chaos of the business world into understandable and manageable chunks of information-to-action.

Effective leaders organize the action of their teams and galvanize their motivation by structuring the chaos of the business world into understandable and manageable chunks of information-to-action. They give direction in the face of change and uncertainty.

Also, influential leaders want to influence people outside their organization. Congregating efforts in the direction of the desired outcome is appealing for them.

Through experience, they understand that they cannot get anything relevant done unless they attract people to their cause and mobilize them to action. A lot of them genuinely care about people and do not see them just as numbers. They want to influence the professional and sometimes the personal development of their employees, colleagues, and partners. And these leaders want to be recognized by the entire company or community as the person who achieved it.

For the majority of CEOs I coach, being the person who transforms people's lives is fundamental.

Position

Tracey Armstrong started as a 21-year-old clerk at Copyright Clearance Center and is currently the CEO. In her spare time, Tracey wrote a marketing brochure when she was a clerk. The marketing department used it and consequently gave her more projects. Tracey achieved recognition for her involvement in managing a big project, which led to the success of the company. And she moved up. She says, "The only boundaries you have are the boundaries you set for yourself."[31]

Leaders don't want to be just a face in the crowd. Standing out is not an option; it's a necessity.

Ronald E. Daley started as a proof-reader at RR Donnelley when he was 17. When he performed it so well that he found it boring, he got promoted to production coordinator, becoming the first African American in that job. He was able to take over a money-losing unit and, within two years, make it profitable. He applied the root cause analysis methods he learned in his colleges. Ronald finished his career as CEO of Oce' USA Holding.[32]

Position matters. The alpha person in an organization is in a distinctive position, a symbol of achievement. In general terms, CEOs care about their reputation, both professional and social. Leaders don't want to be just a face in the crowd. Standing out is not an option; it's a necessity. The alternative is living somewhere down the social or organizational scale. CEOs tend to compare the value they attribute to themselves and others and strive to be on the higher end of the scale.

The specific title of a position matters. "President" is always better than "Director". "Board Member" is higher rank than "General Manager". A director title trumps a manager one. Sometimes you see this motivation in the new hire who negotiates the position title as part of agreeing to accept a position.

Talented people want clear professional growth. They need to progress and moving up the hierarchy is a clear mark of that. If belonging to the executive team is a matter of politics instead of talent, they will be out.

Ambitious, competitive top managers value a progression of significant titles and solid companies on the way up. They want to have the formal acknowledgment they won and occupied a more powerful position each time they moved up the corporate ladder.

Talented people want clear professional growth.

The costs of each behavior mode

Impact, leadership, and position are the three motivations I see more often in leaders at top companies. It's easy to understand why. You need to possess a fair degree of *each* quality to generate the stamina and grit to manage a company.

Climbing the corporate ladder requires a lot of dedication, effort, trade-offs, and losses. This is appealing to those who care about the impact they make, their position, or their leadership because having the CEO position will reward them with ample opportunities.

If you don't care about impact, leadership, and position, you will not find the hard work on the way up appealing. It is because you get those benefits on the way up that the effort and trade-offs become acceptable.

Each of the five behavior modes of the CEO I explained in Chapter 2 – *It's Happening on Your Shift* – has a different effect on these three motivators. The highest level of impact is reached when the top manager is functioning within the Achievement Mode. The other four modes lag at different levels.

Your current *cost* is the difference between the maximum impact, leadership, and position you can achieve and the current one you have. This is what you are losing today.

Compare each of the behavior modes of the CEO for their effect on the three desired outcomes of impact, leadership, and position (see Figure 8).

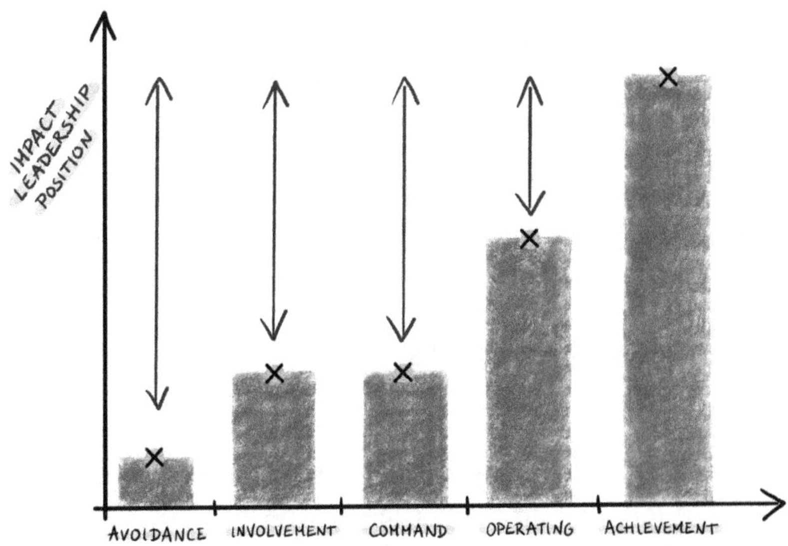

Figure 8 – Different costs of each behavior mode

Avoidance mode costs

Impact

When you are in **avoidance mode,** your impact is low. You are withholding your impact by avoiding dealing directly with the inefficiencies of the management team. This avoidance mode hampers the possibility of becoming the best at what you do, winning the competition, and leaving a personal mark on the company or the market.

Leadership

Understandably, as you are not influencing people to guide their behavior in a specific direction, others will not see you as a leader. At the top level, this means that you will be considered weak and powerless. All other top managers drive their agendas, imposing their style to their departments, and making their decisions their way.

Imagine the confusion this creates. Employees of your company question your effectiveness because there is no common approach, language to describe leadership or even a common corporate culture.

Avoidance behavior mode has the *most significant negative impact and leadership gap* compared to a fully effective executive team. This gap is your cost in Avoidance Mode.

Involvement mode costs

Impact

As you can see in the graph in Figure 8, the Involvement Mode costs are identical in magnitude to the ones of Command Mode, although their relative distribution is different. What you gain in leadership Involvement Mode, by involving your direct reports one-to-one in the decision-making process, you lose impact by not driving a common agenda and approach. There needs to be some clear boundaries to what we are achieving together. Top leaders in Involvement Mode are usually not setting boundaries.

The top leader's impact is severely affected in Involvement Mode due to not setting clear, visible, and agreed ways to reach the vision. There are no boundaries or achievement standards. Even though the top leaders might be leading with boundaries and standards as part of their one-on-one interactions, the *team* has no shared vision of what they are set to achieve in the short or long term. There is no joint agreement about how they want to transform the company. Also, the team operating processes are inefficient, which creates a misalignment among the team members about what and how to communicate down the hierarchy.

Leadership

The leadership aspect of the Involvement Mode is where this behavior is different from the Operating or Achievement Mode. CEOs who use this mode understand the need to involve their direct reports and choose to do this on a one-to-one basis. This makes the team more manageable. In one-to-one relationships, you get to know the other person better. People open more.

As an Involvement Mode leader, you can choose a leadership style and management approach totally adapted to the person you are dealing with. There is no fear that you need to be congruent and do the same with someone else who requires a different approach.

The advantage of this mode is its flexibility in dealing with and influencing individuals' needs. But this is also its biggest drawback. As you assume different leadership styles and action types with each person individually, the team does not know how to figure out what you stand for. This has the potential to create mistrust and, at the very least, to put your direct reports in defensive mode. After all, they do know that you behave differently with each of them. Your leadership is perceived as *volatile*.

Command mode costs

Impact

When you are in **Command Mode,** you *moderately* increase impact in comparison to avoidance. You are driving your style and decisions throughout the organization. This seems to be desirable, right? Why are the impact and leadership levels so low in the graph of Figure 8?

The dimension of impact may be all right. You might be technically competent and know a lot about business and the specifics of the industry. But as I explained in Chapter 1, the increasing complexity of the business world requires that an effective *team* of competent people collaborate to understand the market and design the most adaptive strategies to deal with it.

Making your company the best at what it does requires that you consider all options, possibilities, and drawbacks of each scenario to mitigate unforeseen risks. For this to happen, the Command Mode manager must recognize the need to include other competent people in the decision-making process.

Therefore, the impact of Command behavior mode is lower than most people expect. No one can know all the answers to all the business problems, no matter how good they are. Unless a completely incompetent executive team surrounds you, they should be adding to the solutions. And you should be multiplying the possibilities of that happening.

Leadership

The Command Mode leader requires that decision making be centralized, instead of delegated. You lose leadership effectiveness; people might fear you. They will obey you. And they will adhere to your dictates. They would protect themselves from the possibility of failure, as usually there's punishment associated with Command Mode.

Therefore, the company will not innovate, and employees will not develop professionally or personally. They will perceive you as a tough manager, not a leader. Employees in a rule-driven environment may give you lip service and strictly follow the rules. Still, their commitment to the business lasts only until they have an opportunity to take a position with a different and better-managed company or department. In a full-employment economy, this kind of turnover can be devastating.

The (not so) hidden position costs of the previous modes

As you noticed, the Avoidance, Command, and Involvement Mode descriptions above do not address the costs associated with the position.

Position costs tend to become quite visible. When something goes wrong, losing your position means losing your job. You are downgraded. You descend in the organizational and social scale. It's not fun; it's painful.

I have supported several CEOs in these dark phases. One of them told me during a coaching session, "It seemed as if suddenly I became invisible. People were not willing to pick up the phone or call back. They were less available for social interactions. People I considered friends left me."

Another confided: "My marriage started breaking down after I lost my job. Was this the main cause? Probably not, but it uncovered the real cause of why it was not working in the first place. We had a relationship based on titles. We were living this myth of the successful couple and then I failed to keep up with it."

Losing your job is one of the most stressful events in life. It can provoke anxiety, depression, unwanted weight loss or gain, and sleep disorders, among other symptoms. Our identity and sense of worth are quite connected to the work we do.

Having a job makes it easier for others to find points of connection and relate to us. A title and its ranking are easy ways to categorize people. They also give good indications of what and how much to invest in a relationship with that person, because they set the bar for what and how much to expect from it.

Most people don't consciously assess the value of others with a calculator before speaking to them. But we do have ways to convey the "value" of someone socially. Terms define a specific measure, such as "This is a high net-worth individual", "She is worth x billion dollars."

Why you might lose your job

Position matters, professionally speaking. Losing your job hurts your career, your bank account, and your relationships. To understand how your executive team can help you reduce your position costs, we first need to look at how those costs come about.

CEOs lose their jobs mainly for two reasons: ethical breaches and poor company performance.

Ethical breaches

The Washington Post reports that 39% of CEO firings in 2018 were due to ethical lapses, 35% were due to financial performance, and 13% resulted from conflicts with the company's board. That breakdown is very different than previous findings. For example, as the *Post* points out, at the height of the crisis in 2008, 52% of CEO dismissals were due to financial performance, 35% were due to board conflicts, and 10% were due to misconduct.[33]

Ethical problems are *increasing* as a source of position loss. In their *Strategy & 2016 CEO Success Study,* Price Waterhouse Coopers[34] found the bigger the company, the higher the likelihood the CEO was fired for ethical lapses. And 2018 results show for the first time in the study's history, more CEOs were dismissed for ethical lapses than for financial performance or board struggles.[35]

Consider the famous cases, like Carlos Gosn, Nissan CEO, who was arrested in 2018 and charged for hiding $140 million from investors, using company funds for private purposes, and underreporting his remuneration by around ¥9 billion ($85 million) over eight years.[36,37]

The Sackler family, owner of Purdue Pharma, misrepresented the addictive power of their opioid drug in their marketing efforts, and both made a profit from and fuelled the American opioid crisis. This led to Purdue filing for bankruptcy in September 2019 amid lawsuits and claims for a payment of $10-$12 billion.[38]

Volkswagen's CEO Herbert Diess, chairman Hans Dieter Poetsch, and former CEO Martin Winterkorn were hit with criminal charges in September 2019 for allegedly waiting to tell investors about the automaker's rampant emissions cheating. According to the allegations, the Volkswagen group sold 11 million diesel vehicles that polluted far more than regulations allowed, a scandal that's since become known as Dieselgate.[39]

The massive German automaker masked this fact by installing software on the cars that recognized when they were being put through emissions testing. During these tests, the vehicles would restrict their emissions enough to comply with regulations. But when they were back on the road, they polluted nitrogen oxide at up to 40 times more than the allowed levels.[40]

The Volkswagen "Dieselgate" case cost the company over $30 billion and involved several of its highest-ranking executives from several of its car makes. They were charged with market manipulation connected with a diesel emissions scandal, false certification, and criminal advertising practices.[39]

Elizabeth Holmes, CEO and founder of Theranos, and former Theranos president Sunny Balwani, were charged in 2018 by the U.S. Department of Justice with nine counts of wire fraud and two conspiracy counts to commit wire fraud. These charges stemmed from allegations the two engaged in a scheme to defraud investors and a separate scheme to defraud doctors and patients while at the blood-testing company. The company's shortcomings and inaccuracies of their blood testing technology's ability to perform a full suite of lab tests on a small blood sample were exposed, along with the role Holmes played in covering it all up. Holmes was ousted as CEO, and the company was closed.[41]

Hypocrisy breeds unethical behavior

A study published in 2010 by Joris Lammers and a team of researchers[42] found that as a person's power increases, so does their hypocrisy. They condemn other people's cheating more, while at the same time cheating more themselves. They are also stricter in judging other people's moral transgressions than their own.

It seems as if by moving up the hierarchy ladder, people start believing that what applies to others does not apply to them. These unethical top managers see laws and moral regulations as a must to control everyone else. What they say becomes more divergent from what they do. It seems as if power erodes our sense of what is morally – and even legally – acceptable. "Absolute power corrupts absolutely." Lord Acton.

Consider the case of Mark Hurd, who served as CEO of Hewlett Packard. His aggressive cost-cutting in 2005 resulted in laying off 10% of the workforce, or 15,200 workers, shortly after he assumed office. During the 2009 recession, he imposed a 55% pay cut on all employees and removed many benefits. While he took a base salary pay cut of 20%, the compensation committee increased his bonus by the same amount. During this year, he made a total of $24 million. After an investigation into whether he violated HP's code of business conduct, Hurd resigned his position following claims made by a former contractor (Jodie Fisher). The investigation found that he submitted inaccurate expense accounts, while he did not violate the company's sexual harassment policy.[43]

According to details documented in a letter by Attorney Gloria Allred, HP's board fired Hurd for misusing HP's resources and lying to them about his relationship with Jodie Fisher, an adult movie actress, and reality TV star. Hurd's sudden departure cost HP shareholders billions of dollars in lost stock value and led to multiple lawsuits.[44]

A good executive team protects you and the company from wrongdoings, bad decisions, and poor execution. It reduces the likelihood of ethical breaches because people around you will speak up when they see something that needs to be corrected or not aligned with its values and principles.

Communication about ethical, legal, and moral issues becomes natural as an effective executive team's hallmarks. So also is clarity on acceptable behavior and openness to giving and receiving feedback. People monitor their behavior; they know that being a role model can make or break the company's leadership culture.

If you need to generate more money, you need better management decisions. A Chief Executive Team helps you achieve that.

An effective executive team can help CEOs become self-aware of their own behaviors and align with the company culture, leadership behaviors, and ethical code. After all, we live in a transparent and fully interconnected world. Records of whatever we do are available to anyone, sooner or later. Staying on the ethical side of management is good for business.

Poor company performance

Poor company performance is easier to diagnose and solve than ethical issues. It all boils down to one sentence:

If you need to generate more money, you need better management decisions. A Chief Executive Team helps you achieve that.

The business world is quite simple: your actions either accomplish their purpose or not. And that depends on two things: the quality of your strategy and the quality of its execution. To have a better strategy you need to engage the collective intelligence of your executive team. To have better execution, you need to engage everyone in the company.

In Chapter 1 – *The Elephant in the Room* – I mentioned many gains that a company can generate from having a fully effective and efficient executive team: profitability, productivity, sales growth, market share, operating result, budget compliance, innovation performance, employee engagement, return on assets, return on sales, return on equity, stock performance, and more.

In the end, it's about creating the know-how we need to get things done to be successful and profitable. And in a volatile, complex, and ambiguous market, this requires a Chief Executive Team.

Position costs are higher with the Avoidance, Command, and Involvement Modes because you don't have an effective executive team. Therefore, you get no feedback about the perception, results, and impact of your behavior. These costs are drastically reduced when you move to Operating Mode. There, you will mostly have impact and leadership costs.

Operating mode costs

In Operating Mode your costs decrease substantially as compared to the previous three behavior modes. By focusing the team on what they can achieve through structured processes, you help them solve many of the drawbacks I described above.

When you are in Operating Mode behavior, you impact the management team by structuring their processes and shaping the common agenda of getting things done. You protect the team from chaos and disorder by keeping them focused on productive ways to get things done. As a result, you get them to agree on work processes, rules for time and meeting efficiency, and preferred communication methods. You manage conflict, give feedback, and are clear on what the team needs to progress. And the team starts to provide you with feedback about those same things.

As the team works together by following agreed processes, your voice and actions are amplified down the organization. Therefore, your impact, position, and leadership are increased. This is already a big advantage when compared to previous modes. Your personal cost is as lowest as compared to prior modes. You reduce your cost as you progress to more effective and efficient behavior modes (see Figure 9).

Note how the cost is highest in Avoidance Mode and zero or non-existent in the Achievement Mode.

What is missing in Operating Mode to get it down to zero?

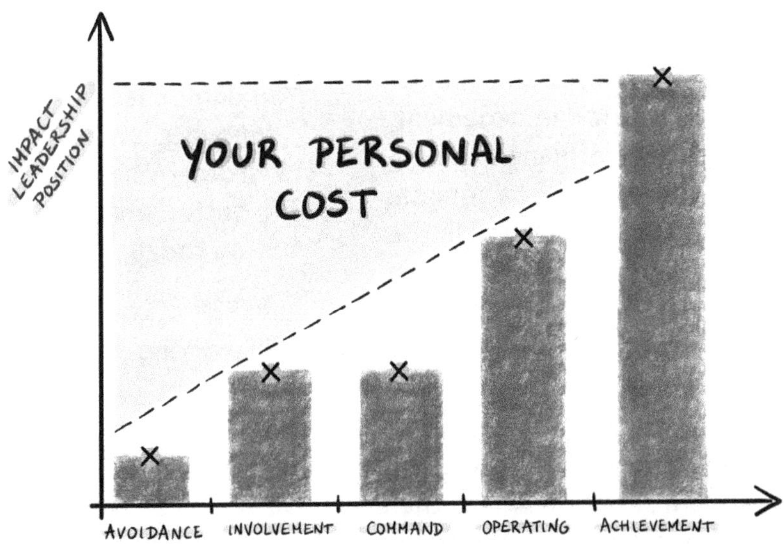

Figure 9 – Your personal cost reduction

Your costs are still relatively high because Operating Mode is about current processes for increasing the team's efficiency. When you focus the team on meeting management, work processes, or communication efficiency, you are getting them to do better what they are doing today. You focus on getting the most out of the current circumstances where the team operates.

This mode's costs are connected to change, innovation, and transformation of the company with and through the management team. You don't change, innovate, and transform by simply doing better what you do today. You need a leap, a stretch, or an almost impossible goal to start with and create the team's right dynamics to achieve it.

This is what you are missing in Operating Mode. This is what you can only get at the Achievement Mode.

Achievement mode costs

In the previous four modes, somehow, the company reaches a plateau, even with a competent management team.

The plateau occurs in results, market presence, innovation, people engagement, or other performance dimensions. You see or feel a colossal challenge forming ahead in the market the executive team does not fully understand, just because the current business model is still working. You know time is running scarce, and the beast needs to be confronted before it starts tearing apart what you have achieved.

You don't change, innovate, and transform by simply doing better what you do today.

Welcome to the future. Achievement Mode is all about creating a situation where the executive team can transform itself while it changes the company. On this journey, you know the starting point. While you also have a vision of the future you want to create for the company, the way to achieve it is through all leadership levels' collaborative efforts, starting right at the executive team.

Your goal is to alter the history of the company and its response to the market. This might mean

- redesigning current processes,
- changing leadership or positions of people,
- challenging attitudes,
- implementing new approaches,
- revamping business models, and
- spreading a new leadership culture.

Achievement Mode is all about creating a situation where the executive team can transform itself while it changes the company.

For this to succeed, you cannot focus on short-term efficiency, which is the only real cost in Achievement Mode. You may notice a momentary lapse of efficiency when you lead the executive team to drive the company to new horizons.

The team can compensate for this in different ways. My clients' most common strategy is to work harder, as they put in the extra time and effort to make something great happen. This is a familiar strategy to top managers and achievers.

In Achievement Mode you can freely use any of the other behavior modes I described above. You may

- choose to *avoid* interference with something.
- *command* the team in getting something done in one specific way.
- *involve* one or several team members individually.
- structure *operating processes* and operating principles of the team.

But you don't stay stuck in any of those modes. They are just situationally-adapted responses to events that require them.

You *can* solve an issue by using avoidance, command, involvement, or operating behaviors in the fulfilment of an Achievement Mode. You are choosing to avoid a specific conflict or use a command to solve a problem. This often happens when the team is stretched to its current limits and is flexibly redesigning its processes to reach an ambitious vision.

For example, you might slip into Command Mode to clearly set the lines if the team has already agreed-upon processes to solve the type of issue that surfaced, assuming the event you face is plainly out of the accepted limits of behavior. Otherwise, you might just let the team deal with it, to see how much they already integrated productive conflict resolution by themselves.

Top managers and executive teams in Achievement Mode transform their leadership techniques as they deal with the challenges. The team members are transforming themselves as they collaborate and learn together how to deal with previously tricky situations. The middle levels of leadership get inspired by the top leaders and are also transformed in the process. The company's potential expands.

The fears of team leadership

In the previous section, I mentioned short-term efficiency as the only *real* cost of Achievement Mode. *Real* was not a spurious word choice. There are imaginary costs in Achievement Mode.

By now, you are familiar with one of the mottos of this book: We have the wrong CEO job description. "Know it all" and "do it all" are not critical success factors. Quite the opposite. Somehow the business world is still delusional about what leadership means. We tend to think these are characteristics of a top leader:

We have the wrong CEO job description. "Know it all" and "do it all" are not critical success factors. Quite the opposite.

- crave being in the spotlight
- speaking loud and over everyone else
- bragging about own achievements

- putting others down
- sticking stubbornly to one's ideas even against new evidence
- being perceived as tough on people

Increasingly, such leaders are being labelled as bullies.

Because bully leaders believe this behavior is acceptable, they fear losing "leadership status" by developing an effective executive team. The truth is that you cannot lose what you don't have.

Leadership is about results, not ego. You might have a great personality and speak well, but if you cannot create the results your company needs, you will be fired. Results are a must. Ego is optional and fraught with landmines. As we've seen so far, having a vast ego can impair leadership effectiveness.

Leadership is about results, not ego. Results are a must. Ego is optional.

Meet Bernard. He is the CEO of a very large family-owned business. He was the first professional manager appointed to the role, after three generations of family members leading the company. As so often happens in these cases, a family can grow in numbers and diversity of interests, competences, and personalities. Therefore, new governance models must be found. Bernard assumed his role when the family realized the need for professional management.

Bernard asked for my help to assist him in his transition to CEO. During our initial meeting, we mapped all his challenges.

- The company had become fat and slow.
- There were established silos.
- The family's brands showed the first signs of losing traction with the new generations of consumers.
- We observed stalled innovation efforts.
- Employees served the boss instead of the customer.

- Indicators showed declining employee engagement.
- It was getting more challenging to attract and keep talent.
- Finger pointing was the norm.
- Everybody was spending too much energy covering their backs instead of getting things done.

Mind you, financial results were good, mostly due to the market share they had been able to grab over the decades and some clever long-term contracts with clients.

Bernard is a visionary, so he could see ahead of the curve. He saw how all these early warning signals were increasing the company's risk. No one seemed to recognize that the company's economic sustainability was at stake. Everybody was happily doing their business as usual because money was still coming in.

During our conversation, it became clear Bernard needed to start creating a new business model and leadership culture, beginning with his direct reports. If nothing got done with the executive team, any change initiative would stall, as was already happening with several cross-departmental projects.

I introduced *The 6P's of Executive Teams®* concept and methodology to him. He was happy to use this structured model to understand his challenges with the executive team, and excited to know and implement the solutions. Bernard asked me for a proposal to include in the strategic plan to present to the supervisory board.

When I next spoke to him, he sounded a bit embarrassed. He said: "Ricardo, thank you for the clear proposal you sent. I know you. I know that your work produces results. This is exactly what the company needs to do right now. But I will not do it. If I start a project like this, immediately after assuming the role, my shareholders will think I don't know how to do my job."

To my surprise, he had not included the project in his strategic plan, having shied away at the last moment. He believed the family shareholders would think he was giving away impact, leadership, and position. He was probably right. They might have thought that because they had the wrong job description for the CEO job.

Objections to changing the CEO behavior mode

"My shareholders will think I am incompetent to do my job" is just one example of the usual fears my coachees have when developing effective executive teams. Others are:

- "I will lose control."
- "I will have to share all the decisions."
- "This will become a country club where no one will be focused on results anymore."

These three fears are interesting and interconnected.

"I will lose control."

Building an effective executive team is not about letting go of control. We don't treat staff like children by deciding everything for them. Instead, we guarantee that people align with both strategy and company culture by ensuring they follow agreed-upon criteria for decision making. In the end, you, as the general manager or CEO, can direct, validate, and decide on those criteria and how to implement them. You are also entitled by your position to revoke at any moment the autonomy from team members who don't play fair.

Don't be afraid. No one will take your position power away from you. Chief Executive Teams increase impact and leadership while allowing you to exercise your position power in more effective ways.

"I will have to share all the decisions."

Being an effective Achievement Mode leader does not mean you relinquish all decisions by delegating them to the team. No team in the world can operate efficiently by joint decision making only. There will be individual decisions, group decisions, and team decisions. What matters is knowing when and how each type is most effective and efficient to reach the maximum impact for the company. Centralizing most decisions at the CEO level is *not* useful. It just creates inefficiencies all over the company.

Our favorite football team either wins as a team or loses as a team. We don't think less of sports stars because they are team players. Quite the opposite.

"This will become a country club where no one will be focused on results anymore."

The third fear mixes different misunderstandings about a team. A team is not about becoming friends with the people with whom you work. No team in the corporate world deliberately tries to under achieve unless it decided to self-destruct.

Our favorite football team either wins as a team or loses as a team. We don't think less of sports stars because they are team players. Quite the opposite. It's the ability to play as a team member that makes our sports stars so liked. If Portuguese-born soccer player Cristiano Ronaldo did not assist other teammates in scoring and focused only on his personal goal count, no one would want him on their team and he would not earn millions a year. Why won't we see it as clearly in the business world?

Other fears come lower in the ranking. They are more frequent in recently appointed CEOs and usually connect to *the impostor syndrome*. This syndrome describes the persistent inability to believe that one's success is deserved or has been legitimately achieved because of one's efforts or skills.

- "People will think I am a fake."
- "When I open up my thinking process to the team, my insecurities will show."

The answer to these objections is simple. If you are insecure about a business decision if you are learning your way into the job you just started, what is better? To pretend you know everything, not listen to anyone, and stick to wrong decisions against all evidence? Or to create trusting relationships with competent people who share the same goals and can design with you the best processes to reach them?

From my experience of twenty-five years of supporting executive teams, I can say that women are faster at developing effective teams. They are more used to working with others to get things done. They are less focused on themselves and more on the results that need to be achieved. They are raised and educated to include and use everyone's best in the family, clan, community, or company. I also see those traits working for them when they become CEOs.

Nothing to lose by being great

You don't lose any impact, leadership, or position by developing an effective executive team with Achievement Mode. You gain more.

Achievement Mode assumes you can do everything from the previous behavior modes. But you deliberately (and temporarily) assume these behaviors only to build, develop, or improve a fully effective management team.

An effective team will understand and even require that you make some decisions alone. Before chaos reigns, you must establish boundaries and guide the team while you are in Command Mode. The team will also accept that in many situations, you will involve each of them to get processes flowing.

And your team will expect you to let go and allow them to solve most of the small problems of daily routine, or even trust them to solve seemingly impossible challenges. They can do it on behalf of the company because they share a clear direction and commitment to its future.

When the team is effective, you can choose to avoid, command, or involve individuals whenever you decide. It is also vital for Achievement Mode leaders that you get the team operating processes right. Nothing of what you do in those previous behavior modes will impair the team's functioning when they are an effective team. Your default mode is now Achievement Mode.

You have nothing to lose by managing within Achievement Mode. The team amplifies your leadership, impact, and consolidation of your position as the person who made it happen. By transforming *why* and *how* you deal with the management team, you boost its effectiveness level and its impact on the strategy's execution. They take care of the *what*. You transform the company and impact the lives of everyone in it. How's that for leadership?

4

BEEN THERE, DONE THAT, AND HAVE THE SCARS TO PROVE IT

"Ricardo is passionate and effective about his work of touching people's lives. His coaching had profound implications on who I am as a person. The transformation I operated as a result impacted both my professional and personal self. My knowledge of myself is deeper and I can serve the people and the business with more versatility than ever. Today I can say with confidence: I am a leader and not a manager."

– Casimiro da Silva Santos | Kemira |
Director Industry & Water South EMEA

TONY MANAGED COMPLEX international infrastructure projects for several years at the top of his career as public servant. After retirement, he accepted a job offer as a general manager of an insolvent company. That was not his dream; the position just showed up at his door. After looking at the accounting books, he decided that the company was salvable and took the job to rescue the friend who owned it.

I will never forget the way Tony approached the job with an interesting mix of skills. Tony was a self-educated top manager who did not graduate from high school. He was unaware of the existence of the concept of "employee engagement." But on his slow hardworking way up the career ladder, he understood his teams needed to wholeheartedly embrace the strategy to achieve their goals.

Because Tony wanted everyone to be as passionate about work as he was, he focused 100% on employee engagement. He communicated with and listened carefully to every employee. Knowing what made them tick made the difference in how he would sell the company's recovery strategy. It was all about purpose.

I learned Tony would take the opportunity of every interaction to galvanize his team against the common "enemy" – the inefficiencies and lack of quality that had provoked the financial crisis. Tony reasoned he should get them to perform at their best, and then focus them on running their processes better and faster every day. Tony was an expert in Operating Mode behavior without having any idea of what that was. Combined with his Uncle Scrooge type budget control, this became a winning strategy to recover that company.

With success behind him, Tony created turnarounds for two other companies. He bought and managed the second company until the end of his work life. After becoming a general manager, Tony used one behavior mode to address all circumstances: Operating Mode.

I find this is typically the case with CEOs and top executives. They have one favorite behavior mode, the one they feel most comfortable with, and that worked for them in the past. And they tend to use it in most circumstances, which is not a problem when they choose Achievement Mode or Operating Mode. The Avoidance, Involvement, and Command Mode behaviors bring more problems.

The other common approach is Bill's. I had a chat with Bill at a client's celebration. He is a well-educated manager who earned a Bachelors and Masters degrees in Management at a reasonably good university. He went through high school with my client. When he learned what I did, he took the chance to tell me that he was very disappointed with people.

"They always ask for something when they need something else. There is no rationality in the process", he said.

"How come?" I asked.

"I find them too emotional. They take things so personally and can't ask for what they really want. And they won't do what I ask of them."

When it is about people, it's always emotional; it's always personal. We don't make the most important decisions in life for rational reasons. People are emotional. As a psychologist, a father, and a husband I know that. Bill also did for sure. But he was not considering this when he made decisions as a COO.

When it is about people, it's always emotional; it's always personal. We don't make the most important decisions in life for rational reasons. People are emotional.

Having read the most essential leadership books, Bill knew what was expected of him. He understood that involving people to get their buy-in was important. Being flexible about the execution phase was paramount for his teams to be proactive in giving suggestions and initiating action.

The only drawback was that some people would not do what Bill expected. And Bill lacked other strategies for dealing with them. He slipped out of Involvement Mode behavior and resorted to Command Mode to demand his team members get things done. They complied, with simmering resentment.

Bill is a classic case of oscillation between Involvement and Command Modes. When time and other resources are available to deal with the challenges, he involves his team to find, define, and decide how to implement solutions. When time and other resources are scarce or even worse became scarce, because people did not follow through, stress reduces his mental space so much that he cannot allow anyone any degree of freedom anymore.

When he later became my coaching client, I discovered his team members considered him a mild case of a split personality. "He goes from Dr. Jekyll to Mr. Hyde in no-time as soon as stress hits him," they told me.

A lot of people are like Bill, used to the most common behavior modes of Command and Involvement. They don't conceive of other options other than those two. It's either black or white, high or low, left or right. By introducing the remaining behavior modes, we help them to become more flexible and choose their options wisely.

One-track mind, two-track mind, no-track mind

Most of us are like Tony or Bill. We are familiar with the behavior modes that maintain the inefficiencies of an executive team. We tend to try one or two alternative behaviors, get comfortable with them, and don't vary in our approach.

Executives may stick to a one-track mind when they say something like, "Focusing the team on processes is my way of doing things." They adhere to a two-track mind when they think, "I prefer Involvement, but now is the time when I should use Command Mode."

As a work and organizational psychologist, I am interested in understanding how individuals make decisions that impact their own and each other's results. The most intriguing question for me is, "Why do we keep these business-as-usual behavior modes instead of just going for what works best?" The reasons are simple and we explore them in this chapter.

So far, I have explained in Chapter 1 – *The Elephant in the Room* – why having an effective executive team instead of a working group of top executives makes all the difference to company results, according to current management research.

Chapter 2 – *It's Happening On Your Shift*– describes the behavior modes of the CEO to deal with the executive team members to develop – or not – an effective executive team.

In Chapter 3 – *And You Will Pay the Price* – I explained the costs for the leader of each of the behavior modes and how they relate to the fully effective executive team results.

In this chapter, we go in detail through the reasons that create and maintain the problem. After you understand them, it becomes easier to break their spell and move forward and upward with your team.

Executive teams are unique. They have their own sets of requirements, restrictions, components, drivers, and processes.

You may have noticed by now that I described behaviors and did not attribute any blame to the CEO for creating the original inefficient situation. The reason is that there are two main types of causes for non-collaborative behavior of C-Level executives:

1. Structural causes hindering collaboration
2. Generic solutions for developing executive teams

Structural causes are inherent to the nature of executive teams, and they usually are the origin of the problems. Executive teams are unique. They have their own sets of requirements, restrictions, components, drivers, and processes. From these unique factors arises a unique set of challenges that no other team in the company has. These structural causes are always present in every executive team of every company, to a bigger or lesser degree. They are:

- Organizational design
- Lack of common goals

- Divergent processes and language
- Corporate politics
- Shareholder interferences
- Runner-up syndrome
- Paradoxes
- Hypocrisy

Generic solutions for developing executive teams are past choices to address the problem of non-collaboration that contribute to maintaining it. As executive teams are unique, their problems cannot be addressed with generic teambuilding approaches. This will only make them worse because when these approaches fail – and they fail more often than not – team members become convinced that teamwork at the top is impossible. This in turn, reinforces the original problems of creating silos and fault lines in the team.

As executive teams are unique, their problems cannot be addressed with generic teambuilding approaches.

Generic solutions for developing executive teams are:

- Time heals everything
- Education
- Instructions
- Feedback and consequences
- Profiling
- Teambuilding activities
- Bootcamps

I detail each of the two types of causes for non-collaborative C-Suite behavior in the next sections.

Structural causes for non-collaborative behavior of C-level executives

Organization design

Multinational companies are structured in ways that do not foster collaboration at the top level. It all starts with the reporting systems. For example, consider the levels of reporting of this COO:

Pierre is the COO of the local operating company of a multinational in Spain. He has a hierarchical reporting line to John, the Europe Middle East and Africa (EMEA) head of operations of his company, in which the local operating company is integrated. John is his formal boss, his traditional "solid line" direct supervisor who sets his objectives and evaluates his performance.

But Pierre also has a reporting relationship to the local CEO, Camile. This is a weaker power relationship than the one with John. Camile has a right to manage part of Pierre's time and resources and to set some goals. But if push comes to shove, John's influence over Pierre's decisions is much stronger. So, we say that Pierre has a weaker "dotted line" reporting to Camile in the matrix organizational chart and a more substantial "solid line" to John. This mix is typical of matrix organizations.

We work in matrix organizations that have us looking 360° around for meaning, input, decision making, support, and deliverables.

But to complicate matters, Pierre also belongs to several teams: (1) the operations team he is managing in Spain; (2) the international project team that is innovating supply chain methodologies in Europe; (3) the cross-functional team that is revamping operations in Spain; (4) the executive team of the company in Spain.

Pierre's multiple levels of involvement are typical. If you have a C-Suite position in a matrix organization, you could likely add a couple more types of teams to which you belong. We work in matrix organizations that have us looking 360° around for meaning, input, decision making, support, and deliverables.

Working in matrix organizations is just the beginning because it only tends to worsen when we mix it with adhocracy, agile, process, and project organizations. Complexity rises like a tsunami in organizational design and operations. In most corporations, daily life is an uphill battle trying to deal with too many priorities while having insufficient resources. The misaligned priorities that come with intricate reporting lines don't support the development of effective executive teams.

Lack of common purpose and goals

Shared purpose and goals are the most critical building block of a functioning team. Without them, there is no need for teamwork. As Pierre's advisor, when we assessed the commonality of goals, one of the teams Pierre belonged to was weaker than the others.

In most corporations, daily life is an uphill battle trying to deal with too many priorities while having insufficient resources.

Pierre has clear goals when he is working under his functional umbrella. The operations' organization is integrated to give visibility and control of KPIs of Pierre's work to John, his regional EMEA "solid line" boss. His innovation project team also has a clear vision of what they are trying to achieve. The cross-functional team he participates in with his executive colleagues also has a strict deadline to deliver precise solutions to consumer needs in the Spanish market. His direct reports evidently deliver the local goals that will further integrate in the international organization.

When we look at the executive team in Spain, we notice something interesting: *only* Camile, the CEO, has *full* responsibility for integrating local goals into a coherent whole. Following Pierre's example, all other executive team members have their performance evaluation and bonuses connected to functional and project KPIs, which are more limited in scope.

In most cases, individual executive bonuses also depend on general financial measures related to growth, profit, or market share of the global company, not the local one. The goals of the local operating company in Spain usually act as thresholds for the bonus payment. They don't stand alone as criteria for bonuses for executives that report to Regional COOs outside the country, as in the case of Pierre, who reports to John in the EMEA region.

Too often, companies create a zero-sum game for budget definition and goals achievement, only to discover later that this hinders the required cooperation between their executives.

As executive bonuses are calculated like this, they are not powerful enough to promote collaboration between executives. Financial KPIs of local operating companies do not work as shared goals.

Even Pierre's performance is evaluated by his formal "solid line" boss John managing EMEA from far away, who can see only his quarterly and yearly results. Camile, his local "dotted line" CEO, can complete or validate the performance appraisal already done by John. Still, she is not ultimately responsible for it, nor can she decide to fully change it. Camile is the one who best knows how Pierre deals with local stakeholders in his function and projects, the quality of what he delivers, and the nature of the relationships he establishes. But this knowledge is not considered mandatory by the company for a performance appraisal.

Pierre's role requires him to display team behavior with the local executive team. But this depends only on his willingness and on the power of influence of Camile, his CEO. Nothing on the goal definition and performance appraisal foster that level of collaboration.

On top of this, sometimes the goals of one functional area, such as marketing, conflict with another area's goals, such as human resources. For one to deliver on their goals, the other must give in, and vice-versa.

The team has shared high-level earnings before interest and taxes (EBIT), profit growth, market share gains, or any other goal that they need to reach to earn their bonuses. But this does not influence their desire to make decisions on behalf of the team that might prevent them from meeting individual KPIs that impact their bonuses.

Too often, companies create a zero-sum game for budget definition and goals achievement, only to discover later that this hinders the required cooperation between their executives.

Divergent processes and language

All members of each department have their ways of doing things. They form a tribe with its sequences of steps, tasks, and cognitive or motoric operations that constitute its processes. Each tribe's functions have different rules, standards, and technical solutions to support them. And most of all, they have specific languages with their jargon and acronyms that only the tribe members understand.

Language does not only describe reality; language shapes the reality of the people who share it.

Some concepts in a company's language are common to all. Most tribes' members in the company will understand the basic idea of profit. Some of them will know what EBIT means. But only the tribe who speaks the financial language will fluently discuss the concept of "weighted cost of capital."

Language does not only describe reality; language shapes the reality of the people who share it. Consider the concept of engagement. For most people, engagement will be an attitude that someone displays. For the neophyte in human resources jargon, it is simultaneously

- an attribute of the relationship between a person and the job,
- a measure of leadership impact and corporate policies,
- an indicator of a company's sustainability, and
- a predictor of stock performance, among other things.

The more a team knows, the more its language increases in complexity to differentiate between concepts. Our jargon *divides* us from others who don't share the same language.

Corporate politics

Political games are about making sure you stay on the winning side of any power disputes in the company. And to do this, C-suite executives tend to play safe. They engage in the practice of not being clear about their convictions or actions. If this happens, others recognize they have already picked a side. That can be too risky. Maximum maneuverability requires a viable exit strategy that allows them to retreat if that side loses.

The more a team knows, the more its language increases in complexity to differentiate between concepts. Our jargon divides us from others who don't share the same language.

Consequently, executives become "flexible" in their positions. They are inconsistent in what they say and do. They may contradict themselves and say something politically correct but act quite differently, assuming no one will see the difference. If someone calls them on that, they will just play dumb, find a circumstantial excuse, and the game goes on.

As you can imagine, this ineffective, over-flexible behavior prevents healthy team functioning. It does not generate trust, nor does it allow for predictability in the deliverables, behavior, and moral conduct. That's the game many companies play, to a bigger or smaller extent.

Executives often don't want to commit to a team when part of its members are on the opposite side of the corporate politics game.

The impact on the executive team's effectiveness can be huge, as these are the people at the heart of most corporate politics. They are the ones who pivot between local and global stakeholders. Career-wise they are the ones who have much at stake by playing this game. And usually, they are in executive positions precisely because they are good players in corporate politics.

Executives often don't want to commit to a team when part of its members are on the opposite side of the corporate politics game. CEOs must deal with all this if they want to develop an effective executive team.

Shareholder interferences

Sometimes shareholders interfere not only with the nomination of executives but also with their functioning. Naturally, executives feel loyalty towards the shareholders who appointed them, but not to the point when it starts interfering with the business.

This interference effectively creates a conflict of interest between the shareholders and the company. One of the situations I frequently encounter in my consultancy practice is manipulating the choice of business partners. More than once a CEO could not use my consulting services because I have a reputation for focusing on the company's goals and interests. By being impartial in defending the company's best interests, I sometimes find myself in no man's land. When the CEO was prevented from hiring me in several of those cases, I discovered later that some of the company's shareholders also owned shares in the consultancy firm that got the contract instead. Thus, they could make sure the "right bias" was applied in the project and earn money at the same time.

More than once a CEO could not use my consulting services because I have a reputation for focusing on the company's goals and interests.

Also standard are the interferences to protect an underperforming executive member. Someone unable or unwilling to contribute meaningfully to the company should have their contract terminated. Sometimes shareholder protection prevents the CEO from giving them the right treatment. Meritocracy starts (or not) at the top of companies. When executives see that someone is dragging the team down and nothing happens, the whole process is discredited and fails. Morale plunges and turnover goes up.

Runner-up syndrome

One of my CEO coachees once told me: "Some of my team members feel that they are being invited to team up with the person who beat them up in a boxing match." He was referring to the runner-up syndrome. When you are appointed to the power chair of a company or corporation, you usually end up being the manager of one or more competitors for that same position. They were not chosen, and you were. They don't like it. I have yet to find a company where this is not the case.

Meritocracy starts (or not) at the top of companies.

Runner-up syndrome leads executive team members to resist or boycott team development attempts by the CEO who got the position they wanted. They are competitive professionals who strive for victory; when they lose, their emotions pull them to the dark side of revenge. They would like to see the winner fail. Sometimes they harbor a fuzzy emotional notion that they might end up landing the job after all. But most often, runner-ups are engulfed in an emotional wave that blocks their rationality and requires payback. I often find this as the source of negative individual attitudes towards collaboration during the implementation of executive teams' development processes.

Runner-up syndrome leads executive team members to resist or boycott team development attempts by the CEO who got the position they wanted.

But there's a catch to this one. The person who competed with you for your job as CEO is the second most prepared to lead the company. The company needs them to continue giving their best, and it's your job to make it happen. It's a delicate balance to get someone who is highly competitive and an excellent performer to give their utmost effort when they might still be holding a grudge about not getting the CEO position. But it needs to happen.

Gaining this person's cooperation can be done. I often see CEOs behave in one of these three ineffective ways to deal with it: letting time pass to see if the runner-up forgets about it, giving them the cold shoulder in return, or threatening them in case they don't change behavior.

The person who competed with you for your job as CEO is the second most prepared to lead the company.

You need to be able to create an alliance with them in the best interest of the company. This is the focus on the *Chief Executive Coaching* methodology I provide.

Paradoxes

Companies are full of contradictions that need to be managed to reap the full benefit of their capabilities to win. Executive teams are the right level of the company to solve these paradoxes.

A paradox is a statement or proposition that seems self-contradictory or absurd but in reality expresses a possible truth. Companies are full of contradictions that need to be managed to reap the full benefit of their capabilities to win. Executive teams are the right level of the company to solve these paradoxes.

Some of the most common paradoxes haunting executive teams are:

1. **Control and don't control.**
   Understand why, when, and how control is indispensable while being able to release power, even when it seems crucial, if the team shows accountability to take over.

2. **Get ahead of each other and get along with each other.**
   We need to make sure everyone has career development opportunities. But these must not happen at the expense of the quality of relationships between team members.

3. **Think originally and generate consensus.**
   Original thinking, as we have seen in Chapter 1, is the basis for innovative behavior and corporate entrepreneurship. But we must strive to arrive at a mutually acceptable decision and integrate diversity to make the best out of it.

4. **Manage for the short and the long term at the same time.** If executive teams think of only one of these, they will eventually kill the company.

5. **Get things done while you learn how to do them.** Executive teams must make decisions in a volatile, uncertain, complex, ambiguous, and hostile environment. Most of the time, they do not know the "right answers." They must learn them while executing a strategy that will become obsolete during its implementation.

6. **Focus on processes and people.** Both are important. Their requirements are often contradictory and must be integrated.

7. **Generate trust while maintaining positive conflict.** If there's a possibility of conflict, there's a possibility of trust. If there is the wrong kind of conflict, trust is gone.

8. **Grow the "me" and the "we".** Team members must differentiate from each other and integrate at the same time, to maximize individuality and team unity at the same time.

We address and solve paradoxes directly by applying *The 6P's of Executive Teams*® methodology. The next chapters provide several examples.

Hypocrisy

As I cited on Chapter 1, Joris Lammers and two other researchers of the Tilburg and Northwestern Universities found out that power tends to generate double standard morals[42]. Powerful people tend to judge more strictly the behavior of others than their own. They condemn other people's cheating more harshly while allowing themselves to cheat. They also judge other people's transgressions as more inexcusable than their own.

Increasing power tenure tends to increase moral hypocrisy. When in power, we don't forgive others for doing the things we would allow ourselves to do.

Not all powerful people get their moral compass broken. But everyone must be aware of the risk. Power increases opportunities for good and bad behavior. And it also increases the possibility of getting away with wrongdoings.

Not all powerful people get their moral compass broken. But everyone must be aware of the risk. Power increases opportunities for good and bad behavior. And it also increases the possibility of getting away with wrongdoings.

It takes only one situation of a double moral standard to kill your company's respect for you. It's even worse. It takes only one problem that *looks like* a double moral standard action by the leaders to destroy their reputation and leadership effectiveness. Reputation is the lifeblood of leadership. Lose your reputation and you lose your credibility as a leader. From that moment onwards, people will smile at you, fear your power. But they will take every opportunity to undermine you and your management behind your back unless they also just want to be as powerful as you to get away with moral hypocrisy. In that case, please delete all communications about company values and culture. Employees will mock these; they know what the leaders value.

When the CEO shows moral hypocrisy, the whole executive team's reputation gets contaminated. Managers and employees of all levels witness the events and think, "Why doesn't someone do something about it?" Everyone around the top leader will be found guilty by association, and whistleblowers emerge to report unethical or illegal behavior.

Developing an executive team under these circumstances becomes an impossible task. Trust is eradicated from the group. No team survives without trust.

Generic solutions for developing executive teams

Apart from the structural reasons that prevent executives from collaborating, some other reasons maintain non-collaboration behaviors at C-level. These are the past attempts at addressing the problem of non-collaboration that ended up contributing to maintaining it.

Time heals everything

Time heals everything, we say. One of the CEO mindsets that I most commonly find is to use *time* as a justification for lack of executive team effectiveness. Usually, this happens when there was a recent change in team composition. Either the CEO just assumed the role or the team is onboarding one or more key team members. In these cases, I often hear:

Reputation is the lifeblood of leadership. Lose your reputation and you lose your credibility as a leader.

- "They need more time to adjust to each other."
- "I just came in and I don't want to disrupt things before I know what's going on."
- "I'm sure the challenges ahead will force the team to collaborate sooner than later."
- "We will get there; people need to mature their relationships."
- "These are competent people. They know how to collaborate and they will eventually understand it's required."

My work is about supporting executive teams to produce fast results. When I hear CEOs speaking about waiting for their executive team to develop, I shiver. It's interesting how top managers who are otherwise so focused in productivity get so complacent about their own team's efficiency.

Janelle is the CEO of a company in Switzerland. She is French and is one of three executive team members that was changed within six months. I coached one of the new executive team members in his previous role in Germany. My contact knew I could help Janelle after he experienced the results of *The 6P's of Executive Teams*® programs. He saw the executive team's efficiency in Switzerland was not excellent and therefore introduced me to Janelle.

My work is about supporting executive teams to produce fast results. When I hear CEOs speaking about waiting for their executive team to develop, I shiver.

In our meeting, Janelle revealed she was aware that the company's management team's effectiveness and efficiency in Switzerland was not up to the requirements. We diagnosed the individual and team needs, understanding the reasons and constraints supporting the team's efficiency level. But when I explained what I could do and the expected results, she said, "I think I need to give them time to sort it out." To which I replied, "Until when are you willing to wait for results to show up?"

Janelle looked at me, trying to probably find an answer in the space above my bald head, nevertheless a bit surprised by the question. She then said in a soft voice, like speaking to herself, trying to clear the doubt, "Three months...?"

"What will be the signs that your team is moving in the right direction?"

"If the current misaligned behaviors of the team disappear, that's a good sign..." she responded.

"What are you going to do differently for that to happen?" I continued.

"Don't you think that me setting the expectations for teamwork is enough?"

I've repeatedly had this conversation in different formats. It always surprises me that executives decide to give a situation or person time to evolve without establishing limits or conditions. I've seen this deteriorate into terrible consequences. When it happens at the highest level of the company, it is even more surprising. But it does happen often enough to create havoc.

CEOs want the situation to change. They even know *what* they would like to have done differently. They trust that with time people will find out what's needed and implement it. But here are the challenges for the team or team member, who must:

- recognize what needs to change
- be motivated to make the changes
- possess the ability to change
- have the fortitude to overcome the usual structural causes for the poor performance of executive teams without even knowing what they are and how to best deal with them.

The case of Kate, an Australian CEO, is the opposite. At her first management meeting of the subsidiary in Italy, she asked the team for feedback on the current level of the executive team's effectiveness and efficiency. The quality level of the information she got was so low that she immediately asked me for a meeting. Forty-five minutes into the meeting, she said, "Yes, let's move on with your process. I need this team to deliver at the highest level this quarter." We worked intermittently over four years, during which the company climbed to the top five position in its market.

Or consider the case of Frederick, the Vice President for Marketing of an Austrian multinational company. I worked with several of his teams over the years. Once, after an incredibly productive workshop, he said, "It's not that the team would not get there without you. We would. But working with you made it happen three times faster and this makes all the difference."

Time is of the essence. Time to market is critical. Concerns about a coming recession, rapidly changing technology, higher regulation levels, and disruptive trends create a sense of urgency. Anything that speeds up the process of getting your executive team to its best effectiveness and efficiency level should be a priority to you.

Education

Sometimes CEOs look for education as a solution for their executive team's efficiency needs. And some or all team members engage in courses and professional skills education. Usually, they choose to pursue a post-graduate management degree at a good university with a good faculty of well-educated and credentialed professors.

Executives seem to value the education provider's social status. One of the top business school names on your CV makes it shine. A good university does an excellent job at teaching executives all about general management and leadership and lectures them on convincing models for how to lead their company and streamline the management of all resources.

Sometimes the course of study also includes soft skills training. These might be:

- conflict management
- influence
- persuasion
- negotiation
- communication

- mindfulness
- emotional intelligence
- resilience
- stress management
- situational leadership
- transformational leadership
- neuro-something leadership

And the team or some of its individuals attend these lectures to be informed and educated.

But regarding team effectiveness, there are no significant changes after one or several team members attend these courses, for several reasons:

1. The educational approach is individual. People attend these leadership and management seminars to be individually educated. Nothing is directed at the team as an entity.
2. This type of intervention does not tackle the structural causes for underperformance of executive teams, let alone each team's specific ones.
3. Management education is usually theoretical. It delivers the most updated models for leadership and hard and soft management skills. Models and flowcharts are quite lovely. (Don't get me wrong. I am a research practitioner; I love them. I use them all over my books and consulting projects.) But they must fulfill two goals: 1) to help understand reality and 2) to help you be more effective in dealing with it. Most academic models are not very good at addressing a management team's effectiveness to help people understand it better or to be more consistently able to change it.

Instructions

Sometimes CEOs clearly communicate what they want. They ask the team members to deliver *teamwork*.

The results might take the form of specific tasks, such as requesting some team members to gather before meetings, generate solutions together, manage conflicts between departments, deliver on cross-company projects, and so on. Or it might take the form of a generic order to the team or individual. "You need to start working better as a team; this level of inefficiency can't go on…" Less often, it takes the form of the CEO giving standards to the team as a benchmark to evaluate the effectiveness of their work together: "These are the standards. This is what I expect you to do together."

These approaches are variations of instructions and encounter the same two difficulties:

1. Teamwork does not happen by decree. No one can tell a group of people to be a better team. After all, they are happily going about their individual goals, processes, projects, interests, priorities, using their jargon, and making the most of their individual resources according to their needs.
2. The second difficulty with delegation, orders, and standards is that by instructing the executives to engage in teamwork, you are effectively taking yourself out of the team. You are not setting the example; you are not driving the behavior. You are not creating the opportunity to discuss, challenge, and agree. You are asking others to do that work for you. Isn't the task of creating an effective executive team yours?

Think of it from the team's perspective: Your boss is asking you to jeopardize everything proven to contribute to your career success to contribute to this abstract thing called the executive team. What an uncertain payback!

There must be a common purpose, agreed upon beforehand, for everyone to be able to establish positive expectations for their effort in creating a team, sometimes against their individual short-term interests.

There are several responsibilities in any job that *cannot* be delegated. Leadership tasks cannot be delegated. It's your job as a leader to create an effective executive team. No matter how competent your people, no matter how much aligned they seem to be, do not delegate this task to them.

There must be a common purpose, agreed upon beforehand, for everyone to be able to establish positive expectations for their effort in creating a team.

They will be able to carry on in your absence, on behalf of you, later. After the team is established, the right processes are in place; the team dynamics are reliable, you can let go and relax. Until then, it's on you.

Feedback and consequences

Sometimes CEOs have a clear picture in their mind about what needs to be achieved. And they even know the practices that need to be displayed by their team members. This should make the alignment of individual team members' behaviors easy, right? Nevertheless, in these circumstances, when you go about giving individuals feedback, comparing the person's behavior with the desired standard, results are usually below expectations. The same response happens when you establish consequences for misaligned behavior.

Leadership tasks cannot be delegated. It's your job as a leader to create an effective executive team.

You might communicate the standards. You might be clear about what happens to people when they don't comply with them. But in the absence of a previously agreed upon purpose and team behavior, it will be mostly your will being imposed on the team. No team dynamics are binding the individual actions; there are no common principles and values to drive the company culture. There's no *us*; there's only *you*.

That's why you feel you have to guide, drive, and achieve. You did not create a team that aligns individual behavior by itself yet.

In the worst instance, CEO feedback and consequences behavior can be inconsistent, volatile, and discretionary, as no common visible norms are guiding it. This happens because you are not able to see and know everything. There will always be misaligned behaviors that go unnoticed. And when that happens, no one will point it out to you. Your team members and everyone else in the company will only wonder why you behaved that way or allowed others' specific behavior. They will assume many negative things about the reason, without giving you the slightest chance to make it right.

That's why you feel you have to guide, drive, and achieve. You did not create a team that aligns individual behavior by itself yet.

Profiling

I am not a fan of personality tests. As a psychologist, I am trained and certified to deliver and interpret them. But I am also qualified to assess their accuracy. And a lot, if not most of them are quite inaccurate.

I am sure you've seen, probably online, one of those Middle Age world maps depicting a flat Earth with few known countries and the sea with edges surrounded by monsters, eager to eat any daring ship that approaches. If you look at your mobile phone now, you can see Google Earth with an aspheric planet, 3D visualization of the terrain, details, and connection to maps, explanations, and whatever else you need to find your way, down to the inch.

My problem with personality profiles is that most of them are like the Middle Age maps. They give you a false representation of reality, based on flawed assumptions, not backed up by research and taking advantage of people's cognitive biases to convince clients the point they are making has sense.

My problem with personality profiles is that most of them are like the Middle Age maps.

In 1948, Psychology professor Bertram R. Forer performed a by now classic experiment. He asked 39 students to answer a personality test he developed, called "Diagnostic Interest Blank". One week later, he delivered their individual profiles back in class asking each of the students to assess how much the description portrayed them.[45]

The average assessment was 4.3 out of 5 points of maximum congruence between the test and their perception of themselves. This is an 86% accuracy rate. Already good. Then Forer asks his students to disclose their profiles to their colleagues.

Brouhaha started in the class when the students were surprised to find all their profiles were the same. If they all have different personalities and the description is the same, how could there have been so much agreement between all of the students and the common profile?

Forer had designed the common personality sketch based on vague statements from an astrology book that potentially apply to anyone. Some of the 13 items he used were:

You have a tendency to be critical of yourself.

You have a great deal of unused capacity which you have not turned to your advantage.

While you have some personality weaknesses, you are generally able to compensate for them.

You have found it unwise to be too frank in revealing yourself to others.

While we all have quite different self-criticism levels, most of us will have had situations where we criticized ourselves. Although some of us have more unused capacity than others, we all tend to believe we have at least some untapped potential. And there are some general rules of life that we all get with experience. We need to compensate for our weaknesses and need to regulate the level of frankness in our relationships to continue living in communities and have a few friends.

Suppose we look for a connection between our experience of our lives and the statements in the test. In that case, our memory immediately finds those congruent instances and we will mark a level of accuracy with the statement. I am not saying how much unused capacity I have compared to the human population; I only have to believe that I have some unused capacity, which most human beings will.

Individuals tend to give high accuracy ratings to descriptions of their personality that supposedly are tailored specifically to them but are vague and general enough to apply to a wide range of people. This psychological phenomenon became more known as *the Barnum Effect* than as the *Forer Effect*.

Although Bertram Forer made the initial research on it in 1948, con artists specialized in the gullibility of people to make them spend money for centuries. And certainly, Phineas T. Barnum, the creator of the Barnum & Bailey circus, ranks as one of the greatest of all times.

For the Barnum Effect to work, the descriptions must comply with three characteristics:

1. The subject believes in the authority of the evaluator. Usually, credibility is built by

   Reference ("One of my friends told me she changed her life because of the aura reading of this expert", "Fortune 500 companies use this tool").

Credential ("It was created by a famous university professor." "I learned it in University twenty years ago.")

Pure belief ("He developed this model from a vision he had during a mystical trip in India", "This is based on the works of Carl Jung.")

2. The description of the traits must be positive (even if the statement says I have weaknesses, it says I can compensate for them, so I find it flattering).

3. And the subject has to be led to believe that the analysis applies to them, therefore attributing personal meaning to the statements ("It's based on my answers to the profile"; "It is calculated based on my date, time and place of birth"; "I choose which of the statements applies to me").

The effect is always the same: We believe that general positive descriptions depict us because we think we are good people and we attribute our meaning to those vague statements. Different studies have successfully replicated the Barnum Effect[46,47,48]. There are no cultural differences in its manifestation.

If someone you believe is an expert tells you that there are nine types of personality, and assesses you on them, you buy it without asking the fundamental questions:

- How did you find out there are nine types?
- What is the data behind it? How much does it describe current real situations?
- Can someone else reach the same conclusion based on independent research?
- Does the profile give the same results consistently? Or do people get different results each time they do it?

These questions pertain to the *validity* and *reliability* of the tests on which the profiles are based.

Validity is the degree to which a tool measures what it claims to measure. If a specific profile is supposed to measure personality types, it would have to

- provide coherent measures of the already scientifically proven personality traits,
- generate consensus among personality experts that it accurately measures personality dimensions,
- be able to predict the behavior of the person in specific areas connected to each personality dimension assessed, and
- be based on a representative sample of the relevant population being measured, appropriate statistical tests, and reliable measurement procedures.

Reliability means the test produces similar results under consistent conditions across time. Knowing that personality is relatively stable, are the results of the test also stable? Or do they change according to the moment and circumstances of the person? Are there errors in the test results?

Don't rely on a test if it was developed without an adequate sampling of the population, the results were not extracted according to the most appropriate statistical tests, and the numbers for validity and reliability are not solid.

We need to stereotype others. Our brains function based on prejudice, impression formation, and quick judgments. Our survival depended on that a hundred thousand years ago.

Malcolm Gladwell's book, *Blink: The Power of Thinking Without Thinking*[49], is an excellent reference on how we form and act on instant impressions. Most personality tests bank on this to create a sense of accuracy when in fact, they assess nothing of the person's personality. They just divide the whole world into four, nine, or sixteen types of people as if reality were that simple.

Using non-valid and unreliable tests ends up creating a false sense of understanding others when in fact, we are just boxing them in labels, thereby preventing the development of the right type of conversations that bring light to the nature of relationships and move them forward.

Teambuilding activities

General team building activities are a big market. There are thousands of companies specialized in delivering all kinds of events in the form of team building activities.

The list of possibilities you can do is endless: team cooking; tracking in the woods; building rafts, imaginary cities, tree houses, shelters; building go-carts and racing them in teams; camping, fishing, campfires, sleeping under the sky; learning basic instruments and playing with an orchestra; fine arts co-creation; playing team sports together with a professional coach and part of a professional team; rally papers; mystery hunters; geocaching; high ropes and low ropes exercises; playing table games; solving riddles; escape rooms; white water rafting; skydiving; corporate social responsibility activities; volunteering to service NGOs; management simulations; playing with Legos, building blocks, wood bricks, structural pieces of any kind to develop creativity and solve challenges, with or without related metaphors; gathering in social activities, fine dining, wine tasting, learning cocktail recipes, and getting drunk together.

These are all entertaining. Within each one's specific limitations, these activities can even support teambuilding for any team in the company. Nevertheless:

- None of these activities addresses the specific needs of an executive team.
- None addresses the structural reasons for executives not working in teams.

- None addresses specifically the behavior modes of the CEO and how they impact the team's effectiveness.
- None is based on the relevant management research.
- None solves the problems.

Bootcamps

Army, rangers, firefighting, marines training facilities are being repurposed to deliver expensive training to civilians of corporations who can afford it. It's an alternative revenue stream to otherwise Spartan-budgeted institutions.

Although aiming at creating team spirit, military-type boot camps do so in a quite different way than general team building activities. They take people out of their natural environment for some days, which allows for stretching their comfort zone and testing their limits, often in physically challenging conditions. But this also creates a suspended reality bubble. Individuals live in this alternative reality where anything that happens will require extra effort to be transferred back to their natural environment.

Also, executives are placed in a follower perspective to feel the benefits of military leadership. They are led and controlled, inside a strict discipline environment, in mechanical institutions in their functioning. Goals are simple; decisions are transparent and indisputable and everything screams linear chain of command.

How can they then transfer their learning to lead an effective executive team in complex, matrix, agile, adhocratic, accountability-based organizations? They encounter moving targets, uncertain environments, innovative products to develop, and competitors who are also partners. They engage with fail-fast-and-cheap missions, challenging professionals who are technically more competent than themselves, employees who ask for purpose and meaning, competence gaps, and conflicting goals. Decisions shift by the minute.

They can't. And they don't.

Executive teams' unique characteristics

CEOs wanting to develop their teams might try some of the activities above, find out they don't produce the desired results and give up. They then resort to business as usual and just make do to deliver the best results allowed by the current team effectiveness level.

It's human. A definition of insanity attributed to Einstein is, "Insanity is doing the same things and expecting different results." So, why wouldn't they give up? They tried what they know and didn't work; they should just stop or do something else.

It's so easy to be wrong because usual team development solutions are designed for every other team in the company, *not* the executive team. The standard team development solutions do help to solve part of the challenges of teams. Sometimes you need to give instructions, feedback, delegate tasks, and establish consequences for behavior alignment. Also, profiling individuals' personality and getting them to do a couple of activities together helps generate a sense of commonality in interests that do more good than harm. And people sometimes find solutions for their problems when given enough time and mental space.

Why are these team activities generally ineffective for executives?

Executive teams have unique characteristics. This might be due to members who operate in a context of complexity and ambiguity, often multicultural, have matrix reporting systems, or follow different processes. They speak different technical jargon, have conflicting goals, compete for the same career opportunities, or side with different corporations' power groups. As I have already noted, they hold grudges and lack trust, share no mutual accountability, have no common purpose, lack social or technical skills to get the job done, or all these together in various degrees.

Therefore, it's so easy to be wrong about it: team building as usual doesn't work for the executive team's unique characteristics. It doesn't address the structural needs of these teams. Using some of the business-as-usual team building methods can often create more negative than positive feelings.

For example, putting your executive team through a group feedback session, without basing it on an agreed structured process and having created a safe context with an end in mind can open a can of worms that no one wants to let loose. That's why executive teams often get resistant to trying out some new teambuilding fads. They have been there, done that, and have the scars to prove it.

Team building as usual doesn't work for the executive team's unique characteristics.

Problems are maintained by failed attempts to solve them

The causes that maintain the problem are threefold.

First, there are the **structural causes** for the poor performance of executive teams that I mentioned earlier in this chapter. These are usually a given. Some will always be there and you must deal with them.

Second, there are the **generic team building solutions** for developing executive teams. This is the combination of all the usual strategies that function very well with other teams in the company and not with the executive team. Your team has likely tried some.

The third level is the **CEO's behavior mode** tried to address the problems on an individual relationship basis with each team member: Avoidance, Involvement, Command, and Operating Mode behaviors, whose impacts I described in Chapter 2 – *It's happening on your shift*.

Structural causes and generic solutions for the underperformance of the executive team, plus the usual CEO behavior modes dealing with them, represent 99% of the difficulties of developing top team effectiveness.

We need to bridge the executive team's structuring process in a way that guarantees success on this slippery way up to produce outstanding results.

This is what I do. This is the methodology I developed over two decades, supporting hundreds of executive teams around the world. This is *The 6P's of Executive Teams®*.

In the next chapter, you will find a description of the full process, its goals, and how the outcomes solve each of the problems identified so far.

The methodology you will learn about is the result of my activity as a research practitioner consultant. This means that I follow an evidence-based approach to solve the performance problems of executive teams. For several reasons, I describe this in general terms. If you are leading an executive team and would like to know what a process could look like for your team, contact me through www.chief-executive.team.

5

THE 6P'S OF EXECUTIVE TEAMS®

> "This is the type of support you need when everything happens at the same time: new business model, new organizational structure, new leadership team, and success can't wait."
>
> – Paula Panarra | Microsoft Portugal | CEO

Show me the money – the "what", "how" and "why" of financial results

"SHOW ME THE money," yelled sports agent Jerry Maguire over the phone, as requested by Rod Tidwell, the wide receiver of the Arizona Cardinals he was trying to sign up. The 1996 movie *Jerry Maguire*, when Tom Cruise played Maguire and Cuba Gooding Jr., won the Academy Award for Best Supporting Actor with his interpretation of Tidwell. The film took this sentence globally.

"Show me the money" is a worldwide easily understandable way of asking for results, questioning impact, assessing outcomes, probing for rationality, demanding simplicity, evaluating risk, asking for data, and measuring outcomes. In the business world, money is a straightforward way to measure different types of results.

You can compare different types of results by translating them to financial gains. Suppose we are discussing sustainability, triple bottom line, social responsibility, and employee engagement. Whatever the key performance indicators (KPIs), you can measure their impact on the financial situation of the company. In the end, most business decisions are about *money*.

In the Introduction of this book, I proposed that most executive teams are leaving a lot of money on the table. And in Chapter 1 – *The Elephant in the Room* – I quoted research that recounts how that is happening. The dynamics of the executive team impact many KPIs of the company. Improve the dynamics and you get more money. Worsen it and you get less money. This seems easy enough to understand. The challenge starts when we try to make it actionable because there are always different causes for current results. Your outcomes depend on what, how and why you do things. Focusing on the causes of your company's results leads you to understand and change the "what", "how", and "why" of financial results.

The dynamics of the executive team impact many KPIs of the company.

What affects your results?

Say you are not happy with the marketing results of your e-newsletter. If you take the first type of cause, you will try to improve the reach and impact of your e-newsletter. Maybe you will make it a video-newsletter. Or increase the list of people you send it to by using different strategies and techniques. You can also tweak its content, make it deeper, shallower, sexier looking. At this level, you will examine the format of your newsletter, focusing on design and content. You focus on the "what" of the newsletter. What is it like? What is in it?

How are you getting results?

The next level of causality is" how." How do you integrate your newsletter in your marketing effort? Maybe the problem is not the newsletter itself. Perhaps you are not researching your target client well enough; you are not keeping up with the market evolution. You might also find out that a newsletter is not the best way to keep your customers close. You are better equipped with a podcast, interviewing clients or thought leaders on your subject. At the "how" level, you will focus on operating principles and processes of your marketing. Focusing on the "how" level can take the "what" level somewhere else entirely.

Why are you doing what you do?

But there's another level, and by now, you guessed what it is. Asking "why" we do things is a deeper level of analysis. If you go for this level, you may discover that you must turn your business model upside down. Instead of selling a service, you will offer it as part of a paid experience. Your marketing strategy is based on alliances and partnerships, and someone else will market you to their clients. The "why" is the level of business assumptions, orthodoxies, and mental models.

Examining your business at the "why we do the things we do" level might be uncomfortable. It is a lot easier to change the "what" and "how" components. In my experience, companies need the assistance of a consultant to help them probe into the mental models supporting the business model.

When results are not satisfactory, you can ask people to do different things. Focusing on the "what" level sometimes helps, but quite often is not enough.

Different levels of causes of executive team problems

Ralph is the CEO of a company that designs and manufactures medical devices. When he called me in, his company was facing a simple challenge. They created an ambitious strategy to revamp the company, but it was not effectively executed. I say executed because it seemed to be clearly defined and communicated. There were enough physical and digital props about the strategy to claim that most people knew the main targets and the roadmaps to achieve them. But blockages in the processes prevented the expected results. Ralph felt there was a lack of skill in execution.

My initial set of interviews confirmed that the strategy was clear; the team had agreed to follow it. Managers at all levels could easily explain what the company was trying to achieve. But many people reported sometimes feeling in doubt about the best way forward. They felt that there were different interpretations of the roadmap at the executive level. Although executives said they agreed with the plan, they did not carry it out.

What could be the causes and the best way to address them?

Following the simple example of the newsletter above, in this type of situation, you can analyze different levels of causes that produce undesirable results:

What we do – Tasks, techniques, and strategies we use.

How we do it – Processes and operating principles we follow.

Why we do it – Assumptions and orthodoxies we take for granted.

If Ralph analyzed the "what" level, he would look for causes of bad strategy execution in the tasks, tools, and techniques people used. He would question the compliance of the team with doing what they agreed to do. As the manager, he would create structures to make the team comply. He would move some tasks from one executive to another to make things more efficient.

At the "how" level, Ralph would review the strategy design and planning, the processes, the embedded technology, the organizational chart designed to make it happen. He would question his directors about how they lead their departments to get the job done. He would work with his executive team on how to participate more, make better decisions, solve conflicts, avoid inefficiencies, and become more effective in streamlining the processes and operating principles of becoming an excellent company.

Focusing on the "why" would mean that Ralph would work with his executive team and his extended leadership team to challenge the company mission, vision, and legacy.

Each level impacts the following ones. If you change the reason "why" you do things, you will have to redesign your business model; then you will look at "how" you translate it to reality, and make sure you are doing "what" it takes to execute it. If you did all well, and with luck, you will eventually get the results you desired (see Figure 10).

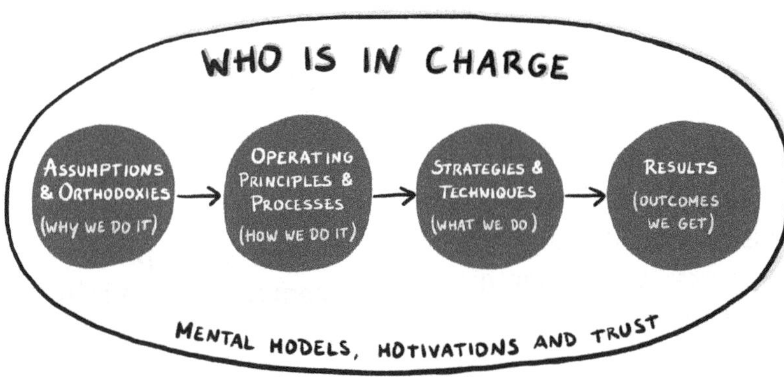

Figure 10 – Levels of causes of executive team problems

The process is unidirectional. You don't have to change business assumptions just because you do different things. You may, but you don't have to. Even when companies stumble into better ways of doing things, they don't rethink their original assumptions. They don't use information from the WHAT level to review and change HOW and WHY they do their business.

Think of Kodak inventing digital photography and burying it away, killing itself in the process. Remember how Deca records rejected The Beatles after auditioning them on January 1, 1962. Consider the multiple publishers who rejected the first book in the Harry Potter series, the best-selling book series in history, and you get what I am saying. When potential success goes against their assumptions, companies pass it by.

Even when companies stumble into better ways of doing things, they don't rethink their original assumptions.

Each of the levels asks different questions in a change management process:

What – Should we be doing different things?

How – Should we do things differently?

Why – Are we doing the right things?

There is yet another level of causality: the people "who" envision, decide, and execute the tasks, thus guaranteeing the desired results:

When potential success goes against their assumptions, companies pass it by.

Who – Do we have the right people to get things done? Who is in charge? What are the mental models, motivations and trust levels in the executive team?

Disrupting a business requires that we have the right people addressing the right questions. This is what *The 6P's of Executive Teams*® allow you to do.

When the executive team is the problem, only the executive team can become the solution

Any effect has several causes and any cause can have several effects. An event can be the cause and effect of itself.

I am not here to assert that executive teams are the only cause of everything in a company. Far from it. As a systems thinker, I believe in multiple and circular causalities. Any effect has several causes and any cause can have several effects. An event can be the cause and effect of itself.

I follow a principle rooted in my experience as a group and family therapist: you need to accept that you are part of the problem to be able to contribute to the solution. If you think that global warming is a problem for others, you will not recycle. Only when you accept that your behavior is part of the problem you will recognize you need to change it.

The same applies here. Suppose the CEO and the executive team members believe that company problems have no causality inside the C-suite. Every negative thing that happens is due to incompetent and misaligned people elsewhere in the company. Therefore, their solutions may fall short of wisdom and impact. At the very least, the executive team's decisions either contribute to increase or reduce the effectiveness and efficiency of current business opportunities. But we want to move way beyond "very least." We want you to be as successful as you can be.

You need to accept that you are part of the problem to be able to contribute to the solution.

If you want something, you take massive action to make success inevitable. Including the executive team as part of the causality of positive and negative results in the company guarantees that executives will do their utmost to get the desired results. Reaching outstanding results as a company always involves C-level decisions and actions. The CEO should make sure that C-level causes are covered in the desired solutions before anything else, saving them a lot of time and trouble later in the process.

If you want something, you take massive action to make success inevitable.

How We Got Here

To get that done, we need to integrate everything we mentioned in the previous chapters about what keeps this problem going. When we understand the current causes, we can propose a different way to address and solve them.

Chapter 2 – *It's happening on your shift* – explains the typical behavior modes of CEOs and how they contribute to the problem's maintenance. Avoidance, Command, Involvement, Operating, and Achievement Behavior Modes have different results, both on the executive team and the rest of the company.

In Chapter 3 – *And you will pay the price* – I went into detail about how much the behavior modes cost the CEOs themselves in impact, leadership, and position. The CEO's behavior can itself be part of the problem or the solution.

The CEO should make sure that C-level causes are covered in the desired solutions.

In Chapter 4 – *Been there, done that and have the scars to prove it* – I detailed the two types of causes that affect results. First, there are structural causes that hinder the effectiveness of executive teams. These are present in all circumstances. Addressing the causes frees the team from restrictions and improves collaboration. Second, we have been trying to solve the problem with a few generic solutions for developing executive teams. The solutions work most of the time with any other team in the company, but they don't respect the executive team's specific needs and constitution. Therefore, they have been failing to deliver what is needed.

As we also established in Chapter 1 –*The elephant in the room* – it makes sense to develop executive teams' effectiveness to result in excellent KPIs.

The question: how do we make sure we get the "who," the "why," the "how," and the "what" of executive teams right to reach outstanding results?

I want to stress the word *outstanding*. I have not been working for the last 25 years with *average* teams. Only once did I support a CEO to get the most out of his less than competent team, in a situation when he had no other choice. And twice I worked with dysfunctional teams.

Let me be clear on this: I work with good teams, very bright and competent professionals, often referred to as top-notch in their market. My clients are fast thinking and intelligent CEOs, with teams currently producing good results. Still, they are not satisfied with their companies being number two or only listed in their market's top 10. They want to be number one. These are ambitious professionals, often individually the best, but still did not find a way to lead their company to achieve its best results.

My job is helping executive teams going from good to great, so they can lead their companies to become outstanding according to their definition. I don't say this in arrogance. It's a mission.

My approach is not right for you if you

- manage a team with mediocre results due to lack of competence of its members,
- think that the job of the CEO is to know everything and control everything,
- believe in management by fear,

- follow carrot-and-stick practices,
- have unethical behavior,
- have a personal agenda that conflicts with the company's best interest,
- want to look good by providing team advisory but want no real change, or
- think that results should come without investment and that investing in people is a waste.

You will be better suited with training or replacing incompetent people, finding technology that allows you to control people better, doing some fun team building activities, and investing in getting a bigger stick and a juicier carrot.

I consider part of my job to challenge assumptions, business orthodoxies, operating principles and processes, motivations, and mental models, to reach a bigger Vision and a more engaging Mission. This approach is working for my clients.

The "invisible" structure of the executive team determines the visible behavior of its members.

Think of it as an iceberg. Above sea level, you see the smallest visible part of the ice, like the team members' observable behavior. You see the daily interactions, their patterns, and trends:

- Susan neglected José's contributions to improve the project.
- Derek tends to be late to work.
- Sandra and Kumar are always bickering.
- We can count on Benedita to have great marketing ideas.

These are visible interactions, behavior that anyone present can witness, see, hear, feel, smell. Below sea level is the bulk of the iceberg. You don't see it, but it determines what part, how much, and in what position the visible tip will appear.

Crack the bottom so that the iceberg tilts sideways, and you will have a different part visible.

The invisible part of the iceberg represents the structure of the team (see Figure 11).

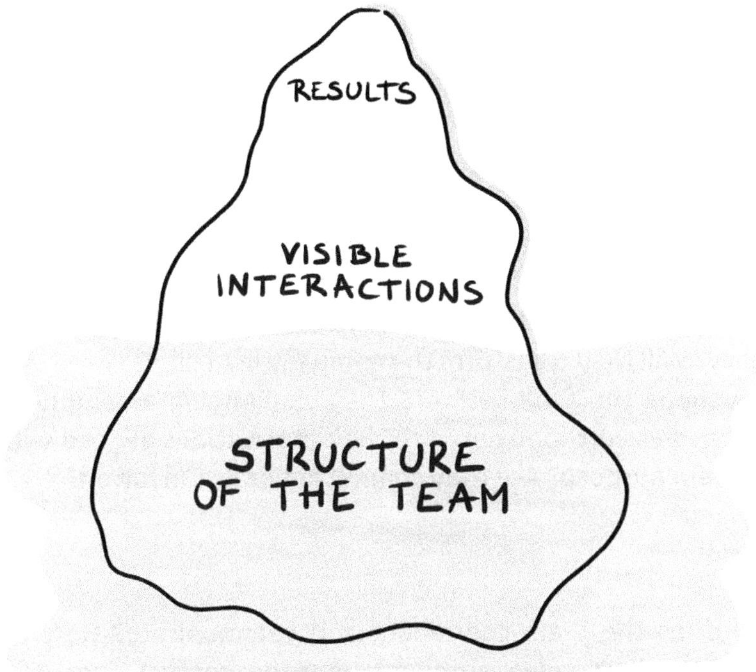

Figure 11 – Team structure determines results

The structure is precisely the "who", the "why", and the "how" of the executive team. If we get these levels right, then the "what" turns out for the best. Below are some questions that allow you to assess how well structured your team is around these principles.

For Who:

Who is in the team? How were they selected? Who is influencing the team even if from the outside? How do the structural causes we saw in Chapter 4 influence this executive team? Do we have the competences to achieve what we propose? Do the individuals in the team have the right attitude? Is there enough diversity? Is it safe for people to be who they are in the team? Is there a level of trust that allows for taking necessary risks? Are team members satisfied with the team's performance?

For Why:

Why was this team brought together? What requires this team to function as a team and not just as a group of individuals? Does the team have a common purpose, or do they just sign up for company strategic goals? Is there an ambitious Vision? Is there a Mission? Are team members contributing to a common legacy? Will they transform the company in positive ways? Will they shape their market? Are they challenging assumptions and business orthodoxies? Are their motivations aligned with the team purpose? Are they committed or just involved?

For How:

How does the team coordinate and communicate? How do team members solve problems, manage conflict, innovate, decide, and evaluate their dynamics together? Is the team able to implement team learning as a process? Are team members self-critical and assess their working processes? What are the operating principles and procedures for all this to be successful? Are they effective and efficient?

Visible interactions are the "what": team dynamics, tasks, operations, individual and group behavior.

It is challenging to create an effective and efficient team and reach outstanding results if your team members are not aligned and working with ill-defined processes to achieve an assortment of individual purposes. This is precisely the consequence of letting an executive team be structured by the intersection of random events instead of being directed by the CEO.

The executive team will obtain mediocre results if it suffers the impact of omnipresent structural causes for poor performance; if the past attempts to improve its dynamics were based on generic teambuilding solutions; and if the CEO's behavior mode falls into one of the three low-impact/high-cost categories.

There is a gap between business as usual and superior results, which I am sure you see – after all, you are reading this book (see Figure 12).

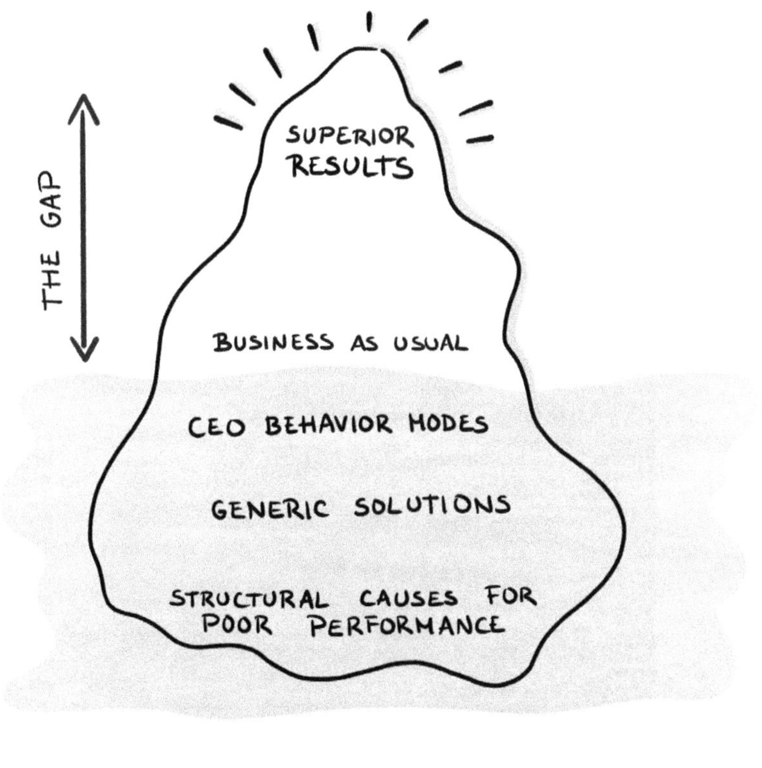

Figure 12 – The gap between business as usual and superior results

As we have seen, you cannot bridge the results gap by focusing on the" what" level: only doing different tasks, activities, and projects. That leads to *business as usual results.*

Revamp the structure of your executive team to achieve outstanding results. That's what *The 6P's of Executive Teams®* can do for you.

The 6P's of Executive Teams®

The 6P's of Executive Teams® is a model for ensuring that a team's structure contributes to reaching the best possible dynamics and highest possible level of results.

In my work with companies, we follow the P's sequence when structuring the team from internal to external focus: Purpose, Processes, People, Problems, Possibilities, and Potential. It is an onion-like structure with layers built on top of each other (see Figure 13).

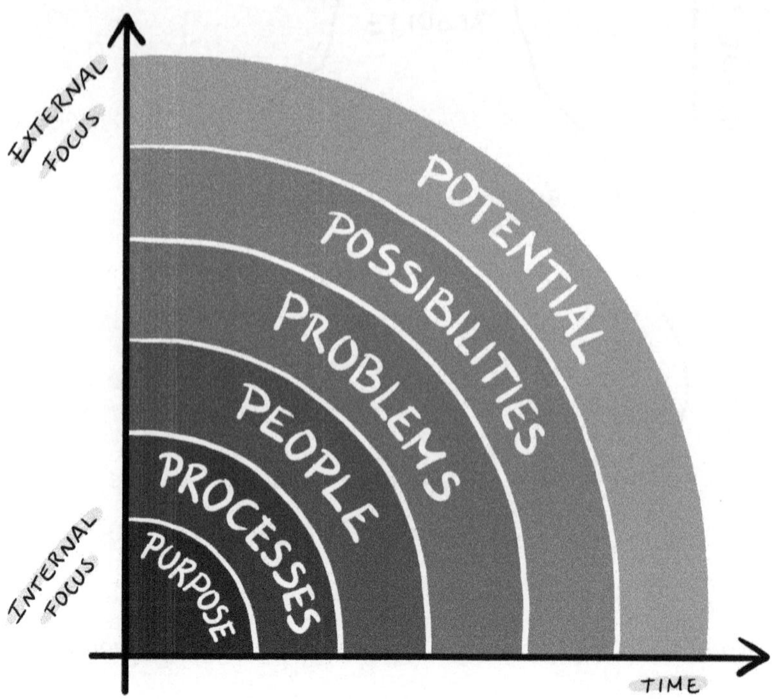

Figure 13 – The 6P's of Executive Teams®

Purpose

The core of the team is a common purpose. Without a common purpose, there's no reason for us to be a team. A purpose can have many dimensions, including financial, social responsibility, transformation, strategic, or other.

Purpose is an *emotional* reason that drives team performance above what all believe currently possible.

Achieving a high level of financial return for your shareholders is not the only viable purpose. That must be the consequence of a bigger purpose. Purpose is more than sales or market share figures. Purpose is an *emotional* reason that drives team performance above what all believe currently possible. The highest level of performance that we consider achievable is limited by the quality of interactions that the team has today. Team purpose must be so bold as to require our best selves to create the superior team to reach it.

At this level we define and agree the team purpose.

Processes

Processes structure the daily interactions and dynamics of the team. These are the ways we work together, the *how* of what it takes to produce something. By assessing these processes, we identify what needs to be changed. Depending on the team's needs, they may redesign many types of processes: envisioning, strategic roadmap, prioritization and planning, workflow, communication, coordination, and synchronization, meeting management, conflict management,

Team purpose must be so bold as to require our best selves to create the superior team to reach it.

problem-solving, innovation, talent management, coaching, people development; you name it.

Following a process is the best way to guarantee that a desired output is consistently delivered and creates effective team dynamics. A productive relationship dynamic, efficient decision making, cognitive diversity, are examples of results that we consider desirable to have consistently. That is what we achieve with the P for Process dimension.

Following a process is the best way to guarantee that a desired output is consistently delivered and creates effective team dynamics.

People

In the P for People layer, we do not ask if an organization has the right people in terms of competences, the right definition of profiles for the executive team, or if the executives we have are filling the jobs' technical profiles. These are questions for average or even lower performance executive teams.

P for People builds on what research shows are the most critical dimensions in creating a team: individual motivations, psychological safety, trust, and cognitive diversity. The challenge tackled here is to improve those dimensions in the executive team to foster individual and team effectiveness to get better company results.

Problems

The fourth P is for problem analysis and solving. Career success means you can solve bigger and more complex problems than before. At the executive team level, you expect to have the worst types of problems a company generates – big, deep, difficult, complex, unstructured,

Career success means you can solve bigger and more complex problems than before.

ambiguous, and expensive. It's surprising how unprepared we are to solve those types of problems. We tend to apply known processes to deal with a reality that does not conform to them anymore and fail to be critical of our thought processes.

As I will show in the chapter for Problems, our education does not prepare us to deal effectively with complex problems in human systems. And guess what? Most problems that get to the executive team are complex and all of them happen in the human system we call the company. At this layer, we make sure the team is prepared to deal with them.

Possibilities

The fifth P is for Possibilities. As the name suggests, this focuses on the executive team's ability to generate new ways of doing things. For this to happen, you need to develop a *learning team*: a group of people who continually enhance their capabilities to create what they want to make. Only when the executive team can do this can they lead the company to consistent growth.

Our education does not prepare us to deal effectively with complex problems in human systems.

At this level, we focus on creating new and expansive thinking patterns, releasing collective aspiration and supporting team members to see how the whole together can be transformed. We revise information selection, collection, and processing patterns as a basis for designing viable strategies.

Potential

The sixth P is for Potential. We aim to maximize the potential for transformation that the executive team can have in the company and its market. What is the limit? How do we know that limit applies to us? The Potential layer usually includes the co-creation of a desired leadership culture in the company.

By aligning all management levels with desired values and behaviors, we maximize strategy execution effectiveness and efficiency. Having a cohesive company with engaged employees unleashes the transformational power of a community. With the right strategy, this is unbeatable.

At this level, we revisit Purpose to understand if what we defined is still valid, or we can make it even more ambitious. Typically, as the team develops, what we believe is possible also expands.

How to take your executive team from good to great by following the 6P's

By following the 6 P's in the executive team development process, we address the Who, the Why, the How, and the What of the executive team.

As the team develops, what we believe is possible also expands.

We make sure that CEO behavior mode is matched to the strategies the team needs for it to be most effective. The CEO moves out of the *push zone* and into the *pull zone*, as described in Chapter 2. This means that by implementing this process with their teams, the CEO's behavior mode goes immediately from Avoidance, Involvement or Command Modes to Operating Mode and Achievement Mode.

We effectively address the structural causes of executive teams' poor performance and neutralize most of their effects. And we even integrate team building activities as part of our process as needed, but never consider them the backbone of the team structuring solution. This ensures that we get out of the box of *tried-and-failed solutions* and into the realm of using activities tailored to this group's needs.

The 6P's Model is a flexible structure that allows for understanding and adaptation to each team and company's needs and constraints. Depending on your team's real circumstances, we might dive deeper or even avoid working on each P entirely.

For example, I worked one full year with a pharma company's executive team on their Processes. We ran one workshop per quarter, as that was their most significant need. With another team, I spent only half a day on that dimension. Most teams find it relatively easy to define an ambitious common Purpose. In contrast, I worked for three days with a team before they agreed on their Purpose. Each team is unique. My job is to adapt to support them.

This also means that the sequence is not always the one I described. There are many reasons why we might start on the P for People, instead of the P for Purpose, for example. Most of them have to do with severe trust issues, diversity and inclusion problems, rigid personal conflict, and difficulties in defining who is in or out of the team. In those circumstances, we must secure the minimum openness of team members required to work on Purpose. But there are also positive reasons to start elsewhere than in Purpose, like the fact that a clear, agreed purpose already exists, or the fact that we need to get People in the right mindset to implement a specific leadership or talent development program, for example.

In some situations, I might go back and forth between some of the Ps. I might need to come back to Processes because new insights emerge when we are working on the Problems dimension. I might need to revisit People because there were changes in team members and a partially new team. But in general, it is possible to efficiently work with an executive team moving from their Purpose to their Potential in sequence.

What makes the model so useful is that it allows the CEO and their team to understand: "We are having this type of problem, but we know its origin and the best way to solve it." Once I asked a general manager: "Does your team have a purpose?" And she said, "Yes, of course." She defined the purpose for me. When I asked the team members, none of them considered that they had a common purpose apart from business goals. An executive team needs to find these differences in perception before they break the team. We clarify all of that as part of the work.

By following *The 6P's of Executive Teams®* as a model for structuring the team, we guarantee that your executive group becomes a Chief Executive Team, thus bridging the gap to produce superior results. This is the aim of this model (see Figure 14).

Figure 14 – Structuring a Chief Executive Team

We want growth, innovation, and leadership, but we cannot do it alone. Not anymore in this century. We need to get the whole company to think and implement the required actions. We must develop the most effective and agile executive team to impact the entire organization and the market. Once in place, we can achieve results that will make everyone shine.

The 6P's of Executive Teams® assessment tool

We want growth, innovation, and leadership, but we cannot do it alone.

Everything in the model I described was based on research right from Frank's team – the first executive team I coached on this path, as I describe in the Introduction chapter. And I kept the model grounded on evidence. We assess how well the executive team is faring on each of the six dimensions. Each P includes the evaluation of a set of variables that impacts team and company performance.

Each P includes the evaluation of a set of variables that impacts team and company performance.

My job is to support the executive team's structuring through the dimensions that science and management research prove are the most effective in generating the best results for your company. Knowing where the team stands on that helps the process.

By using our assessment tool, you can get:

1. **An evaluation of the effectiveness of your executive team.** It doesn't matter if you are the CEO, a Board member, or the CFO. Sooner or later, you will want to be able to analyze the effectiveness of the executive team. Because we use an evidence-based method, you can be sure that our assessment results predict future success and identify problems of your executive team.

2. **Before-after comparison.** When implementing any executive team development, especially *The 6P's of Executive Teams®*, you can use our assessment tool to measure progress and secure accountability.
3. **Ranking of executive teams of local operating companies.** A global executive board sometimes finds it difficult to measure how well each executive team of its local operating companies is doing. Results of the current team dynamics take long to show, and when they do, it might be too late to avoid expensive problems. Also, it may be useful to compare the level of effectiveness of the local operating companies of one specific region (ASIAPAC, EMEA, and so on) to align expectations and strategy.
4. If you are responsible for **global implementation of company culture, values, or leadership practices**, you will need to know if the local executive teams can align with them. Our tool gives you that insight and proposes development paths for each of them.
5. **Benchmark for a specific market or sector.** If you lead a trade or industry association of any kind, you can use our tool to provide a benchmark against which your associates can compare their executive team.
6. **Diagnosis of leadership problems.** With our tool, we can understand how much the leadership team is ready to transform their leadership practices and how much they are aware of the expectations that the whole company has about them.
7. **Finding misalignment in the executive team.** Since we use a 360° rating, we have multi-rater viewpoints on the same subject. If your executive team is misaligned, we will find out and have a clear idea of what to do.
8. **Finding misalignment between the executive team and the rest of the organization**. The tool reveals the issues by analyzing different data from the assessment.

9. **Involvement of extended leadership teams in the development of the executive team.** Having direct reports of the executive team giving feedback to their bosses' team development is an excellent way to create both support and commitment to what needs to get done. Working on the effectiveness of the executive team is not an end per se. We always aim for the improvement of the results of the whole company. Everyone must be committed to that.
10. **Adjusting the 6P's intervention to the specific needs of this team/company.** This is the primary reason why this assessment was created. By analyzing its results, I can design the most suited development process for your executive team.

If your concern is the effectiveness of the executive team, this is the way to address it.

The next chapters

Each of the next six chapters is dedicated to one of the P's: Purpose, Processes, People, Problems Possibilities and Potential. We go in-depth about each of them.

6

P FOR PURPOSE

"The work developed by Ricardo Vargas with the management team was fundamental to achieve alignment and generate change processes, facilitating the existence of a common vision, embodied in visible and concrete actions in the company."

– Afonso Garcia | Novartis | Head People & Organization Global Medical

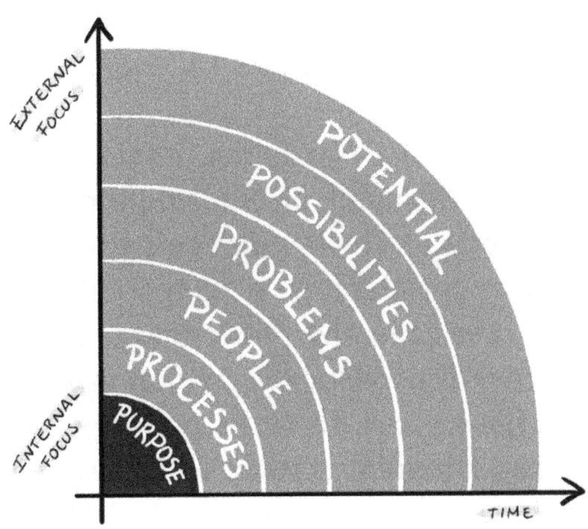

Figure 15 – P for Purpose

Conflicting individual purposes at executive level

JÜRGEN RECENTLY ASSUMED the CEO position for the local operating company of a pharma multinational. He is in his first CEO job after a solid career managing increasingly bigger sales departments in two different companies and running a headquarters position in marketing. He has set the personal goal of delivering two-digit growth based on innovation.

Bill is the oldest of the group and has the highest tenure in the company. He tightly controls sales from his Chief Sales Officer position. Considered old school by many and a bad leader by some, he has issues with Jürgen's appointment as CEO because he wanted that job. Having delivered results consistently over the years, he believes he has done enough to deserve it. He has adopted the strategy of testing how solid Jürgen is so he can get the CEO job. If Jürgen makes a mistake, Bill is watching.

Andrew is a star CFO who landed in this local company with a clear purpose to advance his career as fast as possible. HR assessed him as having high potential, and he knows that if he does things right, he's less than 10 years away from the global executive board. To achieve that, he must take no risks and deliver enough to contribute significant resources to the Western Europe region he reports to, even if local company growth suffers a bit.

As an ambitious pharmaceutical engineer, Anne is currently the General Manager of the single generic medicine factory that the company owns. She feels stuck there because the generic drug business is a commodity that's totally non-strategic for the company. The longer she stays there, the dimmer her career prospects will be. For Anne, the pharma business has to have a soul. This view opposes that of Andrew, the CFO. She had frequent clashes with him about the why, the how, and the what of several projects. With an MBA from a top university, Anne is ready to take on a more visible job, preferably in sales. Her purpose is to get a successor ready to take her role over so that she can move on to Bill's job.

George is the Chief People and Culture Officer. As a competent organizational psychologist, he knows the research backing up the importance of teamwork at the company's top. However, he struggles with the executive team's conflicting goals and desire for each other's jobs. George believes in setting limits in the team for acceptable and non-acceptable behavior. He does all he can to mobilize each team member to join efforts in more productive ways. But Jürgen does not support him, and neither do his peers, who are involved in turf wars with each other.

The remaining three people in the team – Cara, Kelly, and Sean – are more the follower type and want to deliver on their current assignments. They are waiting for Jürgen to be clear about what's next so that they can perform accordingly.

The company's purpose is not the executive team's purpose

George gave me a call. A visionary by default, he wants his executive team to be the best in the region, and he knows they are far from it. An internal survey yielded terrible results for the executive team, and George wants to act on it before the alarms go off at the regional level. He asked me to meet Jürgen and define the best way forward.

Jürgen wanted me to deliver a workshop where I aligned his team members' behavior with more productive practices. "Just get them in line and do it quickly." As usual, the client expected the magic to happen fast.

I started with the qualitative and quantitative *The 6P's of Executive Teams®* assessment. One of the questions I usually put in these initial interviews is, "Does your executive team have a common purpose, clearly formulated?" Jürgen quickly dismissed the question with a strong, "Yes, of course." Later I interviewed all his direct reports and asked them the same question. Most of them said, "No, we don't have a team purpose."

CEOs and their teams often have opposite ideas about what is going on in the executive team. Sometimes there's a high level of denial behind it. Sometimes there's misinformation or coverup. Jürgen and his team had a difference of beliefs and understanding.

Because Jürgen came from the regional headquarters, the global policies and rules had more influence on him than on people from the local operating company.

Jürgen saw the company's purpose as "Innovation in science to improve individual lives", the only motto necessary to inspire everybody to do their best. Also, it ticked his cherished topic of innovation, triggering good emotions, and righteous actions.

When I asked him if the *executive team* had a common purpose, clearly formulated, he uttered the *company's purpose*. From his tone, I sensed he was a bit annoyed at what he thought was my lack of preparation. In his judgment, as a supposedly competent consultant, I should have at least read the company's website, where that sentence shines to inspire the world. As you may have guessed by now, I allowed him to think that badly of me until I had the answers of all the team members.

At the workshop, I presented my evaluation based on quantitative and qualitative interviews. The executive team rated poorly on the *Purpose* dimension of effectiveness.

Jürgen was appalled. Not only he had hired an unprepared consultant to do the job, but also part of his team did not even know the company's purpose. What were they thinking? The team members were also puzzled. Had they misread my question?

They had not. I asked everyone about team purpose, using the same formulation, and they answered with something different in mind. Different interpretations can spell doom in many areas of a team. Just think about strategy execution or product development being interpreted in different ways.

In the case of purpose, we can quickly resolve differences if all involved understand the concepts we are using. Jürgen and two other team members had the company purpose in mind when I asked about the team purpose. The remaining people correctly interpreted my question as being focused on team purpose.

But the real problem was not semantics. Jürgen's team members were pursuing different individual purposes as guidance for their decisions. In the absence of a clearly formulated team purpose, you don't have a team; you have a group of individuals kind of working together.

Now you might be asking why did I not clarify the difference in the first interview with Jürgen? I didn't because the company purpose can, in some circumstances, also be the team purpose. Jürgen could have been right, and he was right according to his work ethic. It all depends on how the company purpose is formulated and the level of explicit commitment the executive team puts behind it. To understand the details, we need to dive into the types of purpose.

In the absence of a clearly formulated team purpose, you don't have a team; you have a group of individuals kind of working together.

There are three different types of purpose in any company: *company purpose*, *individual purpose*, and *team purpose*. They have distinct causes and effects and need to be managed separately to induce outstanding performance.

I explore each of them separately in the next sections.

Company purpose

At the end of the 19th century, Unilever's founder, William Lever, set the company's purpose as "Making cleanliness commonplace." In 2010, the company changed the purpose to

"Making sustainable living commonplace" and set three targets to measure the progress towards this purpose.[50]

1. Improve the health and well-being of one billion people in the world
2. Reduce negative environmental impact in sourcing raw materials in a sustainable way while enhancing livelihood
3. Own different brands, for example, the soap brand, Dove, which took this mission even further

Novo Nordisk is a Danish pharma company that specializes in diabetes care. It defines its contribution as "To discover, develop, and manufacture better biological medicines and make them accessible to people with diabetes throughout the world."50

There are three different types of purpose in any company: *company purpose, individual purpose*, and *team purpose.*

The Body Shop's motto is "Enrich, not exploit." The company committed to enriching people, products, and the planet. They set several objectives, with one being to help 40,000 economically vulnerable people around the world access work. Another is to ensure that 100% of natural ingredients are traceable and sustainably sourced to protect 10,000 acres of forest and other habitats[50].

Anita Roddick, the CEO, says, "Most businesses focus all the time on profits, but I think that is deeply boring. I want to create an electricity and passion that bonds people to the company."[51]

Whole Foods, an organic grocer owned by Amazon, defines its purpose as, "With great courage, integrity, and love, we embrace our responsibility to co-create a world where each of us, our communities, and our planet can flourish."[50]

A recently published study by EY Global Leadership Forecast/Corporate Board suggests that purposeful companies *outperform* the stock market by 42%. Companies without a sense of purpose *underperform* the market by 40%. The ones that rank *average* on the continuum have a purpose statement but don't engage their people around it.[52]

Harvard Business School professors John Kotter and James Heskett published a study based on a decade-long period showing that purposeful, value-driven companies outperformed their counterparts in stock price by a factor of 12.[53]

A recent study by PricewaterhouseCoopers says that 79% of business leaders believe the organization's purpose is central to business success.[54]

The Gartenberg Study, published in 2016, involved over 500,000 people across 429 firms in the U.S. and collated 917 firms' yearly observations from 2006 to 2011. They concluded that firms with employees who maintain strong belief in their work's meaning will experience better performance. Firms that have a high purpose and clarity and engage their employees around it have systematically higher future accounting and stock market performance than other companies.[55]

This research indicates the positive impact on both operating financial performance and forward-looking financial measures or performance measures in the presence of a clearly defined purpose that results in employee engagement. Not only the financial KPIs of companies benefit. They also have more satisfied and loyal customers.

Simon Mainwaring, a *New York Times* bestselling author, reports that 91% of consumers would switch brands if a different brand were purpose-driven and had similar price and quality.[50]

Consumer research by Cone and Porter Novelli shows that 67% of people feel companies need to express caring about them and their families. Seventy-nine percent said they're more loyal to purposed brands. Seventy-three percent said they would defend these brands, and another 67% said they are more willing to forgive such a company for a mistake.[56]

Company purpose easily translates into customer satisfaction, loyalty, and financial results. Your company needs a purpose that is compelling and unique to increase your chances of success. The uniqueness part is the most difficult. Many companies in the same business sector tend to gravitate around the same buzzwords to generate their purpose, in a process that often does not include their employees' contributions.

For Pharma business the key words are life, health, innovation, and science.[57] In this chapter, for confidentiality reasons, I created Jürgen's company purpose from these buzzwords. That purpose does not pertain to any company I know or have worked with.

Why do companies need a purpose?

Why does purpose have such an impact on different types of results? Can't this impact be obtained by business-as-usual operating on strategic targets and goals?

Since the Industrial Revolution, through the Efficiency Movement,[58] and the *Principles of Scientific Management* of Frederick Taylor,[59] management has focused on reducing waste and increasing efficiency. To achieve this goal, the company needs to standardize processes, outcomes, and competences as much as possible, thereby reducing the impact of individual idiosyncrasies in the production system. Methods created include

- assembly lines,
- process management,
- control systems,
- organizational design,
- supply chain,
- strategic planning,

- reporting systems,
- KPIs,
- management by incentives,
- management by objectives,
- business process reengineering,
- total quality management, and
- lean manufacturing, among others.

Most management systems created in the last 200 years focused on reducing the likelihood of one person screwing up the work of many. Together, the combination of these systems allowed companies to grow big and complex. Of course, their implementation also prevents one person from averting the failure of many.

To standardized management, reducing the likelihood of an error or a solution is mostly the same. Any deviation in the designed process is an anomaly to be corrected.

The challenge arises from realizing that we cannot write procedures and standards for everything that people do. The complexity of the market is forcing companies to reopen space for individual initiative and freedom to innovate. Through that space, through that crack in the traditional management systems, purpose comes in.

Organizational purpose gives employees the reference they need to make decisions in uncertainty.

Organizational purpose gives employees the reference they need to make decisions in uncertainty. It's impossible to write procedures for everything, but it *is* possible for individuals to understand how to decide every day according to a common purpose.

Complexity, volatility, uncertainty, and hostility of the globalized world have grown so much that predicting any management initiative's outcomes becomes impossible. Therefore, maintaining process design and compliance against all circumstances becomes suicidal. We always need to ask ourselves, "Are our systems fostering innovation and adaptation, or are they slowing us down?" When the answer is the latter, we must act fast.

Managers were forced to find complementary ways to align individual behavior with a company strategy that is always adapting, a permanent work-in-progress. Purpose is one of the most credible solutions found so far.

How does company purpose work?

Purpose is the reason for which something exists or is done, made or used. Founders create companies to serve their shareholders' intention and function to serve the needs of their stakeholders. Misalignment between these outcomes creates waste and inefficiency.

The simplest way to reduce this source of inefficiency is to make the company purpose explicit. By itself, this is just a declaration of intention. The fact that the managers of company X state a specific purpose doesn't mean that the company already functions as such. Most of its employees must align their decisions and actions by that purpose to make it real.

To effectively align individual behavior, purpose needs to be the single most important criteria for decision making. That means shaping the recruitment, selection, training, development, performance management, and career processes to guarantee that the company has the best group of like-minded individuals to contribute to its purpose. In daily management decisions and operations, when there's no clear process for what and how has to be done next, purpose has to be the source of clarification, guiding actions.

Individual purpose

Companies accomplish their purposes through individuals. Purpose drives individuals and is the "cause" of human behavior. It's the ultimate goal, the motive, the reason why we do things.

The same action can have many different purposes. Let's take marriage as an example. People might marry for various reasons: to leave their parents' home, to improve their financial well-being, to have children, to live with the person they love, to fulfill God's will, to comply with social norms, to become a respected citizen, to avoid loneliness, to punish someone else, and endless other reasons. Sometimes the ulterior motive for our actions and choices is not even clear to us. We have all had the experience of connecting dots about ourselves only in hindsight.

Purpose drives individuals and is the "cause" of human behavior. It's the ultimate goal, the motive, the reason why we do things.

Individual purposes can be broader or narrower in scope, more abstract or concrete. Each of us has a hierarchy of purposes. Even when several purposes determine our behavior, some will be broader or narrower and can be put together as a sequence, from concrete to abstract. I might go to work today because:

I have tasks to do

I want to show my competence

I want to be independent

I am a contributing member of society

I have bills to pay

When we move from bonus to social contribution, we enlarge the scope of our purpose for going to work today. Performing specific tasks is quite narrow and short-term.

Showing my competence pertains to the job role and is medium-term. Maintaining financial independence goes beyond the current job role and my current level of competence; it's long-term. Being a contributing member of society is perennial. If this is my core belief of what a person should be, this purpose will guide my actions in this or any other job and private life.

True individual purpose is this broader, general motive for our behavior that is transformative in all areas of our lives. When we move from short to long-term, from concrete to abstract, from local to global purpose, we also transition between:

Doing something – getting tasks finished

Having something – respect for my competence or independence from others

Being something – a contributing member of society

Each of us usually recognizes a small number of characteristics that a "good person" must have. We will try to fulfill those characteristics with our behavior. These are our individual purposes in life. These overarching motives drive everything we do.

Now imagine that your purpose is to make the world a better place. Therefore, you care for the well-being of unprivileged communities, and you want to reduce inequality in the world. The company you work for has stated the purpose as "To increase shareholder return." You witness how the trading practices of your company increase inequality in communities. Would you be motivated and engaged to do your best in such a company?

Individual purpose is the driver of engagement. Only when there's alignment between individual and company purpose is there full engagement of your employees' hearts and minds.

This alignment needs to happen in everyone's mind, to be able to influence their behavior. Otherwise, company purpose is just a fancy tagline without any real-world significance.

Let's return to the example of the Pharma company executive team at the beginning of this chapter. When the CEO, Jürgen, assumed that the company purpose could also be the executive team purpose, he was missing the fact that team members had their own purposes and a different level of commitment to the company purpose. Consequently, unless it's explicitly discussed and agreed that the company purpose can act as team purpose, it can't. He was assuming it to be a driver of individual behavior when nothing warranted that conclusion.

Executive team purpose

Executive team purpose connects company and individual purposes of its members to the full organization's purpose. It is the missing link between them.

Company purpose needs to be quite general to be as perennial as possible. Unilever kept its initial purpose, "Making cleanliness commonplace" for 120 years.[55] This stability is vital as general guidance, but it's not enough for an executive team.

Executive team purpose connects company and individual purposes of its members to the full organization's purpose. It is the missing link between them.

To get the best from your executive team, you need to generate a team purpose that bridges the perennial "being" of the company with the medium-to-long-term "being" of the executive team. Executive teams are everything but perennial. A 2019 study by Korn Ferry[60] found that CEOs were the only job role with an average tenure above 5 years. Every other C-suite role was below that mark.

PricewaterhouseCoopers' strategy consulting business completed a "2018 CEO Success Study," a 19-year analysis of the world's biggest 2500 companies.[61] It reports a record high 17.5% CEO turnover in 2018, above the last decade's norm.

When CEOs join a company, they also like to shape the C-suite as much as possible according to their vision and strategy, increasing other team members' turnover who find the environment no longer hospitable or consistent with their own ambitions.

With CEOs having a short average tenure at C-level of about three to five years, there needs to be a clear executive team purpose that can be achieved by the current team. Without this, C-suite executives will only care about their own immediate goals and the bridge between their individual purposes and company purpose will be missing. This disconnect is what we see in most executive teams, and it provides the basis for their misfortunes, as we have seen in previous chapters.

Most company purposes are no more than a dull description of what the company does. Much like a documentary of old lifestyles, they don't excite us to discover and create new universes. The executive team's purpose needs to merge team members' individual purposes in a powerful enough statement to build on the company purpose and inspire all employees to a different level of commitment.

So, the question is: what is an effective executive team purpose?

Characteristics of a good executive team purpose

These are the characteristics of a good executive team purpose:

1. Appeals to individual motives

A good team purpose must appeal to the individual motives of the people who espouse it. For that to happen, it needs to contain possible links to different motivators.

"Profit" and "shareholder return" by themselves appeal only to the shareholders. "Becoming a market leader" might be interesting for the sales area of the organization. "Innovation in science to improve individual lives" might be important for someone who wants to make the world a better place and to the ones connected to the research and development unit.

As people have several types of basic motivations, their behavior will be triggered differently by the same purpose. Therefore, we can't assume a purpose works for a team if we don't discuss and agree with it.

2. Challenging

Don't bother to write a single sentence for *Purpose, Mission,* or *Vision* of your company if the outcome is boring business as usual. There must be a reasonable degree of challenge to force us to become the better versions of ourselves and achieve the best possible performance together.

Challenge can be simultaneously personal, collective, and organizational. Take the following example:

> "We are recognized by customers as the best team to boost categories growth, deliver the best execution in store, and interpret consumers' needs."

This statement raises the bar for company processes, team behavior, and individual competencies at the same time. By assessing the clients' perception of the company's delivery on growth, in-store execution, and understanding of consumer needs, the executive team will receive valuable information to improve their own decision making, strategizing, and execution processes.

3. Defines a legacy

What will be left when your executive team dissolves and a significant part of it is replaced? Will some tangible signs prove you made a real difference together? Did you leave the company better prepared than when you joined it?

Consider these purposes:

> "We establish OurCompany as a thought leader for digital transformation reinforcing innovation and disruption to aim higher."

> "We ensure the success of OurCompany by making it the best place to work, to attract, and retain the best talent."

> "We will diversify our product portfolio and develop category X to rise above the penetration and per capita consumption of the last 20 years."

Each of the previous purposes can be measured at the end of the term of the executive team. Did we leave the legacy of our company being the thought leader on digital transformation? Did we become the best place to work, and did we improve our talent pool? Did we diversify the product portfolio? Did category X go above per capita consumption of the last 20 years? If so, we have a legacy.

You can look at these sentences as normal strategic targets, and they are. The difference is that to reach the company goals and strategic aim, the team does not need to do these specific things. Not screwing what is already working is a good enough approach to deliver what is expected in many circumstances.

It is precisely the whole team's optional challenge as a purpose that generates the extra effort and requires reaching different levels of effectiveness and efficiency. Suppose we don't need to increase per capita consumption of a category to meet our business targets but choose to do it. In that case, this legacy becomes a challenge connected to the team members' different motivators.

4. Transformational

Challenges can be big but still inside the bubble of who you are and how you do things. Sometimes you need to burst that bubble and go in new directions for your company to remain successful. A bold company *Vision*, to be achieved in the challenging period of five years or a decade, gives a hand to the process. But sometimes, you want to produce a real transformation.

Robert is the CEO of a local operating company in Belgium. Previously he managed three local operating companies in different countries for the same multinational. The business faces several challenges:

- It needs a revamp to adjust to a new consumer profile.
- There are supply-chain restrictions provoked by the suspension of international trading.
- New market needs were created by the pandemic.
- The company needs to recover from a couple of unsuccessful product launches.
- There is a requirement to improve penetration in new demographics, and a couple of other challenges.

When we discussed the company's strategic roadmap in a workshop, Robert's executive team had two choices:

- either to improve the way they traditionally did business to allow a solution for those challenges, or
- to transform the business practices and model to create a more modern company, adapted to the 21st century.

We identified several management paradoxes that would justify creating a new level of "management consciousness". The team understood that keeping business as usual could soon become quite detrimental to the company's success.

The issue was that the shareholders of their very traditional ninety-year-old company did not see business model transformation as the staple of the day. Any changes in those dimensions could negatively impact the emotional connection between consumers and their brand. They were right as well. Robert and his team needed to be both careful and fast in making changes.

The executive team found that the solution was to address the management paradoxes head-on. They created an overarching executive team purpose:

> "We lead as a team to perpetuate the history of OurCompany and create its next century."

They complemented this purpose with more specific sub-purposes connected to each paradox initially identified: short- and long-term results, maintaining company identity and changing its content, local roots, and global organization, financial and social impact, growth, and profitability.

Any executive team purpose must verify the team's agreement on:

Why we need to be a team

What we want to achieve in the next three to five years

The type of decisions we will have to make

The management paradoxes we will have to be conscious about and manage

Criteria for strategic and operational decision making

How we will measure our collective success at the end of our tenure

The answer to all these points creates a solid compact on why we need to be a team and who we want to be. That's your executive team purpose.

5. Connected to the company's Mission and Vision

You absolutely must make sure that your executive team's purpose aligns 100% with the company's Mission and Vision (when explicit). Design it in a way that bridges the motivational gap between company purpose and individual purposes: first the individual purposes of the C-level team, then the individual purposes of the rest of the company's members.

A good executive team's value is that it introduces a new layer of meaning, challenge, concreteness, and emotion between the company and the individual layers. It creates a renewed identity of the executive team, which will foster new decisions, actions, and achievements.

How to get to an executive team purpose?

I usually run a workshop where we discuss with the executive team the answers to the many questions you read in this chapter:

1. Are we a team or a working group?
2. Do we need to be a team?
3. Are there things we can achieve as a team that we wouldn't as a working group?
4. What do we want to achieve in three to five years?
5. Is this evolutionary or transformational, compared to the company's business model and operations?
6. If we identify a transformation, is it warranted by the Board and Shareholders? How much are we supported to deliver on it?
7. How will we measure our collective success at the end of our tenure (for ourselves as a team, not for the advancement of our careers.)
8. Do we have a clear legacy we want to leave behind? How can we best describe it?

9. What are the most mission-critical decisions that we need to make in our journey?
10. Are there any management paradoxes making those decisions difficult? Which?
11. Can we decide on strategic and operational decision-making criteria upfront?
12. What is the executive team job that arises from the company's Mission and Vision that we still did not address?
13. How can we make the company's strategic intent more intelligible for our employees?
14. What initiatives would help our associates understand better the company's strategy and become emotionally engaged with it?
15. What motivates each of us? What is the difference that each of us wants to make in the world? How can we connect these to the tasks at hand?
16. How can we become better leaders?
17. What are the leadership practices required to deliver on the overarching purpose?
18. What type of professional will I be (individually) when I deliver on this?
19. Do I feel energized by what we decided, or is it just a sequence of bland sentences?
20. What is the final level of commitment we have with our purpose?

Through purpose, people connect emotionally to a bigger entity.

You don't need to answer all of the above questions to get to an excellent executive team purpose. Some will be more relevant than others for your quest. Most of the time, a good, facilitated discussion only needs one question to ignite your team members' passion and deliver the desired results.

No purpose, no team

Successful companies embody the importance of purpose. Through purpose, people connect emotionally to a bigger entity. They assume a collective identity and develop a sense of belonging. True purpose has a human impact. Purpose means making a positive difference in the lives of others. Your purpose leads you to do the right thing, reinforced by the work of others who share and practice the same purpose. This benefits people and businesses, as it releases discretionary energy that your associates can put on the job and increases their satisfaction for producing something meaningful.

True purpose has a human impact.

My experience of over two decades supporting executive teams in getting to their purposes is that there is a before and after team purpose definition. If you as a team member feel an emotional release, clarity of intention, and togetherness that you did not feel before, you have a purpose. Most CEOs are unaware of how important this leadership tool is. It releases the extra commitment and energy that your team members can decide to put on the job.

If you don't have an explicit common purpose, you don't have a team.

If you don't have an explicit common purpose, you don't have a team.

7

P FOR PROCESSES

"Brilliant! Ricardo has scientific evidence proving the transformational impact for companies of his practical experience and organizational knowledge. The scientific evidence supporting his programs makes them highly credible and top class, and raises all clients' expectations."

– Pedro Abreu Rodrigues | Eurobic | Director

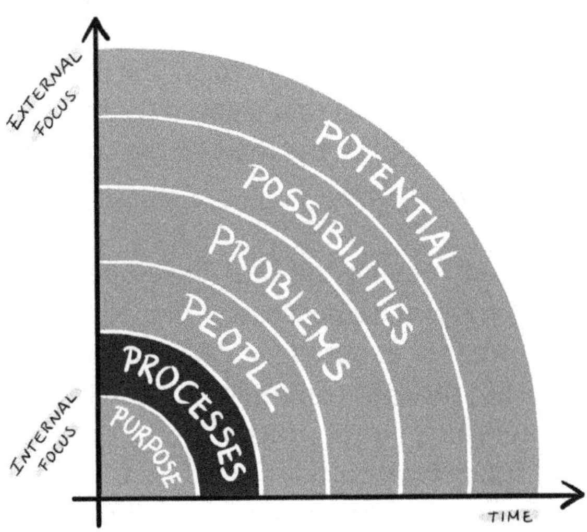

Figure 16 – P for Processes

JOHN AND MATHEW are co-founders of a start-up in the entertainment business – XCT/ZON. Mathew is the product wizard, the idea man who created the first successful product that took the company from concept to scale-up in five years. He occupies the Chief Product Officer position.

John is the CEO. He has been instrumental from the beginning to create the context that brought Mathew's ideas to life. He is a soft-spoken man who convinced investors to back the company from seed capital to series C funding and manages the company without ever raising his voice. Valued at $250 million, with a solid base of global clients and a product pipeline that keeps investors hooked, the business is growing fast.

The executive team has five other people:

- Andrea, the Chief Commercial Officer
- Rudy, the Chief Technical Officer
- Ana, the Chief Financial Officer

Andrea, Rudy, and Ana have been with the company since the initial funding.

- Thomas, the Chief Marketing Officer, came later into the team, replacing a previous person.
- Mara is the Chief People Officer. She is the latest addition to the team, in a role created for her. With the war for talent going on in the market, the company requires her skills for success.

Attracting and keeping the best developers is critical for XCT/ZON. These are quite successful individuals. They know all about their areas of expertise and have proven their worth.

John, the CEO, thought continuing to feed the pipeline and successfully launching one product after the other to grow the company to $500 million quickly should be a "normal expectation." He announced an aggressive growth plan for the next five years but accomplishing that goal was not so easy.

The first sign he saw was team meetings lacked the efficiency he wanted. There were too many side discussions and magnification of small problems. Mathew (CPO) and Rudy (CTO) tended to engage in arguments that escalated quickly into the blame game. Both were serial entrepreneurs.

For Mathew, XCT/ZON was his second start-up, for Rudy the third. Both are quite eager to bring their previous experiences to XCT/ZON. They were confident they knew what works and what doesn't, what to do and what not to do. Their convictions result in arguments that Mathew tends to win, given his co-founder status. Rudy nurtures his grudges and retreats to develop new arguments.

Andrea (the CCO) works well with Thomas (the CMO). Sharing the job of bringing money from different revenue streams, they clarify each other's contributions for a bigger pie.

When yet another sidetracking discussion starts in an executive meeting, Andrea rolls her eyes, and Thomas raises and lowers his eyebrows while grunting in acknowledgment. They just need to get great products to make money; it shouldn't be so challenging to get the pipeline moving with so many brilliant people in the team.

Mara is not happy. Her talent attraction and retention goals are not met because the company's leadership behaviors don't align with what younger Millennials and Generation Z expect from their managers. She sees the impact of Mathew and Rudy's little turf wars affecting the teams in their departments. Mara understands how the Andrea-Thomas coalition creates an "us-versus-them" atmosphere in the executive team that contaminates the rest of the company. She tries nicely to get her colleagues to understand the bigger context of their actions, but it's not working and, lacking tenure-based credibility, she must be careful.

Ana (the CFO) is on a mission to prepare an IPO and keep investors happy with what they get. An experienced executive, she's the only one in the team over fifty years old. She sees how the dynamics of the executive team drain company value.

If their effectiveness was higher, the company could launch more and better products earlier, generating more cash to scale it further. She continually presses John to act and align the executive team.

John expected to be able to focus on the business. He has a company to scale, international investors to please, numbers to deliver, and people to inspire and lead. He set up this executive team to support that, but they seem to create new problems.

Concerned about the team dynamics' obvious and subtle signals, John invited me in as advisor. He is frustrated because some company processes are not efficient enough to deliver the desired results, although he expects his executive team to have sorted that out already.

As part of my initial assessment, I asked him about his executive team—who they were, their behaviors, and dynamics. He described the non-verbal reactions of Andrea and Thomas, and the issues I referred before. He receives input during spontaneous interactions with team members. They complain about each other.

I also inquired about his goals and previous initiatives to deal with the perceived team inefficiency. With frustration in his voice, he said, "You put together a team of six aces on a mission. You expect the result to be at least ten, and in our case, it's five. We are delivering less value collectively than we have individually."

Synergy: when 1+1=3

Synergy is a property of systems that occurs when the interaction of elements combined produces a greater total effect than the sum of the individual contributions.[62] Best known through the 1+1=3 formula, it means that two competent people working together can produce a better result than the same people working individually and summing up their results in the end. This concept also opens the possibility of its opposite, the

Executive teams tend to underperform when compared to the potential individual contributions of their members.

1+1=1 formula, where two people working together reduce the contributions of each other.[63]

When John said he put together a team of six competent people and anticipated a result bigger than the sum of the individual contributions, he meant he expected a synergistic effect from his team. That was not happening.

This is one of the observations I most frequently hear when interviewing executives. Executive teams tend to underperform when compared to the potential individual contributions of their members. If synergy is not happening, you don't have a team; you have a working group.

If synergy is not happening, you don't have a team; you have a working group.

In Chapter 1 – *The Elephant in the Room*, I explained the differences between a team and a working group. You can narrow it down to three elements:

1. Teams have a common purpose and goals.
2. Teams have common processes to achieve their goals and realize their purpose.
3. Team members consider themselves mutually accountable for common purpose, goals, and processes.

Conclusions are easy:

> If you don't have a common purpose, you don't have a team.
>
> If you don't have common processes, you don't have efficiency.

If you don't have mutual accountability for purpose and processes, you don't have synergy.

I dealt with purpose in the previous chapter. I deal with processes and accountability in this one.

Before we go into the details, let me point out the obvious: defining clear processes and systems is the best way to secure that your executive team is resilient enough to withstand the loss of a charismatic CEO [64]. Your team is also effective and adaptable to market changes[65] and resistant to the effects of external shocks. Trusting your team is easy when you have the right processes in place.

Work management processes versus relationship management processes

When we speak of processes, most people immediately think about workflow. Workflow is "an orchestrated and repeatable pattern of activity, enabled by the systematic organization of resources into processes that transform materials, provide services, or process information. It can be depicted as a sequence of operations, the work of a person or group, the work of an organization of staff, or one or more simple or complex mechanisms."[66]

Trusting your team is easy when you have the right processes in place.

Most people think processes are a sequence of tasks and activities that become patterns subject to continuous improvement. This view is right according to the definition above, but it lacks substance. It loses a significant portion of what processes are and what they can do for your executive team.

To effectively manage team processes we must distinguish between two kinds:

Work management processes[67] determine the way people organize themselves to perform work. They describe what needs to be done, by whom, in which sequence and pace. If you organize a project plan, you get work management processes defined.

Relationship management processes[67] determine how people relate to each other while they are performing their jobs. They determine team effectiveness and define the type of relationships developed and maintained by communication, participation, conflict management, and change management.

Going back to the example at the start of this chapter, if John's executive team must decide between continuing to fund a product or killing it, a *decision management process* would be to:

1. choose a decision-making process
2. decide the relevant information for that process
3. take turns in providing said information
4. follow the decision-making activities as described in the process
5. arrive at a conclusion and evaluate its validity.

Half of John's team are engineers, including himself, and all are bright people. Why are they not doing it naturally? After all, they know everything about process engineering, rationalization, workflow, and continuous improvement. But it simply doesn't work like that.

Even when the decision-making work management process is clear, each team member might have a quite different definition of relevant information. Domination of the team by one or two members might unbalance the method of taking turns to provide information. Subsequent decision-making activities can become bumpy due to the resistance of some team members. One individual might not find the conclusion acceptable for many reasons. These are but a few of the difficulties involved.

When it's about people, it's always emotional and it's always personal.

People are not machines, and there can be many variations in how activities are done. Individual variations that people bring to their jobs account for huge differences in what they achieve. The discretionary energy, initiative, attention, effort, creativity, and commitment that your people decide to put into the job are the real game-changers. If they *only* do *what* their supervisor tells them, *when* their supervisor directs them, and how their supervisor conveys the message, your company is doomed.

When it's about people, it's always emotional and it's always personal.

If you want to release your employees' discretionary energy to propel the company's purpose, you must not focus on *work management processes;* you must focus on *relationship management processes.*

Work management processes allow you to manage the process or *what* is done. They answer the questions:

- What are the goals?
- What are the tasks to achieve them?
- What is the most efficient way to organize them?
- What is the process?
- What are the required skills to perform these activities?
- How do we train people or machines to perform them?
- How do we monitor and control execution?
- How do we evaluate results?

Relationship management processes allow you to manage *how* work is done. They answer the questions:

- Do we have a common understanding of our goals and how they concur to a common purpose?
- How can we all support the process?
- How can we make sure everybody participates and we have no bystanders?
- Is the way we relate to each other the most productive one? How can we improve that?
- Are there some topics that fracture the team in subgroups? Why? How can we address those topics without fracturing the team?
- What is the relationship level during our activities: transactional or transformational? How do we increase the transformational level when relevant?
- Do we understand the sources of conflict between goals and roles and how to keep them under balance, so we don't contaminate our relationship's quality?
- How do we create and maintain a high-performance team culture?
- How do we align unproductive behavior to foster team improvement?

To create a Chief Executive Team, we must take care of the two types of processes: work management and relationship management. If we only address work management processes, we focus on activities and we aim for efficiency at the cost of effectiveness and synergy. If we only address relationship management processes, we focus on effectiveness at the expense of efficiency and synergy. We need to manage work and relationship processes to generate synergy.

We need to manage work and relationship processes to generate synergy.

This was the challenge for John's executive team. They all knew what they needed to get done (goals and tasks) and their importance (purpose). They had different ideas about the best way to organize the tasks (work process management) and communicate with the organization as they got it done (relationship management processes). The result? Instead of 7 X 1 = 10 (I included John in the formula) they got 7 X 1 = 5, the *opposite* of synergy.

The most important processes for an executive team to develop synergy, as shown by management research, are:

- Role clarity
- Decision making
- Meeting management
- Conflict management
- Communication
- Participation
- Team effectiveness

I dedicate a section to each of them. But let me address the following: all these processes have an impact on relationship management. Although some of them are work management processes (mostly role clarity, decision making, and meeting management), I explore them from the relationship management side. Traditional management literature usually describes the work management dimension.

Role clarity: from job description to accountability

The concept of a management group at the top of an organization is old. It dates back to the time when markets were predictable, stable, and slow. Workers in general, were less educated. The few people with university degrees enjoyed an intellectual advantage that could be maintained for a generation. The complexity of management tasks was low as was their uncertainty. One person could keep updated in their area of expertise by applying the same mental operations for the same type of problems for decades.

Fast forward to today. Education levels have been steadily rising in the world. Each generation is more educated than the previous one. Also, science and technology are advancing at an unprecedented pace. Markets are hostile, unpredictable, and react fast. No company can maintain a clear advantage for long in the face of the exponential growth of complexity and uncertainty.

Half of what you know becomes obsolete in a couple of years. We all struggle to keep updated in our fields of expertise. There is a constant production of more knowledge than we can assimilate. If you rely on applying the same mental operations without constant revision and self-criticism, you become outdated fast.

The composition of executive teams reflects the need for having different viewpoints for every single complex problem. Suppose you want to go into a new market or get better at exploiting your current opportunities. In that case, you need the collaborative effort of people with financial, marketing, human resources, supply-chain, and sales skills, for example.

The problem is that assembling a team with these competencies does not guarantee success. Even if you describe their job profiles with (supposedly) clear areas of responsibility and processes or parts of processes, many gray zones will emerge from market changes and normal business operations.

Most companies don't even bother to write job descriptions anymore. It's impossible to keep them updated, and they generate more bureaucracy than results. Ironically, their best use is to protect someone from taking blame for a mistake – as in "But in whose job description is the responsibility for that?" – or as an excuse for not doing something – as in "That's not in my job profile." The phrase in a job description, "Performs all other duties as required", covers the ambiguity.

Role clarity is a clear understanding of who is going to get a task done. It requires having information about behaviors associated with each role performed in the job, how those roles interact with other team roles, and types of responsibility associated with each of them.[68]

As an example, you might have a well-designed innovation process, but if you don't have role clarity that enables people to commit to its implementation, the innovation performance of the company will suffer.[69]

As the market increases in volatility, the responsibilities of executives become ambiguous. We might have a customer experience project that "belongs" to the sales department, the marketing department, or the IT department. It depends on how it is formatted.

Business reality is too fluid to conform to a fixed job description.

Almost half of the transformational leadership projects I've designed and implemented with a company's executive team, as advisor, in the last twenty-five years originated out of the HR/ People / Culture / Talent Department. The most impactful ones included C-level executives of several functional areas, flexibly sharing responsibility that evolved along with the project. Business reality is too fluid to conform to a fixed job description.

Job descriptions are dead. Long live accountability.

As complexity and uncertainty increase, so does the importance of accountability. Accountability is the expectation that others can ask me to justify my beliefs, feelings, or actions.[70,71]

Executives cannot have in their job description: "You will have to justify how much you believe in the effectiveness of your executive team and how you behave to make it real. And, by the way, your emotions as you do so might be part of the conversation as well." But this is what accountability for the executive team's actions means.

When roles are not clear, we might have a situation where no one feels accountable for something, or several people feel

You don't solve an executive team's dysfunctionalities by lecturing them on high-performing teams or by taking them through some fun team-building activities.

accountable for the same thing. This tends to happen in teams with silo mentality, where all are focused on their functional area and defend their own interests without regard to the whole. Territorial fights or blame settings occur as a result, and unclear roles become weapons in these conflicts.

Team effectiveness and role clarity are positively correlated. They allow for focused discussions and alignment of different contributions to the common goal.[72]

C-suite leaders call me to rescue dysfunctional executive teams. You don't solve an executive team's dysfunctionalities by lecturing them on high-performing teams or by taking them through some fun team-building activities. The only way out of the pit is to address how they behave towards each other, how it feels working in the team, and what they believe the future will look like.

Bad CEOs don't want to deal with other people's emotions but force everyone to deal with theirs.

Sometimes the words *feeling* and *emotion* provoke a negative reaction when people read it on a book page. We believe the good CEO is as cold as a machine and objective as a microscope and that emotions have no place in business. If that was so, the same people who believe in this myth should never get frustrated, enraged, or happy about company results. Bad CEOs don't want to deal with other people's emotions but force everyone to deal with theirs. Leadership cannot function without emotional engagement.

Accountability for what?

Apart from guaranteeing role clarity in the team, CEOs must also include accountability for developing a Chief Executive Team as part of each executive's role. Every person must be made accountable for the actions, thoughts, and emotions that bring the team to a higher performance level. Collaboration must be part of it from the beginning.

Accountability for the team's success is one of the major gaps in executive teams' job descriptions. Traditionally, these only cover functional areas of responsibility and technical roles. No one gets informed that they must collaborate to develop the best possible Chief Executive Team. Your role definition should state this clearly and include leadership accountability. Leaders set and communicate the company's long-term strategy, motivate and coach employees, create the company's desired culture, and create an environment of execution and accountability for the people they are leading.[73] This should be expected by default.

Who's deciding this one? – Decision-making processes

In *Chapter 4 – Been There, Done That, and Have the Scars To Prove It*, I presented the most typical structural problems that challenge executive teams and foster non-collaborative behavior:

- Organizational design
- Lack of common goals
- Divergent processes and language
- Corporate politics
- Shareholder interferences
- Runner-up syndrome
- Paradoxes
- Hypocrisy

Altogether, they account for many conflicting interests of executive team members that make any decision-making difficult. You must add to that the individual differences in values and motivations that bring extra biases to information collection and processing, apart from directly influencing the decision-making process.

When you factor in all this, you might wonder how people can make decisions together. Many teams do it poorly. Most decision-making processes at the executive level are as inefficient and ineffective as they are further down in the hierarchy. Cognitive and organizational biases contribute to frequent performance shortfalls, such as the significant cost overruns that affect 90% of capital projects.[74]

The most common problems I encounter in executive teams' decisions are that they:

- Take too long
- Analyze too little information
- Generate winner-loser feelings, contributing to break the team in sub-units

Teams can avoid these problems if the decision-making accountabilities are clear, which often does not happen.

Five types of decision-making processes

I characterize executive decisions at top levels according to two dimensions:

1) how much the CEO is willing to *consider information* contributed by other people (information-sourcing) and
2) how much the CEO is willing to *distribute the power* actually to make the decision (power distribution).

If we graph these two dimensions, we find five types of decision-making processes, as you see in Figure 17:

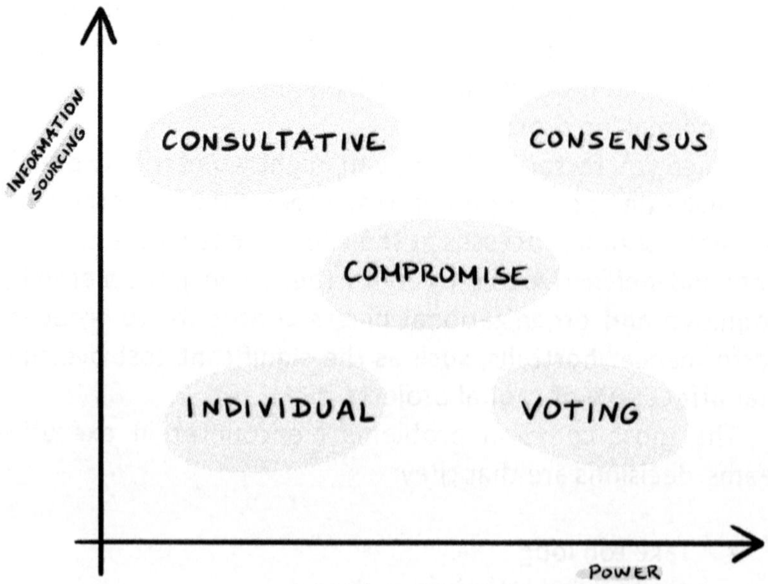

Figure 17 – Five decision-making styles

Individual decision-making

Individual decision-making happens when CEOs use information mostly collected by themselves (company data, experience, market information, intuition) and decide alone. This is probably the default decision-making method in most organizations. Research shows that the more power people have, the less likely they are to listen to other people's advice.[75]

More troubling, the same research also showed that this level of confidence in the person's own judgment is coupled with a *decrease* in the accuracy of the decisions made. As I have stated since Chapter 1 of this book: The world is too complex for one person to understand it and design effective strategies based solely on their knowledge and information.

Consultative decision-making

The CEO also makes consultative decision making alone after considering information provided by other team members. Even if a C-Suite leader consults one person, we consider the decision type as consultative. The CEO might also consult with an advisor who is external to the team or the company. Information sourcing is more diversified than in an individual process, but the decision power remains centralized.

Voting

Voting is a process with maximum power distribution (one person, one vote) but not necessarily with the highest integration of diverse information. A group of people can vote after listening to an expert presenting the pros and cons of a set of alternatives, or even based on their own information and experience. Voting does not require that we solve our differences before deciding because it does not require any sharing. The voting process is by itself a way to solve differences. This explains why it's so tempting to use it when there's a deadlock in teams.

Compromise

Compromise happens when decisions are made by finding a middle ground between opposing alternatives. If you want to invest $10 million in a brand revamp, and I think we should invest $0, the decision to invest $4 million is a compromise decision. Compromise generates winner-loser feelings that can create or increase "us-versus-them" attitudes in the team.

Consensus decision-making

Consensus decision-making is when a team discusses alternatives and reaches a common decision acceptable to all. This is not the same as the "middle ground," where we have to partially give in in order to reach a compromise. An acceptable common decision by consensus might be to develop a new approach, with elements of the previous ones, or to decide not to act at all and do something else instead. There are many forms of consensual decisions, but they all share being acceptable to all and being made together.

Variations and dangers of decision-making in executive teams

An executive team's types of decisions vary from short-term operational decisions to mid-term tactical decisions to long-term high-impact strategic decisions. The choice of decision-making process must accompany the kind of decision.

The more strategic a decision, the more it needs to be made by consensus.

The more strategic a decision, the more it needs to be made by consensus. Consensus decision-making reduces conflict, aligns the team for the execution, generates commitment with the solution found, and considers the maximum amount of information possible. It has the big *disadvantage* of requiring more time and information. For this reason, for tactical decisions, we should aim for *consultative decision making*.

When all consensually agree to the strategy, a smaller team of experts can refine some parts of its tactical definitions much more quickly, producing a recommendation the CEO or the C-level responsible executive can then make. Consultative decision making in fact, is a variation of individual decision making that considers more information.

Complying with a decision is not the same as committing to make it work.

Unless a novel problem emerges, all operational decisions involving the business' daily running don't require the team's entire or even partial involvement. Individual decision making is the best option when speed and clarity are of the essence (see Figure 18). If routinely used by the CEO also for tactical and strategic decisions, though, individual decision making will prevent the development of a team identity. It will reduce the commitment of all with the decision made. Complying with a decision is not the same as committing to make it work.

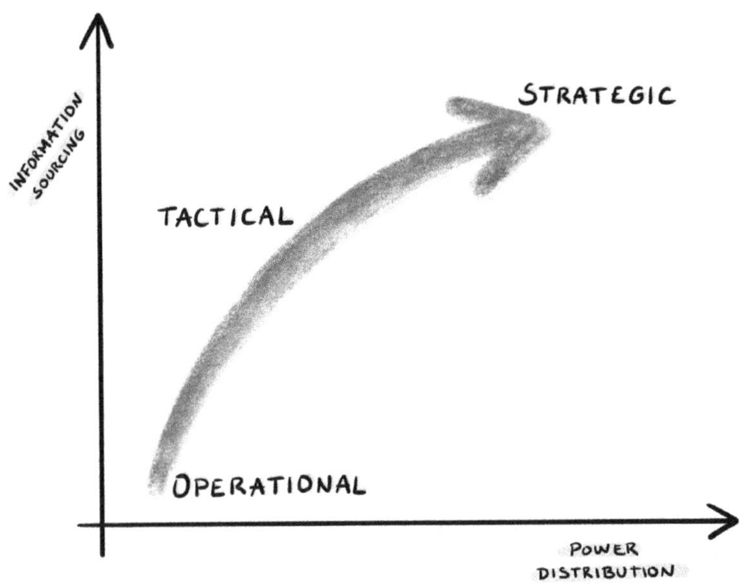

Figure 18 – Relationship between types of decisions and strategy level

You might have noticed that I did not mention *voting* and *compromise* as decision-making processes to match the three types of decisions an executive team needs to make. Executive teams should avoid these two decision-making processes at all costs.

Voting is useful when a big group needs to decide, and neither the time nor the opportunity are available to source and process all the information required. Executive teams never grow to be big enough to require it. Voting is not a rational process and does not consider that some people – namely the subject matter experts – might have more accurate and relevant information to make the decision. For these two reasons, executive teams must never use this process.

Reaching decisions by compromise leaves everyone with a bitter taste of having given more than what they got in return. It is a lazy process, whereby the team fails to consider enough information to generate a good enough consensual decision. Avoid this at all costs because it creates a vicious cycle. It drains commitment to the decision's implementation and contributes to fracturing the team into subunits. Overall, it leads to less alignment in the team members' behavior. Teams with less aligned/integrated behavior tend to generate and process less information, consider fewer alternatives, and reach poorer decision outcomes in unstructured situations.[76]

If you superimpose Figures 17 and 18 you will find that the arrow between operational and strategic decision-making in Figure 18 goes around compromise and completely avoids voting in Figure 17.

If the team cannot make a strategic decision in consensus, then the CEO should make it individually. If the CEO collects and processes all the relevant information and the CEO decides alone, this is consultative decision making.

The title of this section: "Who's deciding this one?" refers to the fact that quite often, executive team members have mismatched ideas of the current decision-making process. You will behave in very different ways if

1. you believe that you are being consulted for a decision,
2. you are negotiating a middle ground between alternatives,
3. you expect to generate together the best possible solution, or
4. someone else decides this one alone.

Different understanding of the CEO's expectations concerning decision making is one of the main productivity and energy drains of executive teams. When I assess executive team effectiveness, I often find contradictory ideas of how decisions are made and the resulting general sense of frustration with process efficiency and effectiveness.

Using techniques to neutralize cognitive biases in decision-making processes improves decision outcomes. The C-Suite needs to address unclear areas of the process by defining decision-making frameworks.[77]

The first time a philosopher asked, "What are we doing here?" he was not thinking of the Universe nor the meaning of life. He was, for sure, in an executive team meeting.

Decision-making efficiency results from clarifying the decision type and the decision-making process of the decisions we make in each meeting. But these factors are not sufficient. We also need to have an executive team purpose (Chapter 6), trust (Chapter 8), and understanding of the complexity of our problems (Chapter 9). I cover this in the next chapters.

What am I doing here? – Meeting management

The first time a philosopher asked, "What are we doing here?" he was not thinking of the Universe nor the meaning of life. He was, for sure, in an executive team meeting.

Don't get me wrong. I believe meetings are essential and indispensable for many things. There is so far no better way to get a group of people to share ideas and produce a common outcome than an effective and efficient meeting. The problem is that most meetings, at all levels of a company's hierarchy, are neither effective nor efficient. A survey conducted with 635 leaders found that 75% of them poorly evaluated their meetings on these dimensions.[78]

Why does this happen? Of all people, C-level professionals should be able to grasp the need for being efficient and effective. And they do. But they direct that understanding to the actions of everyone else in the company. When it's about them, they allow the structural problems that challenge executive teams – that I mentioned earlier in this chapter – to stand between them and meeting efficiency.

Inefficiency of Meetings

Meeting inefficiency at the top level has three causes: incompetence, personal interests, and ego.

Any C-level professional should know by heart the rules of effective and efficient meetings. These are: what to do before, during, and after the meeting to produce the desired results with the least use of resources possible. I find an appalling lack of knowledge about this in executive teams. The people who spend most of their working time in meetings know too little about making them efficient. While they may be competent in their jobs, they are not fluent in an effective meeting's dynamics.

Avoid at all costs allowing personal interests – significant for some members but irrelevant to the goal – to hijack the meeting into long discussions. Yes, the team needs to discuss and align many different interests, paradoxes, and views to make the team functional. But after setting aside a bit of time for these discussions, the meeting agenda must focus on the goal of the meeting, rather than members repeatedly returning to personal interests that drain energy and time from the plan.

Finally, ego. There are three types of people in meetings:

- the ones who speak to be listened to
- the ones who speak to listen to themselves
- the ones who speak because others are also speaking.

There are three types of people in meetings:

- **the ones who speak to be listened to**
- **the ones who speak to listen to themselves**
- **the ones who speak because others are also speaking**

Be the type of person who speaks when you have something relevant to say. Keep focused on the goal, listen, think, and ask.

I do not dive into meeting management rules and logistics in this book. There are hundreds of good books about it.[79,80,81,82,83] When I support executive teams improving their meeting management processes, I prefer not to follow a template. Instead, I start from the team's needs and facilitate a collaborative design workshop to find the best processes to improve meeting effectiveness. However, I share with you my overarching principle for meeting management:

Having less meetings, with less people, less topics, and less time, equals more results.

Nothing beats a good argument – Conflict management

Joshua is the head of Regulatory and Quality Affairs in a pharma company. I welcomed him into my online meeting room. The conversation had already gone for twenty minutes, exploring his views on the executive team's effectiveness when he paused for five seconds. Joshua made a serious face and said in a grave tone, "I know what my colleagues think about me. You've interviewed several of them already, so you've heard it. I want you to know that I am aware of what is going on."

Having less meetings, with less people, less topics, and less time, equals more results.

I smiled, leaned forward, and asked, "Exactly what do you mean?"

"They see me as the main block to the team's progress. The official narrative is that Sales and Marketing would do a great job if it were not for what they call my petty considerations of how we must conduct business. But my job has two important dimensions: to guarantee that the company follows all the applicable regulations, and to reduce the risk in grey situations by making the necessary decisions."

For the reader less familiar with pharma company functioning, it is typical for Regulatory Affairs to have veto power over other executives' decisions, except the CEO. After Joshua made a string of decisions preventing some marketing and sales strategies and correcting some research approaches, part of the team reacted emotionally in a meeting. One shouted, "You are blocking the functioning of this company! You are breaking the team apart!"

Why was this happening? Joshua was right about how others saw him. His colleagues revealed to me that he was the main source of team conflict. All decisions, discussions, proposals, and interactions with any legal component inevitably ended in a strong emotional debate in the team.

The half of the team who had their bonuses directly affected by sales results was quite vocal about it. "Joshua is taking money out of my pocket!" The other half, who only suffered the indirect impact of sales goals on their bonuses, was also not happy but less vocal.

The CEO, Gaia, tried to steer the clash to calmer waters for the last six months without evidence of success. At that point, she asked me to assess the team and solve the issue.

My quantitative and qualitative assessment made it clear that conflict management was one of the team's poorest effectiveness and efficiency areas.

After some months of vetoes and pushbacks from Joshua on marketing and sales tactics, the team said, "Joshua prevents us from doing things our competitors are doing. It cannot be that we are the only company that is 100% right in the market, and everybody else is wrong. He is inflexible. His stringent interpretation of rules and procedures is harming the company. Without his interference, we could sell a lot more and do more for our clients."

There are three types of conflict in executive teams: process, cognitive, and affective.

Gaia had a balanced approach. Her view was that Joshua meant well; protecting the company from risk and liability was good. Still, the way he was enforcing his decisions created the perception he was overpowering everyone else in the executive team and was uncooperative. The impact of the "Joshua against all" dispute on the team's efficiency and effectiveness was getting out of control. And at the end of my assessment, I knew why.

Types of Conflict

There are three types of conflict in executive teams[84]: process, cognitive, and affective.

Process conflict

Process conflict happens when the rules and procedures a person in one role must follow to accomplish tasks, generate outcomes, and meet goals clash with the rules and procedures a person in another role must follow. In general terms, this occurs due to company organizational and process design. Some level of process conflict inevitably exists in all organizations because there are always more goals, processes, and tasks to harmonize than is possible. Process conflict naturally emerges from the structural causes for non-collaborative behavior of executive teams that I mentioned in *Chapter 4 – Been there, done that, and have the scars to prove it.* The executive team has the role of resolving these paradoxes to minimize process conflict and maximize the company's efficiency and effectiveness.

Cognitive conflict

Cognitive conflict happens when we have different opinions, viewpoints, knowledge, and proposals to reach common goals. Whereas process conflict arises from *conflicting* goals, cognitive conflict assumes a *commonality* of goals. We are clear we want the same purpose, but we want to achieve it in different ways. Cognitive conflict emerges from cognitive diversity. This is the good type of conflict you want to have in your team because it increases decision quality.[84] The absence of cognitive conflict means we are all thinking the same way and proposing the same solutions for our current challenges.

Process conflict is about goals and rules. Cognitive conflict is about ideas. Affective conflict is about people.

Groupthink is an occurrence whereby a group comes to a unanimous decision about a possible action despite the existence of fact that points to another correct course of action. Social psychologist Irving Janis derived this term. [85] This is hardly a way to adapt to an ever-changing environment.

Affective conflict

Affective conflict happens when we feel we are incompatible with each other as individuals. We are annoyed, upset, disgusted, or enraged by others' contributions, proposals, or simply by their presence. Interactions become personal.

a) Process conflict is about goals and rules.
b) Cognitive conflict is about ideas.
c) Affective conflict is about people.

The paradox is that *cognitive conflict* contributes to increased quality of decisions, but, left unmanaged, it might also fuel affective conflict, which hinders the quality of decisions.[86] *Process conflict* is inevitable but needs to be managed to stay low. *Cognitive conflict* is desirable and needs to be directed to produce results. *Affective conflict* spells *doom* for your team.

When trust is gone, you don't accept others' proposed solutions. You need an intervention.

If one team member thinks about another: "YOU are preventing ME from doing my work and reaching my goals", it's not difficult to see what will happen next. There will be no collaboration in your executive team; cognitive diversity will fuel disrespect instead of productivity. The team will build moats and walls. Good luck with increasing results of any kind in those circumstances.

This is what was already happening with Gaia's team. The inevitable process conflict between Joshua's role and the rest of the group was not well managed from the beginning. It created a level of animosity between team members that provoked a level of affective conflict that no one could manage internally. Trust is the key factor in managing conflict in a group.[87] When trust is gone, you don't accept others' proposed solutions. You need an intervention. Despite Gaia's best efforts and carefully considered interventions, the damage was done.

Teams can avoid breaking relationships by agreeing on ground rules for managing conflict and addressing the conflicting situations early enough.[88] This is not done in most cases. Therefore, we typically have an escalation of affective conflict in teams that the team might have avoided. To defuse affective conflict once it's been established, you need a specific intervention, as defined below.

Some of the usual components of effective interventions include:

- understanding the sources of conflict
- defining how organizational design and processes generate process conflict
- recognizing how to effectively manage different causes of process conflict
- defining and identifying affective conflict
- implementing tools to deal with affective conflict
- maximizing the use of cognitive conflict while keeping it at an efficient level

After a couple of workshop days with me, focused on repairing relationships and rebuilding trust, including all the steps in the previous paragraph, the team could behave in productive ways to deal with all sources of conflict. The team moved toward collaborative behavior and properly identified cognitive conflict as a continuous improvement driver instead of a personal attack.

When no one thinks because no one speaks – Communication and groupthink

I find it valuable to collect newcomers' initial impressions before they get corrupted by the official company culture narrative. "Beware of first impressions, they are usually right," said Socrates.

I am interviewing Luca as part of the qualitative diagnosis of his executive team. He is the CTO of the Romanian company of a FMCG multinational. Having joined the team two months before our call and coming from a consulting background, he has a fresh look at how things work.

When I asked Luca to describe the communication patterns he observed in the executive team, he said: "In one word, people are too diplomatic."

"What do you mean?" I probed.

"Things are not said. Some people don't contribute at all in some meetings. They don't voice their opinion. And when there's dissonance, they put it in such a diluted argument that we don't understand how important the difference of approaches is, or how big its consequences might be. And it seems as if we all agree all the times, when probably it's not the case."

What Luca was referring to is a process we call groupthink. Groupthink happens when the group fails to analyse different alternatives and agrees on one suggestion without discussion. The team gives up critical thinking to adhere to one option without due consideration of its implications.

Groupthink happens when the group fails to analyse different alternatives and agrees on one suggestion without discussion.

If you think that this plague can afflict only inexperienced CEOs of small companies, think again. Research by the Independent Evaluation Office analyzed the IMF's performance during 2004-2007, leading to its less than efficient dealing with the financial upheaval of that era. They linked the IMF's failure to several factors, including groupthink.[89]

Groupthink was also at the root of the January 28, 1986, tragedy of the Challenger space shuttle. Specifically, the loss of seven lives occurred due to failed communications in the face of public pressure to proceed with the launch despite dangerous conditions.[90]

The suggestion of the CEO or of the most competent person in a specific knowledge area usually triggers groupthink. This might sound logical. After all, if someone knows more than you about something, you should probably shut up and listen instead of speaking up. But there are several glitches with this thinking. Even when you are not the expert, you might:

- Have relevant information contradictory to the proposal, even if you cannot defend it technically or even relate it fully with the proposal. You should then put it forward for the group to analyze it.

- Have a hunch or instinct the decision is not going in the right direction, although you can't explain it rationally. It would be best if you asked the team to support you in revealing what might lurk behind that hunch. Intuition is an experience-based input, and usually, with some questions, one can get to its significance.
- Want to support the group's "agreement party" and go along with it even if you know it will not work. (I know this sounds strange, but it happens a lot for different reasons.) In this case, you should invoke the right to positively interfere with any team agreement to ensure the team is factoring in all consequences.

Groupthink happens when disagreement is seen negatively or taken personally. People are afraid to be tagged as opponents or ridiculed as incompetent, contribute to the team's fracturing, or simply have professional confidence issues.

Groupthink is poison.

Groupthink is poison. It destroys the team's effectiveness and cohesiveness in a nutshell. All of *The 6P's of Executive Teams®* are antidotes to it.

1. By having an explicitly agreed common *Purpose*, we align intention.
2. By defining relationship communication *Processes,* we validate the right behavior.
3. By working on the *People's* psychological safety and trust, we create a context where groupthink is unnecessary.
4. By defining the best *Problem* solving approaches, we eliminate the emotional part of the idea clash that leads to groupthink.
5. By defining learning methods for a team to create new *Possibilities*, the whole team goes in the "us" box and deliberately fights against groupthink.

6. By defining the *Potential* impact of our team in the company and market, we create a culture where groupthink is eradicated from our company.

As for the impact of relationship communication process on groupthink, I highlight three things:

- Groupthink is born of fear. Keep this in mind. It's your fear of losing face, being misinterpreted, or any other thing that prevents you from speaking up. Look that fear in the eyes and confront it.
- You are accountable for the team's effectiveness. If any team member or the team as a whole fails, you fail. It's your responsibility to speak up.
- If the team culture is promoting groupthink, you should address it directly with your CEO. If you are the CEO, change it now. Communicate about it, and communicate better to avoid it.

For the sake of effectiveness, factor in all relevant information in the team's decisions. If this makes you the spoiler, so be it.

Some of us already checked out – Participation and team effectiveness

Did you skip the introduction of this book, where I invited you to join the leadership transformation that needs to happen at the top level? If so, it might be a good idea to go over it, before the next paragraph. This will help you place my first client, Frank's team, in the context of what I describe next.

Frank and his CEO were surprised at the first action I proposed to do with their team. I did not suggest running a strategic workshop with graphic facilitation, as we used to do in 1997. I did not propose to bring them to a retreat with outdoor bootcamp activities. I did not invite them to see me perform on stage in front of a big audience event (actually, they had seen that already). But most surprising to them was the fact that I did not even want to interview all the team members individually. That was the second project task I would do.

The first thing I asked for was to observe a full executive team meeting, to just be there like a fly on the wall.

And there I sat, during a full morning, with a paper pad on my hands, silently taking notes. Of course, Frank informed the team of who I was and what I was doing. They knew there would be some form of intervention afterward. As soon as they dove into the meeting topics, they soon forgot about me and slid back to normal team interaction. Frank confirmed that at the break. That's what I was there to observe.

Both Frank and his CEO were surprised that I did not want to comment or give feedback at the end of the meeting. I declined with a smile, explaining to the team that I would interview each of them individually to complete my understanding of the situation before volunteering any assessment, or proposing any action.

Frank's surprise became pure shock after the meeting. We had a brief chat in his office, and he took a peep at my notepad. Each white page represented the individual positions sitting at the table, and connecting them were arrows, loops, and codes for each meeting topic. There were no "normal" written notes, no standard "diagnosis," no "behavior problems" identified. My notes only showed interactions and had words like proposal, offer, instruction, coalition, blockage, disqualification, withdrawal, support, and dominance.

I saw shock turning to horror in his face. I could read the speech bubble above his head: "How can I abort this process before Ricardo destroys my team? What was I thinking to bring this lunatic for an intervention? How will I get away with this?" I smiled at him. I reassured him that I knew very well what I was doing and that the observation had achieved all my goals.

What Frank could not appreciate was that I had already nailed it. I had mapped the most relevant team processes and had identified improvement points for all of them. I had it. Once I included the content of the processes, I would have a detailed, colorful map of his executive team. And that's what the individual interviews would give me afterwards: a detailed description of how the team life felt for the team members.

Processes make the structure of a team. *Content* gives it liveliness. Together they define what a team is and how it functions. But if you can only go for one of them, always choose *processes*. You can always change the content of what you say, the examples you use, and your tone. But once a specific process becomes rooted in the team's functioning, it establishes a pattern of relationship that is very difficult to change. The more you see the processes, the more you can understand and change your team's reality.

***Processes* make the structure of a team. *Content* gives it liveliness.**

Well defined processes reduce team asymmetries

Even in less diverse teams, with members who share many demographic characteristics, there are two sources of asymmetry to consider. People differ in their interests, mostly due to their personality and education, which prepare them to select, collect, and interpret different data types. They also differ in the types and amount of information they get and process as part of their job, mostly due to their role in the company structure.

The asymmetries of information and interests generate an unbalanced relationship between team members.

The asymmetries of information and interests generate an unbalanced relationship between team members. Whatever the decision, some team members will be more prepared, informed, and willing to make it than others. But even if some of us might be more informed and prepared, that does not mean that the others' contributions are not relevant or even critical.

It's often the outsider who brings a fresh perspective and spot-on questions that shed light on the issue. Usually, it's the person least emotionally involved with the subject who can force the required objectivity to make the best decision. Often, it's the stupid question that triggers the right answer.

Defining and agreeing on clear work and relationship management processes promotes as much as possible a symmetrical distribution of information and interests among the team members. This, in turn, guarantees the best usage of the team members' competences.[91]

Often, it's the stupid question that triggers the right answer.

If we don't have clear relationship management processes, some team members will dominate, and others will withdraw, depending on the subject. The *worst possible scenario* happens when some team members dominate the interactions no matter what the topic being decided. If this happens in your team, ask for help.

In an effective team, there is no stable dominance. We ask for all relevant inputs to make the best possible decision. Commitment is all about process and participation. This translates into an attitude of "we are in this together," where everyone has got each other's backs on critical decisions. A team like this, with the required level of competence, is unbeatable.

In an effective team, there is no stable dominance.

Only strive to become the best you can be, nothing more

Tony Dungy became the first African American football coach to win the Super Bowl. After that, he wrote a book that became a *New York Times* bestseller, *Quiet Strength: The Principles, Practices, and Priorities of a Winning Life*. Tony Dungy refers to how he was influenced by Coach Chuck Noll's philosophy. One quote by Chuck Noll is a founding principle of Dungy's success: "If you want to win, do the ordinary things better than anyone else does them, day in and day out."[92]

Chief Executive Teams excel at designing and improving their operating processes.

That's it. There are a set of processes that any executive team must master to become a Chief Executive Team. I highlighted in this chapter the most important ones, according to my experience and management research. Chief Executive Teams excel at designing and improving their operating processes. Be it work or relationship management processes, they focus on improving them, day in, day out.

8

P FOR PEOPLE

"When you move from "I don't trust you" to "I don't understand you," you eliminate filters and have meaningful productive conversations in the team. Working with Ricardo facilitated that process."

– Francois-Xavier Mahot | Grupa Żywiec | CEO

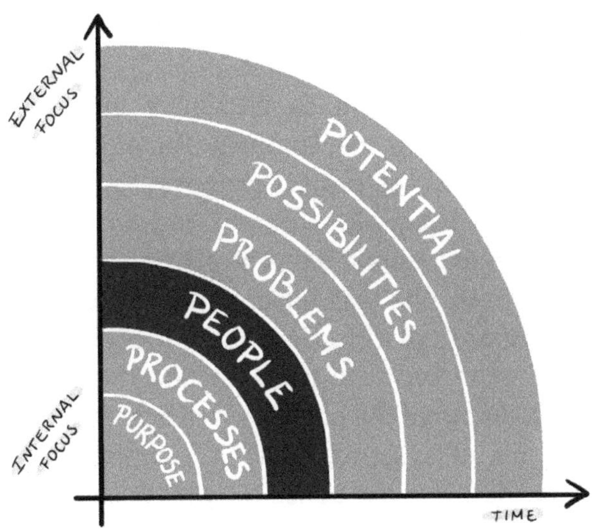

Figure 19 – P for People

USUALLY, WHEN I speak about the P for People (see Figure 19), my workshop participants, or the people who are interviewing me, think this refers to having the right people in the team. It *does*, but what makes them "right" encompasses more than you might imagine.

"P for People is not about competence, matching skills to jobs, having functions performed to *at least* the minimum required level of quality and performance, and *optimally* to the best performance level required by the company. I'm not talking about ideal levels of education or previous training.

"P for People" is not about search and selection. It is about making sure that the people you already have in the team *become* the right people for the team, in any relevant dimension. Let's begin with a real situation.

Managing executives is like herding cats

Birgit, the quite seasoned Chief Commercial Officer (CCO) of a communications company, asked me to advise her on becoming more effective at her role. When we designed her strategic game plan and mapped her stakeholder relationships, we understood one series of events as the focal point for her feeling of low effectiveness.

Birgit had been trying to introduce business process reengineering (BPR) in the company for almost two years. When she presented the project proposal to the Board, they rejected it twice. Even with a forecasted positive return on investment, and immediate gains of efficiency and profitability, it did not pass. She was unsure why this was happening because the Board's justifications were irrational when compared to the expected results. It seemed the top managers didn't want to improve the company's efficiency.

Using a mix of systems thinking techniques, we implemented a method to make sense of what occurred. She filled in the gaps with descriptions of the interactions she had with the Board during the period of the two rejections, in and out of the room. We then analyzed possible meanings and causes for the rejections. When we put together all the pieces of the puzzle, it became clear that the CEO, Hugh, had decided to block the BPR proposal because of the negative influence of the Chief Operating Officer (COO).

David, the COO could not admit that anyone but him would lead a BPR project. "Processes are part of COO territory", he said. Therefore, in his mind, the only real reason for Birgit to try to advance this project was to gain power over his operations kingdom. David would always fight that.

We mapped the causal web of interactions between the other Board members and Birgit. We understood how everyone's behavior contributed to the rejection of the BPR initiative, including Birgit's. She was acting in ways that could scare David, her COO colleague. Birgit had achieved excellent success managing operations in another subsidiary of the same holding company. She was also more experienced, older, and had a reputation for being tough and confrontational about her beliefs. Birgit was a quite competent and straightforward manager.

David was fearful of being minimized and having his career prospects reduced. Birgit bringing a BPR to restructure the whole company looked like she was handing a certificate of incompetence to him. In his mind, his position depended on killing that project.

Hugh, the CEO, did not want to stand between Birgit and David. After unsuccessfully moderating the discussion about the BPR project, when seeing that his two direct reports did not reach a minimum consensus, he did not make a final decision. He postponed the project's discussion, asking Birgit to solve the information gaps in the project.

On the second occasion, the same rejection occurred, this time postponing the project without a set date. Why did Hugh do that? Because Birgit was his biggest challenger for the CEO position. She was at least as prepared as him to run the company.

Birgit has a stainless-steel work ethic. Her only interest was the greater good of the company. Both David and Hugh missed Birgit's proposal's real intention, therefore dismissing its value as a smokescreen of hers to gain power.

Birgit reacted personally to her values being misjudged by her colleagues on the Board and responded accordingly by overpowering them in other decisions that exemplified the same values. She wanted to draw a clear line. This, in turn, increased the perception that she was an inflexible power addict.

Armed with the systems thinking of how the management group organized to reject Birgit's proposal, we defined alternative ways to address the situation and give it another try. The blockage was not about business rationality. It was all about emotional power struggles, misinterpreted intentions, and errors of communication.

Birgit implemented a plan to increase her flexibility in the relationship with her colleagues. We discussed how to deal with the perception that the CEO and the COO developed about her intentions. Through a series of interactions, resulting in implicit and explicit guarantees, she reassured the COO that she did not want his job or to manage his area. She influenced different key personnel to feed the CEO with information that would create an urgency for change. She pitched the project to a supervisory board member to get improvement feedback, gaining an insider ally in the process.

At the third attempt, Birgit got the BPR project approved and budgeted. After execution, the project's results were *above* the expected return, delivering savings of $400,000 in the first year, increasing subsequently, a great outcome for an investment of three days of my consulting.

This anecdote has several points.

1. **Executive teams tend to be the worst team in the company, exactly where you should have the best one.**

Qualitative research led by Hambrick involved interviewing 23 CEOs of major companies headquartered in the USA and

Europe. The data showed their concerns fell into five categories: inadequate capabilities of a single executive, common shortcoming of several members of the whole team, harmful internal rivalries, groupthink, and fragmentation.[93] Welcome to the real life at the top.

2. The CEO's behavior mode is instrumental in maintaining the problem.

As I underlined, Hugh deliberately didn't want to take a side or decide to solve the dispute between Birgit and David. This is one of the malignant examples of avoidance behavior mode I mentioned in Chapter 2 – *It's Happening on Your Shift*. Hugh, the CEO, had a horse in the race. He was also fearful of Birgit's competence and drive, as she could easily have his job. He decided not to intervene for his own protection, allowing David to fight the war for him and collect the benefit without exposing himself. Hugh was oblivious to the fact that he might be hurting the company in the process.

There are better ways to deliver results with an executive team. You just need your group of executives to become a Chief Executive Team, a little effort with a big payout.

3. Data does not argue for itself.

Information about the project's importance was there from the beginning. David and Hugh did not want to integrate it into their analysis of the business case. This is entirely normal. We have a process called "selective attention"[94] that unconsciously filters information that enters our brain and decides which should be processed and used. The limbic system in our brain influences this process,[95] the areas that govern emotions.

If you don't have the right emotions, you can't select and process the relevant information to learn from experience. Suppose we don't generate the appropriate mental states in the executive team. In that case, we will impair its ability to learn, especially in unstructured, volatile, hostile, and complex situations that are the most stressful.

When it's about people, it's always personal, and it's always emotional.

4. Birgit is a woman.

Birgit was the only woman on the board. According to the research I cited in Chapter 1 – *The Elephant in the Room*, we know that any distinctive individual characteristic might become a source for identifying someone as one of the "others" and fracture the executive team into subgroups of "us" versus "them." Age, education, ethnicity, nationality, religion, and gender are some of the most common and visible individual characteristics that alienate others.

Birgit became used to demonstrating more competence than her male colleagues to progress in her career and get to the Board. She had the grit to do it, but she also developed a toughness level in communication that others perceived as a constant fighting mode. She never brought the gender dimension of the situation. Part of her development strategy was not to regard it as an issue. She just considered any barrier for what it was: an obstacle that could be surpassed with the right amount of effort and display of competence. But there were some signs that the boys were excluding the girl from the ball game.

Diversity in an executive team is essential. But it's not enough to create it; you also have to put it to work. That is your job as CEO.

5. Mistrust destroys a team.

A substantial cause of the issues in Birgit's executive team was the mistrust between the team members. David and Hugh did not trust Birgit's intentions. Birgit also didn't trust theirs. She questioned the CEO's competence to make the decision and his neutrality in management. She questioned

David's willingness and capability to develop a sound BPR project and improve its efficiency. There was mistrust all over the place. Can you build a team on that? No. That's the topic for the next section.

The four dimensions of trust

"P for People" is about making sure team members can come together as a cohesive group that collaborates to realize a purpose. In a word, this is all about trust.

Trust is the glue that binds people together. It holds the relationships among all team members and allows the team to go through adversity, challenge, conflict, difficulties, lack of resources, and crisis without breaking up.

Without trust, people will start bearing grudges against each other and create mutually negative perceptions. They will assume the worst about others, and they will split the team between "us" and "them." The team will fragment.

"P for People" is all about generating the maximum level of trust in the team. To do it, we need to understand the four dimensions of trust in an executive team.

I trust that you know what you need to know

Usually, you get to the top of a company because you worked harder, studied more, were more consistent, competent, productive, creative, and smarter than any other competitor for the job. You are supposed to know a lot more than most people in the same field. You should consistently know or find the answers to the challenges the team faces in your knowledge area.

That's what every other executive team member expects from you. They expect that your answers, reports, communications, and opinions are free from technical mistakes, errors of judgment, and omissions. Your executive team needs to trust that when you say something, you know what you are saying. You will not be right all the time. No one can do that. But what you say must be technically sound, evidence-based, and thought through according to the current level of knowledge on the topic.

You must be on top of your game to gain trust at executive level. Technical competence, i.e. your credibility, influences how much others trust you.

But seldom is this the dimension that fails in executive teams, according to my experience.

I trust that you will deliver what you commit to

You commit. You give your word. You say you will deliver the task or result on the deadline. You miss it. You miss the next one and another one later. What happens?

When you commit to a result or deadline, you create an expectation that something will happen. The team will plan, decide, and execute their work, counting on having your output by date x. This expectation becomes a benchmark against which to measure your delivery.

A sequence of broken expectations means that people will stop believing you whenever you commit. They will stop trusting you. They will create systems to monitor, anticipate, and control what you do. They will lie about deadlines and start asking for things earlier than needed to keep buffer time to protect themselves from your regular failure to deliver.

Once such patterns are established, it becomes quite challenging to reverse the process. Whenever you deliver on your promises, they will think, “He only did it because I controlled that outcome.” When you don’t deliver, they think, “There he is again, failing” and increase control to make sure you don’t let them down again. You don’t want to enter that vicious cycle.

Consistently delivering on your commitments, i.e. your reliability, influences how much others trust you.

I trust you mean well

We are all guilty of it: mind-reading. An essential part of our brain, the pre-frontal cortex, automatically forecasts outcomes for our actions. It's all about making sure we manage our resources efficiently. Our ancestors were so short of resources that they needed to make sure they were hunting the right buffalo, carrying the right gear, and building the right shelter. To save resources, be more sustainable, and increase survival chances, they needed to assess how others, animals, and elements would behave before deciding to put resources into action.

This means that whenever we interact with someone, we need to predict how much we should invest in the relationship. This investment of time, energy, knowledge, and emotions, is dosed according to one factor: How much do I trust that you care about me, that you mean well, that you have good intentions towards me?

Any signal that can be interpreted as "You have an ulterior motive to do this" or "You are trying to [insert negative action] me" or, even worse, evidence that "You lied to me," will trigger a proportional disinvestment of resources in the relationship.

When you get to this point, it doesn't matter what you say to justify yourself, because, in the mind of the other person, you could be saying anything to trick them again and further exploit their resources.

Even if this is sometimes unfair, because other people don't have access to our real intentions and are guessing them from our actions, we need to take their interpretation as their "real" assessment of us. And we must dig deeper to discover what signals we might be sending that create a negative perception of our intentions. Only then can we understand how to transform their negative perception of our intentions. Relationships are a lot about perception.

Manipulative people with negative intentions towards others do this by default. They are very aware and actively manage others' perceptions of them. That's how they thrive in life. This book and my work are not for them.

The degree to which you care for other's interests, i.e. your benevolence, influences how much they trust you.

I can be vulnerable with you

The first three dimensions of trust exist from the first moments you interact with a colleague. In the first executive team meeting, you already start assessing your colleagues' knowledge, commitment, and motives to understand if you can trust them. And they start assessing yours. But there's a fourth dimension of trust that takes a bit more time to develop.

What happens when you trust someone? You open up. You share your doubts, your unanswered questions, your concerns, and your fears. You admit your mistakes; you apologize; you strive to be better. You ask for help; you offer help; you go out of your way to meet their needs. You share reasons and emotions for your behavior that you don't share with people you don't trust. This makes you vulnerable. The trusted person can use all that information against you, either within your relationship or in the context of other relationships.

The easiest way for vulnerability to be risk-free is for it to be mutual. When two people share their fears about the future, both know each other's fears. Both trust enough to be open. Both can use information against each other. This reduces risk. But there are situations where a relationship is unbalanced, and one person can trust another with their vulnerability, and the other doesn't. This has to do with the individual capacity for empathy and how quickly they decide to trust.

If you think that vulnerability is about "being emotional" in the workplace, think again. Admitting you don't know the answer to the next strategic decision and asking your

If you think that vulnerability is about "being emotional" in the workplace, think again.

executive team for input is a quite vulnerable action that a CEO can take. A VUCA (volatile, uncertain, complex, ambiguous) world needs it. If you are not familiar with the work of Brené Brown on this, it's a good time to read her research-based book on vulnerability.[96]

Giving positive space and answers to other people's concerns, i.e. welcoming vulnerability, influences how much others trust you.[97]

Where there is risk, there must be trust

If we knew with 100% certainty how someone would behave, we would not need trust. Trust is all about taking the risk of depending on someone else's behavior.[98] If I am confident that you will do what you commit to, deliver precisely what I expect, and have been doing it flawlessly in the past, trust is not an uncertainty in our relationship.

As we are all human, sooner or later, we fail. Trust exists because we recognize risk, and we have uncertainty and doubt about a person's behavior, but we decide to believe that that person will do everything to deliver.

Trust is a form of belief that the person most likely will behave in a certain positive way. Exceptions could include extreme circumstances in which people's behavior may change dramatically. However, under normal, even difficult circumstances, I trust that the person will not willingly and deliberately do something to harm me or my interests.

Risk is *unbalanced* in a relationship. One person risks more than the other in the trusting process. "I trust you will give me what I need" means that I will be negatively affected by your failure. Trust is *unidirectional.*

The fact that I trust someone does not require that the person trusts me back. I might trust that you will be a good partner for this project because you are the best expert on the subject, you always deliver, and you think of the company's best interest, which includes compensating for my lack of competence. This does not require you to trust me back. I might be a dummy riding along. You feel burdened and need to prevent me from destroying the project. But I still trust you 100%.

Trust provides an assessment of how much risk you are assuming when depending on someone else. To move forward with a decision, project, or action, a team needs to overcompensate for the situation's perceived risk.

Trust is always personal

If your project is to cross the canyon on a tightrope, whom will you trust more to manage that project for you?

Roberto, the person who consistently did it for the last twenty-five years and successfully helped hundreds of others crossing that same canyon?

Or a company that provides many activities, some with tightropes, and has different people doing it?

Most people in this situation would prefer Roberto, with a consistent track record and the right work ethic, with whom you can share your concerns about the crossing, and who will have no-nonsense answers. A brand, a logo, or a big organization are not very useful when you walk over the chasm and wonder how much the guy who screwed the security bolts knows about it and realize that you don't know his name.

Even when we say that clients place a high level of trust in an organization, a team, a methodology, or a concept, in the end, it's about who represents that company, brand, team, concept, or methodology.

Trust is a personal issue; it's a personal dimension. We can lend it to the brand, the company, or the team we represent, but it's my behavior with this client, team member, or colleague that will make that person trust the brand or the company I represent.

An interesting question arises when we compare Roberto, who's been supporting others crossing the canyon for twenty-five years, with your friend, Joe. You already trust Joe from other interactions. He knows a lot about outdoor activities in general but not specifically tightropes over a canyon. The trust matrix as seen in Figure 20 would be a perceived draw at the starting point:

	Credibility	Reliability	Benevolence	Vulnerability
Seasoned expert	✓	✓		
Friend Joe			✓	✓

Figure 20 – The trust matrix

You know that Roberto is more knowledgeable and reliable than your friend, Joe. After all, he has been doing it for decades. But you don't know how much the expert cares about your goals and safety. On the other hand, you know that Joe cares about your interests, and you already established a relationship where you can voice your concerns and emotions. But you don't know how much he can learn about the tightrope-over-canyon project. This is the starting point before meeting Roberto in person.

Whom would you choose to support you in crossing the canyon on a tightrope?

This might sound as a surprise, but a lot of people would choose exactly the opposite answer that you did, whatever it was. From my international experience, it depends a lot on the country's culture.

Some cultures place a lot of value on a personal relationship.[99,100] People only do business with friends. According to this view, you need to get to a certain depth of relationship before trusting someone with your business. This happens in countries where the value of contracts and agreements is a general indication of future intention, that might be complied with or not. It is not conceivable for these cultures to openly share your goals and interests, doubts, and concerns when you still do not trust the person. That's why it's only natural to trust their friend, Joe, over Roberto and hope Joe can learn fast enough to secure the tightrope. Sometimes he does.

Other cultures value agreements, contracts, and work ethics over personal relationships. According to this view, people need to be competent and reliable in the business dimension for me to do business with them. They separate personal and business dimensions of life. For these cultures, if the seasoned expert has been in the market for twenty-five years with a proven track record, this means you can trust Roberto's work ethic and competence. Clients will perceive that it is in the best interest of the seasoned expert to care for their individual interests and give space and no-nonsense answers to their concerns. A flawless track record requires maintaining a lot of personal effort.

Therefore, they schedule the meeting with Roberto and voice their concerns as a natural part of the process. That is how they test if he can be of service to them. If they feel their legitimate interests and concerns are understood and thoroughly answered in that first meeting, the seasoned expert bridged the gap for benevolence and vulnerability, and they trust him. Life can be easy sometimes.

Trust is a situational rational-emotional process

When you trust, you assess, and you feel. In the professional dimension of our lives, we tend to assess first and feel after. In the first seconds of interaction with someone, we create a lasting impression of who they are and what we can expect of them by inferring personal characteristics from their behavior and appearance.[101]

We do this type of trust assessment automatically, unconsciously, as we ask and answer as quickly as possible the following questions:

> "How much does this person know about the subject?"
>
> "How much can I trust that they will deliver on their commitment?"
>
> "How much do they care about our common interests and my individual ones?"
>
> "How comfortable do I feel in sharing work concerns, doubts, and errors with them?"

If the answers to these four questions overcome our perceived risk of the situation, we *feel* we can trust the person for that one situation. We might not trust them for other situations where they are out of their knowledge and experience depth or have vested interests. Trust is situational because it depends so much on limited areas of competence in our professional lives.

When we have a hunch that something is off, and we can't trust someone, we can also use the four questions above as tools to understand where the feeling comes from. Is it their credibility, their reliability, their benevolence, or the space they give for vulnerability? We will find a gap in one or more of these dimensions for sure.

What got you here prevents you from getting there

Why do executive teams tend to have lower than needed levels of trust?

In *Chapter 4 – Been There, Done That, and Have the Scars to Prove It*, I covered two types of reasons for executive teams' low collaborative performance. Structural causes hinder collaboration: organizational design, lack of common goals, divergent processes and language, corporate politics, shareholder interferences, runner-up syndrome, paradoxes, and hypocrisy. Some generic attempted solutions for solving those structural causes do more harm than good: time heals everything, education, instructions, feedback and consequences, profiling, team building activities, and boot camps.

These two types of reasons impact the level of trust an executive team can attain. But another factor erodes trust directly. Let's have an example.

Mary was a quite competent and ambitious marketing manager. She managed a team of ten people in a FMCG company. Marketing tends to be a critical department in this business sector, an excellent path to the C-level and ultimately to CEO. Mary knows and wants this.

As a good manager, she can get her teams to a high level of performance. As an intelligent person, she can sell her team's results as an outcome of her strategies. As an ambitious person, she knows how to get credited for work, including the work of her team to land the sequence of promotions she needs for her career.

She understands that everyone interested in top positions plays the same game. You step up in your career by showing that you are better than anyone else, by taking personal credit for strategizing your team's initiatives, by selling your skills and commitment in a smarter way than anyone else.

As there is a limited number of positions at the top, Mary needs to beat her other colleagues competing for the Marketing Director position and the Chief Marketing Officer and CEO positions. After playing the game following these rules for ten years, Mary becomes the CEO of her multinational's local operating company.

By now, everything is about her, individually. And now people expect her – the hero – to have all the answers, and she can't because it's impossible to have all the answers in a volatile, uncertain, complex, and ambiguous world, through crisis, digital transformation, lockdowns, trade wars and everything else.

Mary understands that she needs to change strategy and develop an effective team. However, her direct reports, her executive group members, are still fighting the good fight to get to CEO position. Why should they cooperate with the very people they need to split budget, resources, exposure, impact and influence with? It's counterproductive for their careers as much as it was for Mary's before. They are sure she understands that, and asking them to team up is only something she says to look good. She surely doesn't mean it. She probably got it from a book or a webinar.

C-level executives reach the top *because* they were highly competitive for decades. This behavior tends not to generate high trust, either between team members or between managers and team members.

The set of learned behaviors that got you to the top won't serve you once you're there. But this is not one of those "What got you here won't get you there" situations. It's worse.

> **What got you here *prevents* you from getting there. The learned set of behaviors and beliefs that brought you to the top position of a company will quite likely prevent you and your executive team from performing at its best.**

What got you here *prevents* you from getting there. The learned set of behaviors and beliefs that brought you to the top position of a company will quite likely prevent you and your executive team from performing at its best. You need to reverse strategies, assumptions, beliefs, rules, skills, ingrained patterns of behavior, and leadership models, to unleash the potential of your executive team and the full company.

Becoming CEO is not winning the game. You did not become game master. You are the wild card in a new game with infinite matches. And the first match is about transforming yourself.

What got you to the top is preventing you from transforming the world. You must change the way you see and act to impact the world.

Do they trust you as leader?

When we speak about trust in executive teams, we need to consider that not all team members are equal. The CEO has a different level of accountability. We need to consider four different relationships of trust in an executive team:

- Trust among executive team members
- Trust between executive team and CEO
- Trust between each executive and CEO
- Trust of the organization in the executive team

To develop a Chief Executive Team, you need to work on the four types of trust relationships. In this section, I will focus on the importance of trust between the CEO and the team and between CEO and team members individually. Still, the following questions can assess any of the trust types above.

To assess how much your team members trust you, ask yourself the following questions:

1. Are you credible in what you say concerning:
    - your role,
    - your competences,
    - your business knowledge,
    - your team leading skills?

2. Are your predictions and opinions more often right than wrong?
3. Do you deliver on your commitments to the team and the company?
4. How consistent is your track record of fulfilling agreements made with people?
5. Do you make time as a team to discuss the team's collective needs?
6. Do you attend to your team's needs?
7. Are you attentive to the team dynamics and able to interpret them? For example: What is the primary emotion in your team at a given moment?
8. Do you take into consideration the individual team members' needs?
9. Do you acknowledge your team members' desire for career advancement as fair? Are you willing to prepare them to take over your job?
10. Can people open up with you about their concerns, doubts, and mistakes, or do you kill the messenger?
11. Are you open to vulnerability, or does it trigger your killer instinct?
12. Do you consider it a weakness to discuss personal issues or emotions of your team members?
13. Do you make time to discuss your team members' individual needs?

After you answer all these questions for yourself, ask your team members the same, and compare the answers. Creating a trusting atmosphere in the executive team usually requires some effort, but the following research shows that the payoff is immense.

A study revealed that the level of CEO trust in their teams, measured in how much latitude for influencing decisions they allowed, increased return on assets, return on equity, and return on sales of companies in turbulent times.[102] In volatile market situations, dominance of CEOs (meaning they allow little influence from their executive team members) correlates with *worse* financial performance of companies in those KPI's. Dominant CEOs who control the team and determine what happens, when it happens, and how it happens can only make their companies successful in situations where context and market are relatively stable. When was the last time that happened?

Dominance means someone is confident of their knowledge. As we have seen before, in turbulent environments, cognitive diversity yields better results.

You can improve performance and reduce waste of resources by developing trust in the executive team, the fourth type of trust relationship I mentioned above. A study found that the executive team's perceived trustworthiness is negatively related to the negative emotions of employees and consequently their turnover. The more your employees trust their top management, the fewer negative emotions they have connected to work, and the more they want to stay with you.[23] You will save a lot of money in recruitment, onboarding, loss of performance due to lack of people and competencies, training, mentoring, etc.

You are so different; how can I trust you?

Trust has a worthy opponent in executive teams: diversity.

Diversity of executive teams is essential for the performance of companies. It's easy to understand why. As the world becomes more complex, hostile, and unpredictable, you need to have different perception and processing styles and other experiences to draw from to understand the world, decide, and act on that decision.

More diverse teams tend to perform better, manage work stress better, and have higher satisfaction and commitment than less diverse teams.[103] They solve problems faster,[104] consider a greater range of perspectives to generate more high-quality solutions,[105] have more productive debates, make more comprehensive decisions, and positively impact sales growth and profitability.[106]

A study of 180 publicly traded companies in the USA, France, Germany, and the UK, found that those with senior teams in the top quartile of diversity (e.g. more women and foreign nationals' participation) had 53% higher return on equity and 14% higher EBIT margins than the ones from the bottom quartile.[107]

A study with venture capitalists (VCs), examining tens of thousands of VCs' decisions found that diversity in executive teams (e.g. in ethnicity and school backgrounds) significantly improves financial performance on measures such as profitable investments and the individual portfolio-company level and overall fund returns.[108]

But diversity can also hinder performance if it becomes a reason to break the executive team into subgroups by demographic characteristics. Groups like this tend to disintegrate, feel less satisfied, and increase turnover[104]. The relationship of cognitive diversity with collective intelligence is an inverted U shape. Too little and too much diversity can hinder the collective intelligence of a team.[109] The right amount of variety makes the executive team more collectively intelligent.

Any distinctive dimension that people have can be a basis for division. Sometimes we don't even need to have any characteristic at all. It just suffices that someone we already trust gives them a label based on an arbitrary characteristic, such as yellow versus red team.[110]

As the indie rock band, Gogol Bordello sings in "Illumination", "Of course there is no us and them, but them they do not think the same." Anyone can become *one of them*, based on our perception. As soon as we tag others, they become "them," as opposed to "us."

Trust is *the* enabler of diversity. With trust, your team thrives on diversity. Without trust, diversity becomes the slayer of your team.

Diversity + Trust = Increased performance

Diversity – Trust = Impaired performance

Diversity is a double-edged sword for your executive team. Its impact is too good to miss and too dangerous not to be controlled. As a CEO, you must create and purposefully manage diversity to create outstanding results.

The diversity that matters is in the mind

We have seen in the last decade several pro-diversity movements in the business world. In general terms, their aim is that people with different characteristics have an opportunity to get to the upper echelons of companies and that demographic diversity in ethnicity, religion, age, gender, university of origin, etc., are not exclusion factors in your career.

Trust is *the* enabler of diversity. With trust, your team thrives on diversity. Without trust, diversity becomes the slayer of your team.

This is important from the civilizational point of view. Demographic diversity in management means that our critical decisions about human potential become as free as possible from prejudice and stereotype. We need to have it because our societies are in many ways destroying talent that would be instrumental for common progress.

A recent analysis by the National Bureau of Economic Research of the USA shows that about 25% of the GDP growth per capita of the last 50 years can be attributed to the progressive entrance of white women and black Americans of both genders in highly skilled occupations.[111] A report by Catalyst shows that Fortune 500 firms with the highest proportion of female leaders had higher returns on equity, sales, and invested capital.[112] McKinsey found that European publicly traded companies are more successful when they are more diverse.[113]

Although I understand the importance and fully support the advance of demographic diversity, this is not my fight. I think we must go a step further or deeper.

Why is demographic diversity important at the executive level? Because we expect people from different educational backgrounds, ethnicities, countries, gender, ages, and religions to have more cognitive diversity than those who are similar in all those characteristics.

Cognitive diversity, also known as *deep diversity*, refers to the range of ways your employees can use to think and solve problems.[114] Cognitive diversity partially overlaps with demographic diversity but must not be mistaken for it. The overlapping is much smaller than usually believed.[115]

Individuals think differently because they have different life experiences. And because they think differently, the team is aware of more types of data and uses different processing strategies, which results in better strategies and increased performance.

We still take demographic diversity as a proxy for cognitive diversity. Only when demographic diversity does not bring us apart can we focus on the most important type of diversity: cognitive. If you can think differently, you are more valuable to the team. Individuals with cognitive versatility, i.e. who can tackle tasks and problems using different thinking patterns, can mitigate adverse effects and increase the positive impact of diversity (measured in team size) on team performance by increasing process learning.[116]

You cannot lead if you cannot transform

Executive teams are fascinating. There's such a great variety of events to observe and participate in. To a bigger or smaller extent, I witness all kinds of turf wars, rash judgments, misinterpretations, grudges, coalitions; you name it. Life is never boring in the executive team. The examples I gave in this chapter are mild ones. I've seen much worse.

No one thinks that the executive team needs to transform itself to lead the transformation of the company. People believe all it takes is a dominant CEO to make change happen.

I have seen technology implementation, business process reengineering, and innovation programs boycotted to prevent someone else from getting to CEO position. I have seen mergers and acquisitions, culture change, and organizational transformation projects failing due to executive team dynamics. I see digitalization and digital transformation projects stalling for lack of purpose, divergent executive team processes, and mistrust.

And if you think that the issue is lack of expertise, that if the projects were technically well designed this would not happen, think again. My clients are multinationals. Some of those projects were designed by the best of the best, the world guru in the field, the person who wrote the book on it. I found no single technical flaw in most of them. The problem is: No one thinks that the executive team needs to transform itself to lead the transformation of the company. People believe all it takes is a dominant CEO to make change happen.

Change requires trust to happen. People need to go out of themselves to transform themselves. This requires a massive amount of trust. And it must start at the executive team level.

Once I witnessed how a negative trust dynamic created a $3 million problem in twenty minutes. I have been called to solve these types of situations, save the heads of board members, rescue dying projects, and support CEOs revamping their companies. I sometimes get late evening phone calls to board a plane to meet an executive team and figure things out. Sometimes I get there too late to be effective, unfortunately. Some leaders are deluded by their self-importance, only to discover that their executive team was the neglected critical success factor.

Significant projects are blocked, stopped, boycotted, and sabotaged to better fit someone's agenda.

Significant projects are blocked, stopped, boycotted, and sabotaged to better fit someone's agenda. When I say that business as usual is destroying value and creating the wrong performance culture in your company, this is what I mean. All the unproductive, sometimes even pathological, relationship dynamics that executives have with their peers and leaders result in diminished returns and disengaged people. If we don't reverse this familiar modus operandi, company sustainability is at risk.

I know, this sounds too harsh, exaggerated, unbelievable even. This could never happen in your company. But it happens in other companies with which I work. Yes, I am sure this would never happen in your country, but it happens in all other countries in which I work.

As Richard Rosen and Fred Adair found in their research,[117] CEOs tend to rate their performance better than the teams themselves do. CEOs tend to be the last to know about what is not going well in their teams.

To improve the effectiveness of your executive team, first, you need to see and accept reality. Seeing is the problematic part. The executive team's interactions and behaviors happen in one-to-one meetings, confidential conversations, and direct text messages, below the radar of the CEO. CEOs only see the tip of the iceberg of their executive team's dynamics (the tip that everyone else wants them to see.)

You cannot lead if you cannot transform. And you cannot transform what you don't know.

While you are focused on executing strategy and KPIs, your executive team defines the company culture that determines if and how the strategy will be executed and results produced.

Therefore, you need a tool to catch the subtle, the informal, the hidden relationship, and work patterns that make up your executive team's life. You need to go beyond the official narrative of "who we are" that people repeat to please you and face reality.

You cannot lead if you cannot transform. And you cannot transform what you don't know. Knowing the reality of your executive team's dynamics is the basis of your CEO leadership program.

The 6P's of Executive Teams® assessment captures the reality of your team. Based on management research, it measures dimensions of the executive team functioning found to impact company performance. And it captures perceptions, attitudes, behaviors of different management levels, concerning the executive team. Because it is a 360° assessment, it triangulates and compares viewpoints, allowing for richness of information and layers of interpretation.

Often, when I present the assessment results, CEOs are surprised by the real situation they were oblivious to. These are the well-meaning CEOs who want to improve the company's results and understand that their executive team is crucial in the process. Others know exactly what they are doing to divide and conquer and could not care less about the damage, at least while good times keep rolling. But these are not my clients.

I'm a psychologist with a systemic family therapy background. I became an accredited expert in social, work, and organizational psychology, and an advanced expert in psychological coaching. I dedicated the last 25 years of my life to learn the science, the rules, the conditions, and the motives for individual and team transformation. I do what I do because I believe people can transform themselves and their contexts. That is my mission.

I am fortunate that my work is to multiply positive transformation in the lives of people with who I interact.

I love people and I want them to improve because life is too short to realize one's vast potential.

That's why I was a therapist; that's why I have been a trainer, a coach, a consultant; that's what I do. I love people and I want them to improve because life is too short to realize one's vast potential.

But you don't need to believe in what I do to start the journey of becoming a better CEO and develop a Chief Executive Team. Even if your job is only about money and power, I hope I have made the point by now that you also get those effects if you focus on their determining factors. If you look at this objectively, you will see that management research points to Chief Executive Teams as a driver of company performance.

9

P FOR PROBLEMS

"Ricardo's work is not a 'nice to have.' It impacts the strategy and results of the company. He combines emotional inspiration, rational understanding, and effective tools to deliver transformation, all based on a deep understanding of human dynamics. Really unique."

– Antonio Mariani | GB Foods Italy | General Manager

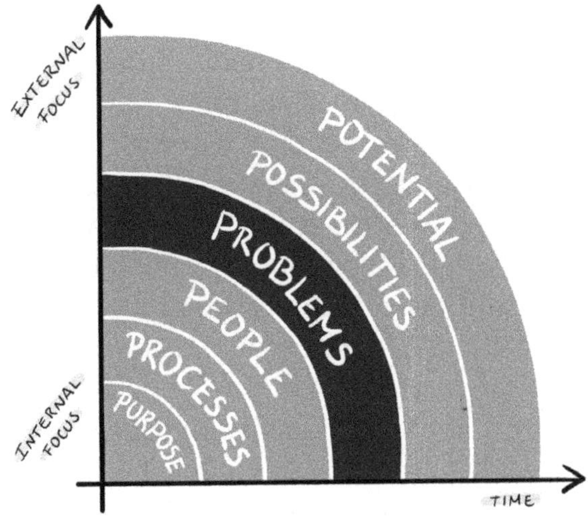

Figure 21 – P for Problems

YOU ARE READY to begin your day at work. You start your laptop, but it seems to be dead. The battery ran out. You plug it in and get your tasks done. After a couple of hours, you check the battery symbol, and it's still at 0%. You check the charging cable; it's well plugged. You need a new battery; this one is gone. You buy a new battery, replace the old one, computer works, problem solved.

Our parents, school, and media educate us with the wrong idea that what I described in the paragraph above represents problem-solving. When there is a malfunction, anomaly, breakdown, gap, disruption, problem, you simply need to find the cause, fix it, and have peace of mind again.

Let's think of a different example. A family has a daughter with anorexia. Her anorexia causes different types of problems in the relationship with her two siblings, parents, and extended family, apart from the obvious health problems for herself. If we apply the same principles, we just need to replace the girl with another one with similar characteristics, and the family functions well again, right?

I know the example seems too stupid to feature in a management book but bear with me for a moment. We agree that applying the same problem-solving philosophy does not work, but why? Why don't we think that replacing an element of the family works just as well to solve family problems as replacing the mechanical item in your computer?

We would readily agree that we must use a different approach when we address human problems because people are not objects and we should not treat them as such. This is an ethical stance that I follow, but my point still holds valid. As a mind experiment, what if there were no ethical barriers to replacing the girl in the family? Would that even work to solve the problem?

The answer is no. And the main question is still why. Why don't we think that replacing an element of a family solves problems just as well as replacing a mechanical item?

It's because a family is a human system, not a mechanical one. Replacing one element of a human system transforms the system. Regardless of whether it functions better, it becomes something different. The family will never be the same without "their" child. We all see it, and that's why we don't believe in solving family problems that way. Even apart from any ethical consideration, it just doesn't work. So, what do we do instead?

We keep the same girl as daughter but try to fix her. We do our best to make her functional again. This might sound a bit harsh, but in my life as a family therapist working with drug addiction and anorexia, I saw it countless times. A father or mother enters the therapist's office and asks, in various formulations, "Please fix my son/daughter so we can have peace of mind again." The underlying request is: "There's something wrong with him/her; please fix it so we can go on with life as usual."

The child in this example is what we name the *identified patient* in family therapy. She unconsciously represents in her behavior larger issues going on in the family: conflict, betrayal, lies, neglect, or substance, emotional, physical, or sexual abuse, for example. By focusing the family's concern on their self-destructive behavior, children simultaneously voice and disguise larger underlying issues going on in the family. A family systems therapy approach defends the principle that the "identified" problem or person is a manifestation of family issues and that *all* family members should participate in treatment to increase effectiveness.[118]

I know, this is counterintuitive and even insulting for some. The notion that a teenager is using drugs because he cannot deal with his father being abusive makes absolutely no sense, does it? Using drugs is solely the teenager's responsibility, not his family's. He chooses that behavior by himself, doesn't he? He should function perfectly even if his father is abusive or his mother is too addicted to prescription medicines to care for her children. This is what a lot of families think.

When we try to bring the whole family in to discuss and find solutions, often we get answers like, "Why do I have to go? The problem is him/her. There's nothing wrong with me; I am a good provider/ caring mother/ responsible sibling."

You'd actually expect a good father, mother, sibling to step forward and say: "How can I support?" The fact that so often they don't is an interesting contradiction.

Yet, bringing the family together for therapy works [119,120,121] exactly because it considers that people are not objects. You cannot just "fix" someone and make them functional again if there are underlying causes of dysfunction in the human system where they operate. You can detox addicted teenagers to the point of stopping the physical craving. Still, once they are back in their natural environment, all the contextual triggers and causes push them towards using drugs again. To secure the treatment's positive result, you need to address the context where it happens – the system.

The idea is that all human systems develop structures to become more effective and efficient, as they function.[122] The ones which don't become obsolete and eventually disappear. These structures can be physical, determining the space where the systems' activities happen and how they happen: walls, open versus closed office and living plans, light design, technology available, etc. But they can also be symbolic: roles distribution, access to resources, hierarchy, mental representations of the problems we face, habits, language we use, and so on.

Without addressing the structures that determine behavior, we cannot succeed in solving the problem. Instead, the problem returns. The existing structures influence the new elements in the system to perform according to old behavior. A change in the program does not affect system structures.[123] This is why systems thinkers speak about structural fixes[124] versus cognitive fixes, when solving a problem.

Mechanical versus human systems

There are two types of systems: mechanical and human.

1. Mechanical systems are simple systems such as your laptop, your car, or your mobile phone.
2. Human systems are complex systems, such as families, communities, companies, and teams.

They differ greatly from each other in the way they are built and operate. Therefore, problems in each type of system have distinctive features and require different approaches to be solved.

Using simple systems approaches to solve complex systems problems usually has one of the following effects:

1. It does not impact the problem.

Did you ever attempt to solve a problem and your actions had no effect on it? Or maybe they even backfired and made the problem worse?

2. It makes the problem recurrent.

Did it ever happen to you that a solution only worked temporarily? After some time the problem came back exactly as before? And you applied the same actions again and the cycle restarts?

3. It creates new and worse problems downstream.

Did you ever solve a problem only to find out that you had created unpredicted problems in other areas of the situation? That some attempts to solve a problem seem to create a multitude of other issues that might blow out of proportion?

This is what happens when we apply mechanical type of solutions to human systems. By doing so, we ignore that all complex systems have the possibility to amplify, deflect or neutralize any attempt to change them. And that those features might be at play against our attempted solutions at any given moment.

To effectively solve human systems problems, we must understand the differences between the two types of systems and use them to model and solve our problems in companies.

There are many differences between the two types of systems. In the next section, I choose to explain the ones I use most in my work with executive teams.

Characteristics of simple systems

Objects, machines, buildings, and all other manufactured non-living things have these characteristics.

1. Known delay between cause and effect

You don't wait three hours for your computer to start. If it doesn't work after a few seconds, you know there is a problem because you know how long the delay should be between pressing "on" and having the expected result. This only happens in simple systems.

2. Energy based

All simple systems work on energy: electric, combustion, hydraulic, or wind. There's an energy flux that crosses the system to make all its parts work. If you cut that source of energy, the system shuts down. Simple systems can be turned on and off at will.

3. Functional connection between individual parts

There is no special link between that individual battery to the other parts of your laptop. You change one element for a similar one, and the simple system works. All that matters is the function performed by that single element, not its unique characteristics and individuality.

4. No free agency

Mechanical parts of a system don't have free agency. They are designed, assembled, and operated according to instructions. They mindlessly follow instructions to perform discrete tasks. Your laptop battery cannot decide to perform a different function or the same function differently in its mechanical system.

5. Material

A simple system exists only in the material world. Destroy the matter that constitutes it, and you eliminate the system forever.

6. Self-disorganizing

Mechanical systems tend to disorganize themselves as they function. They become obsolete, deteriorate, and malfunction to the point where they stop working. They require outside maintenance, management, and organization to keep running. Entropy takes over.

7. Finite

Simple systems are finite. They have a finite number of parts or elements, each performing a limited role, with a finite number of operations. Simple systems also have a finite duration.

8. Linear causality

For every effect, there is a cause; for every cause, there is an effect. Simple systems work like that. Cause always precedes effect, and there's no effect without a cause. After a quick test (plugging in your laptop), you know the cause of the problem: Everything works perfectly except the battery. Linear causality seems to be a law of nature, but it's only a law of simple systems.

Characteristics of complex systems

From those involving a few people to those including all humankind, human systems of any size have these characteristics. Biological systems also share most of them.

1. Unknown delay

Your sales team's results for last month are not what you expected. You decide to introduce new products, change product bundles, make a promotion, and redesign sales processes. Two weeks go by, and results are not clear either way. You're getting nervous. Should you act to correct the strategy or wait another week? How long will the new strategy take to produce its full effect? Maybe your salespeople need time to adjust and ramp up some competencies to make the new processes work. It might take a bit longer than just business as usual, but how much longer?

In human systems there is an unknown delay between action and result, strategy execution and effectiveness. Most of the time, we decide to correct our strategies not because we are sure they will not produce results but because we can't wait for results anymore. Or, worse, because we already wasted too many resources waiting, even if we still believe in the original strategy.

2. Information based

Complex systems are information-based. There are always fluxes of information between elements of a human system. For us to be able to live and work with each other, we need to communicate. People decide and act based on the information they have available. This is our way of informing others in the system what we expect of them, what we can provide for them, our function, what we would like the system to be, and so on.

We continuously send, receive, and interpret "packages" of information about our life in any system: family, company, group of friends, and community. Information is essential for us to perform our activities that keep the system running. And no one controls 100% of the information fluxes in a human system.

3. Personal connection between individual elements

Human systems are individually connected. It's not just about a person's function (being a father, a manager, a coach). The person's individual characteristics may make a huge difference on why and how they perform that function. What happens when you replace the company founder with a professional CEO? Or the first generation of a family-owned company with the second one?

If you take out the cherished coach of that team, founder of that company, or leader of that community, there will be consequences. If you remove the star player of a sports team, there will be an impact. Replacing a person does not guarantee that the system will work better or the same with the new one. A lot depends on the new person's unique connection with the rest of the system elements and how the system structures influence their behavior.

4. Free agency

Humans have free agency. Even if most of our decisions are unconscious, we make hundreds of purchasing, professional, and behavioral decisions every day.[125,126] Peer pressure, advertising, thought leaders, government, bosses, and social media influencers might influence us. But these outside factors cannot unilaterally determine our behavior. Unlike machines, humans can decide to rebel, resist, or react in unpredictable ways. And often, we do, even against our own short-term benefit. Sometimes we do this only to prove that we keep the freedom to do, think, and feel what we want, against external determinants.[127]

5. Symbolic

In human history, powerful authorities destroyed political, religious, and criminal groups. People died (think of the Roman empire crushing the first Christians), and yet those groups came back. They had a cause, a unique form of connection, and specific processes that brought people together around a purpose.

You can destroy most of the materiality of a human system, and it might continue despite that. If there is some form of memory of why, how, and what the system was, people will be able to re-establish it. We store this symbolic memory in books, on the internet, or in a person's brain.

Ray Bradbury's 1953 novel, Fahrenheit 451 provides an example of people's role in preserving knowledge. In this novel, a future evil dystopian society decided to outlaw books, so firemen burned the books. To counter the loss of knowledge, people memorized books and became their living representations.

If it remains somewhere, the system can reenact itself. Human systems have a symbolic representation that outlives their materiality.

6. Self-organizing

Because of the previous characteristics, complex systems are homeostatic and self-organizing. They react to shocks and attacks by adjusting internal conditions and changing the external context to survive. This is homeostasis: "the tendency of a system, especially the physiological system of higher animals, to maintain internal stability, owing to the coordinated response of its parts to any situation or stimulus that would tend to disturb its normal condition or function."[128]

Self-organization, also called spontaneous order, "is a process where some form of overall order arises from local interactions between parts of an initially disordered system. The process can be spontaneous, not needing control by any external agent."[129] In a complex system, any element can contribute to the organization of the whole, bringing information that repairs and improves the system. This is what makes decentralized human organizations so robust and able to survive disruption.

7. Infinite

Because of the previous characteristics, human systems can add more operations, more elements, integrate with other systems, and have no limited duration. As each of us belongs to several systems, we transport information from one to many. We can decide to perform new roles in the old system or old roles in a new system, integrate and separate. There is an impossible-to-calculate number of possibilities because they depend on the agent's creativity.

8. Circular causality

In a human system, cause and effect are not always easy to distinguish. Circular causality describes "a sequence of causes and effects that leads back to the original cause and either alters or confirms it, thus producing a new sequence, as in a feedback loop."[130]

A single effect can have many causes; many effects can have a single cause, and any combination in between is possible. Cause and effect can become intertwined in human systems because they are information-based, symbolic, self-organizing, and their elements have free agency. Something can be cause or effect of itself.[131] This is a core property of systems that allow for new structures to emerge through the combination of self-organization, free agency, and information processing.[132]

Mental models and the illusion of objectivity

My usual client is a multinational company with a global presence and a spot on the Fortune 500 list. I support these companies to increase the effectiveness of their local operating companies' executive teams. I help CEOs to solve problems faster by developing Chief Executive Teams.

Executive teams of multinational corporations, or large local companies, are made up of competent, intelligent, sensible, and well-intentioned people. However, when we bring them together as a team, the result is often not greater than the sum of the parts. It's often even lower, as I described in Chapter 7 – *P for Processes.* And the reason is simple: The mental models that people design to deal with complex challenges limit their interventions' effectiveness.

A mental model represents the real situation, which allows us to perform simulations of "causality and impact" of different possible solutions.[133,134] The mental model is built on pre-existing information, to which it applies accepted thought processes. And this is where the problems begin. The thought processes accepted by a group always contain evaluative assumptions that determine the quality and quantity of information necessary to understand the problem and the type of solution to be adopted. They are affected by cognitive biases that reject useful information and operate irrational processes on it.[135,136,137]

Objectivity is an illusion in complex systems with even a moderate level of uncertainty.[138] Often, the resulting decision only produces the desired results by chance, although our cognitive biases will convince us otherwise.

If you see complex systems like machines you will destroy any human system with your attempts to change it.

This happens because people model complex systems as if they were simple ones. If you assume the reality you are dealing with works like a machine; when it has the characteristics of a human system, you will make very wrong decisions.

If you see complex systems like machines you will destroy any human system with your attempts to change it.

Let's analyze an example you are familiar with to see how simple systems approaches can backfire when applied to complex systems problems.

Problem-solving lessons from Covid-19 pandemic[1]

Covid-19's topic carries strong emotions, deep-rooted beliefs, ideological polarization, rushed judgment, unfair behavior. Somehow it seems to bring out the worst of people. This Is not new to me. I've seen all those characteristics displayed in C-level decision making, especially when the company faces a life-or-death problem.

A pandemic is an oversized problem in an über-complex system. It's ideal for seeing in an overblown version all the small mistakes we humans make when managing problems in complex systems. We cannot miss pandemic-size mistakes because of their huge impact on people's lives. Small mistakes ordinarily go unnoticed in most circumstances.

In the case of the Covid-19 pandemic, it is easy to identify the source of decision-makers' assumptions that shape their mental models: ideology and personal interests.

---

1 I am writing this book during lockdown. This chapter is an example of how to map a complex system of variables to make better problem-solving decisions, using Covid-19 as an example. I am not advocating for any specific approach to solve this problem. Not knowing what the outcome of the pandemic will be, or the measures taken to mitigate it, I choose to use this example as the best proxy for decision making at executive level in a VUCA world. If in two years from now, some of the things I write seem foolish to you, bear in mind the amount of information existing in August 2020 about each variable presented.

- Suppose the new coronavirus infection is perceived, through ideology and personal interest, as a threat to the credibility of the government. In that case, we silence the doctor who identified the disease, and we hide the epidemic numbers.
- If it is perceived as another country's problem, we do not prepare our country for the outbreak.
- If a powerful political figure sees the pandemic as thwarting his desire to get re-elected, he minimizes the problem to keep it hidden for as long as possible.
- If it is framed as a mild disease like flu or a cold, we aim for fast herd immunity.
- If there are only a few cases we think will disappear on their own, we do nothing.
- If it is seen as a lethal disease that can decimate the population, we lock down.

In truth, the complexity, volatility, and uncertainty of the disease outbreak determined that no one could be certain about what this pandemic was in March 2020. And in the absence of applicable evidence-based knowledge, we need to use a model to understand and act in uncertain complex situations. Models are a representation of reality. They might fit the data but never fully match reality.

Covid-19 is neither a lethal disease that kills everyone nor a light cold. It is neither a threat to the state nor other countries' problem. It will neither go away nor terminate humankind. These are cognitive tags we put on the disease that give it a specific model to operate on the problem. But our tags do not adequately describe the problem, the operations we design to solve it will also be ineffective.

Assumptions might fool you

Within companies, assumptions may be less evident because political ideology is less important, and polarization is considered less useful. But assumptions are present in all decisions made by managers. By influencing how decision-makers develop their models of reality, they limit a company's effectiveness in dealing with internal or market challenges.

The questions we need to answer to model (i.e., "understand") reality and decide on company strategy are not so different from the ones a disruptive virus poses.

- What is the meaning of a new competitor? If we see it as a lethal opponent, we need to prepare for war. If it's a bunch of incompetent kids making a computer in a garage, we just wait for them to crash.
- How do we deal with potentially disruptive technology? If it's just a fad, we will wait for business as usual to resume. If it's a complete disruption of our business model, we need to transform fast to survive.
- How do we understand our growth of market share in a market in constant decline? If it's an opportunity to generate cash to transform our business, we will protect earnings and invest heavily. If we see it as "competitors worse than us are going busted in a difficult market," we will happily jeopardize our survival by spending resources.
- How important is employee engagement? If we think it's about perks and fun, we will treat it quite differently than if we perceive it as a predictor of company performance and map the variables it impacts.
- What does a company acquisition mean? If we see it as a simple purchase of market share, we will plan and execute it differently than if we perceive it as a threat to our current company culture.
- What is the impact of a pandemic on our business? If we see it as a fast and unique event, we will design business continuity differently than if we see it as a slow-moving disaster.

Values, assumptions, information deficits and, consequently, mental models that can fit reality or not, influence management decisions. The discrepancy between how we model reality and how it works is the most significant source of errors in decision making. Most of the mistakes we make are not due to lack of information but rather because of the misconceptions we have of how others might react to our decisions. We create subjective interpretations of how the world works and act based on those interpretations and not on objective information we might receive.

We all have cognitive biases that prevent us from seeing reality as it is and force us to see reality as we want it to be.

Naturally, this should happen. We all have cognitive biases that prevent us from seeing reality as it is and force us to see reality as we want it to be. These are automatic mechanisms of unconscious processing that fulfill adaptive functions for the species. Cognitive biases are fully proven by scientific research in psychology.[139] From the point of view of decision making, their effect is apparent: they reduce the ability to understand and effectively deal with reality.

No mental model is perfect, but some are a better fit to reality than others. It is the executive team's responsibility to ensure that their company does not suffer the consequences of deficient modeling of reality.

Executive teams tend to use implicit models as a basis to make decisions and execute them. These phrases or words are full of implicit valuations of what matters and how to make things happen in your company:

- intuition
- professional experience
- technical knowledge
- we always did it like this

Reality has no inherent quality. It makes no mistakes and adapting itself to our models is not in its plans.

By *not* making these assumptions explicit, you can't assess how sound they are, test them as you go, and improve your strategy's accuracy. Your decisions will be influenced by a load of factors you don't even know exist.

Implicit models do not guarantee the quality of decisions. They just give you the illusion you know something while they prevent you from understanding it. Your assumptions distort reality to please you.

Reality exists, but you don't know it

Sars-CoV-2 virus is a reality. It cares not who it infects. It simply does its job – find a host and replicate. Like the virus, reality is neither left-wing nor right-wing. It is neither believer nor agnostic; it is not conservative nor liberal. It is not fast nor slow, it is neither good nor bad. Reality has no inherent quality. It makes no mistakes and adapting itself to our models is not in its plans.

Reality simply *is*, and in human systems, it is complex. It has characteristics that make it unpredictable. Almost everything that is human was created or exists today in a complex, globalized system with various relationships between local and global elements. Different types of material or symbolic benefits, communication, and network channels intersect, but which run on different languages and sometimes antagonistic values.

To deal effectively with reality, you need to understand and accept it. The education system in most countries does not prepare professionals to understand the reality of human systems. It remains attached to a mechanistic view of reality, in which for each effect there is a cause, and for each cause, there is an effect. Causality in human systems is circular and multiple. There are many causes for each effect, many effects for each cause, and cause and effect are not linear over time.

When you don't adequately understand the causal links, you will not have the minimum required understanding of reality to be effective.

Decisions can create the effect before the cause

In Lombardy (Italy), the order for lockdown in February 2020 provoked the widespread stampede that it intended to avoid and spread Covid-19 throughout Italy.[140] Decision-makers did not anticipate that the effect would come before the cause because it was not in their public health or regional management manuals.

If like the authorities in Lombardy, you make a decision that 16 million people will perceive as negatively affecting them, you will have:

1. Unknown delays between your decision and its execution, between execution and its impacts. You might believe you can communicate it on the following day, and it will work, but the reality is that you don't know if this is true. You also don't know if and when it will work after executed.
2. Some people with a personal connection to others will warn them about it to protect their close connections from the negative impact. Those, in turn, will be personally connected to some others. Rumors, speculation, and misinformation quickly spread to the population in general.
3. Information flowing at the speed of light mobilizes the system to act.
4. The symbolic meaning of restricting citizens' constitutional rights and the material disruption of personal lives has an impact.
5. Sixteen million people simultaneously try to protect their interests.

A system self-organizes to neutralize your decisions' perceived negative impacts by using ordinary and creative approaches to create unexpected options (i.e. emergent behavior) in an infinite game.

Consequently, Lombardy's lockdown decision provoked the opposite effect than was intended even before officials carried it out. The effect came before the cause because, in a human system, people anticipate each other's actions and pre-emptively act based on their own perceptions of others' future moves. Machines don't do that. Yet.

If it were not tragic, it would be comical to see how most governments and health authorities applied this linear causality thought of "command and control" to communities that are moved by collective dynamics based on the perception of personal effectiveness and need to protect their interests.

Self-organization is an emergent property of human systems that explains seemingly incomprehensible mass phenomena. In this case, it can account for a lot of what has been happening in Covid-19 times.

Many management decisions are ineffective or produce opposite effects because the model on which they are based is black and white, whereas reality is colorful.

Because companies are smaller groups of humans, and their action time is shorter, decisions' effectiveness can more quickly be measured. The result can be equally tragic. Many management decisions are ineffective or produce opposite effects because the model on which they are based is black and white, whereas reality is colorful.

It's the system, man

A human system has specific characteristics that, once understood, allow for more effective decision making. Solving a complex problem does not necessarily require complex decisions or actions. Sometimes the combination of several simple actions is enough. But these must be based on the understanding of the complexity of the context that originated the problem. The interventions must interrupt the circular causality that sustains the problem. Otherwise, they may produce more negative than positive results.

The simple actions of locking down the entire population of a state to their homes do not solve the pandemic problem. Neither does letting the virus go rampant in the population and kill at will.

A pandemic is a complex problem with many dimensions: physical health, mental health, political, economic, legal, ethical, ideological, environmental, and technological. And each agent sees only its part of the system, advocating solutions that aggravate the other dimensions of the problem for other agents. Neglecting the economic dimension aggravates the health issue later. Neglecting the death toll today slows down the economy tomorrow. Not supporting employees' mental health through the crisis worsens future physical health and reduces company productivity.

Moving one variable of a system affects all the others. This is the nature of complex systems and all human problems, even if we do not want to see it when we are making daily business decisions.

To be effective, an executive team must adequately model the system it manages – the company – and the context in which it operates – the market.

This requires knowledge and application of systems-thinking concepts to decision making in management. Understanding a system means

1. Critically distinguishing variables, target groups, geography, or territories;
2. Qualifying relationships between individuals, groups, and variables;
3. Mapping agents' perspectives; and

4. Understanding the context of the system in which everything occurs.

These four actions allow you to model each measure's impact, test on a small scale, learn from the feedback, and progressively adjust the intervention measures to the problem. This is how you innovate successfully, both during Covid-19 and in everyday business challenges.

The learning: traditional decision making doesn't work

The most positive consequence of this pandemic is demonstrating that traditional decision-making models are too weak to deal with complex problems. Anything based on linear cause-effect, sequential in time, isolated in space, ignorant of the processes and contexts of occurrence, will fail because human interaction dynamics are complex.

The only goal to declare an emergency state and restrict individual freedom is to reduce the complexity of decisions by eliminating individual will and the possibility of spontaneous social events. Authorities lock down to manipulate human interaction and temporarily suspend some variables. Decision making is simplified by artificially reducing complexity and postponing the consequences of this reduction. By locking down, authorities try to turn a human system into a mechanical one.

The most positive consequence of this pandemic is demonstrating that traditional decision-making models are too weak to deal with complex problems.

Apart from monopolies or illegal manipulation, companies do not have the power to determine what happens to their markets. Therefore, they must be much better than governments and health authorities at understanding how their internal and external environments work.

It is easier for an executive team to perform this task because the degree of complexity of business decisions is lower than the management of a pandemic.

Causal loop diagrams

We understand better mental models and complex systems when we represent them in some form of graphic design. We can use many types of representations of systems to understand them better.

In this section I will use causal loop diagrams. I have found them useful in supporting executive teams to generate better understanding of variables that they need to monitor, change, or stabilize while solving problems. A lot of people are visual thinkers, and these maps allow them to comprehend in one sheet of paper the most relevant variables they need to act on.

You don't need to be able to make a causal loop diagram to solve problems in complex systems. I usually guide the executive team through the process while they find better ways to deal with their biggest challenges. But understanding what they are and how they foster flexibility in thinking and originality in solution helps a lot.

If you find that this specific systems-thinking tool is not for you, just skip this section and go directly to the next one – *Benefits of systems thinking models*. There you will read a summary of the benefits of using this and other tools.

A causal loop diagram is a display of the causal relationships between the system's most important variables.[141, 142, 143]

Each variable is a node of the system; an arrow represents the influence between them. Each node must be stated neutrally, without any positive or negative interpretation.

In Figure 22, we mark each arrow with + (plus) or – (minus) according to its impact on the following one. Do not confuse

+ with *positive* or – with *negative value judgments*. There are no value judgments associated with the symbols. The signal + or the letter P (for positive correlation) means that the two variables will increase or decrease together. An increase in variable 1 provokes an increase in variable 2. And a decrease in variable 1 produces a decrease in variable 2.

The signal – or the letter I (for inverse correlation) means an inverse relationship between variables. An increase in 1 decreases 2, or a decrease in 1 increases 2. They covary in different directions.

When we design a human system's causal diagram, it always closes itself in several feedback loops. This is what we mean when we use the term *circular causality*. Wherever you start in the system, that's an efficient cause for actively maintaining the current problem. All nodes in the system are causes of the next one. All nodes are effects of previous ones. Any node is simultaneously cause and effect. Because the loop closes, any cause will be an effect of itself and any effect a cause of itself.

The importance of mapping factors that influence health promotion in the multisectoral health system, as a basis to design better policies, was established by a team of researchers in Australia.[144] We can use the same principles to draft a simple Covid-19 causal loop diagram, only to understand the immediate impacts of the decision to lock down a state.

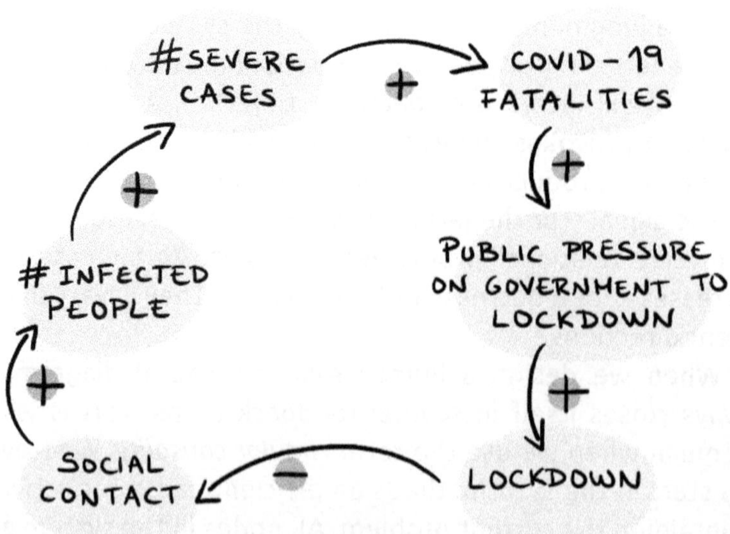

Figure 22 – Lockdown Causal Loop

If you map some of the variables, you see in Figure 22 that lockdowns reduce social contact, thereby reducing the number of infected people, which reduces the number of severe cases of Covid-19, thereby slowing down the fatality rate and the public pressure on governments to lockdown. The idea is that lockdowns will reduce Covid-19 fatality rate to a level where the people will be asking their government to unlock the state. Conclusion: lockdown is a good solution.

If you want to dig deeper, you might add some other variables and find out that by reducing the total number of infected people in a population, you reduce both the severe cases and the mild/asymptomatic ones.

You might also see that, as with any other virus that does not kill all its hosts and the survivors develop immunity, the number of immune people in a population increases proportionally with the number of infected people.

The more immune people you have in the population, the less infected people you will get in the future. Having a higher ratio of mild/asymptomatic cases increases immunity in the population without burdening hospitals and increasing the fatality rate. Having a higher ratio of severe cases increases the burden on ICU beds and the fatality rate.

If we could guarantee that through infection all asymptomatic people, and none of the risk groups, got the disease at once, the population would be immune to the disease without any fatalities. This is what effective and safe vaccines do. They can act as external determinant of immunity that does not increase fatality rate of the disease because it provokes asymptomatic immunity in all groups.

There are usually four causes for viral immunity: severe infections, mild/asymptomatic infections, effective vaccines and pre-existing immunity from similar viruses. Because they have different impacts on the fatality rate, they should be mapped separately (see Figure 23).

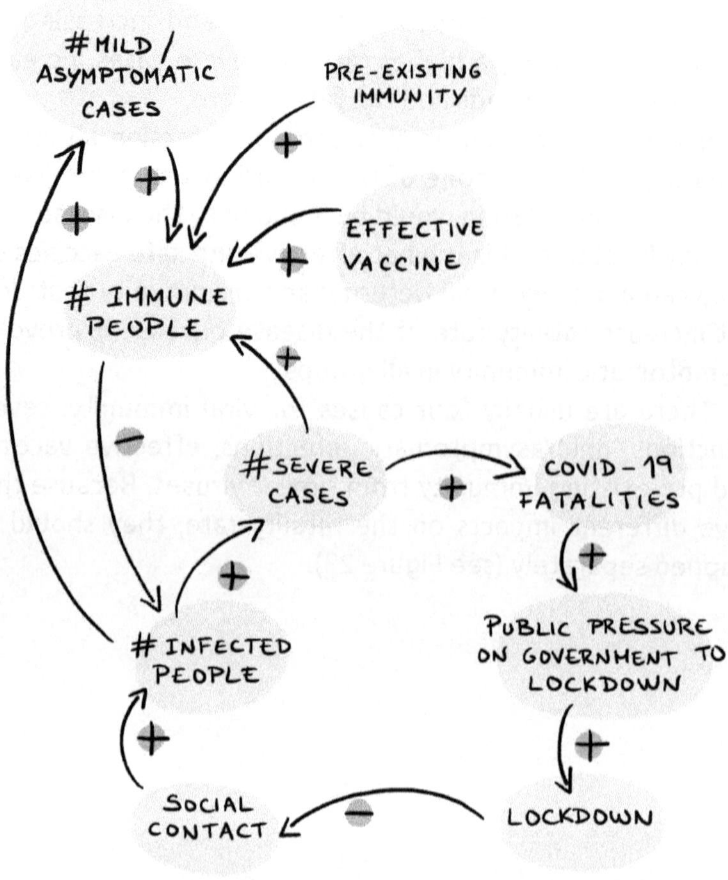

Figure 23 – The different causes for Covid-19 immunity

Creating the highest possible rate of asymptomatic cases in a population helps protect the elderly and other high-risk groups, until a safe and effective vaccine is created. Therefore, we should map separately the "closed schools" variable. This has a clearly distinct value from other lockdown measures by impacting mild and asymptomatic cases with only a marginal increase in severe cases (see Figure 24).

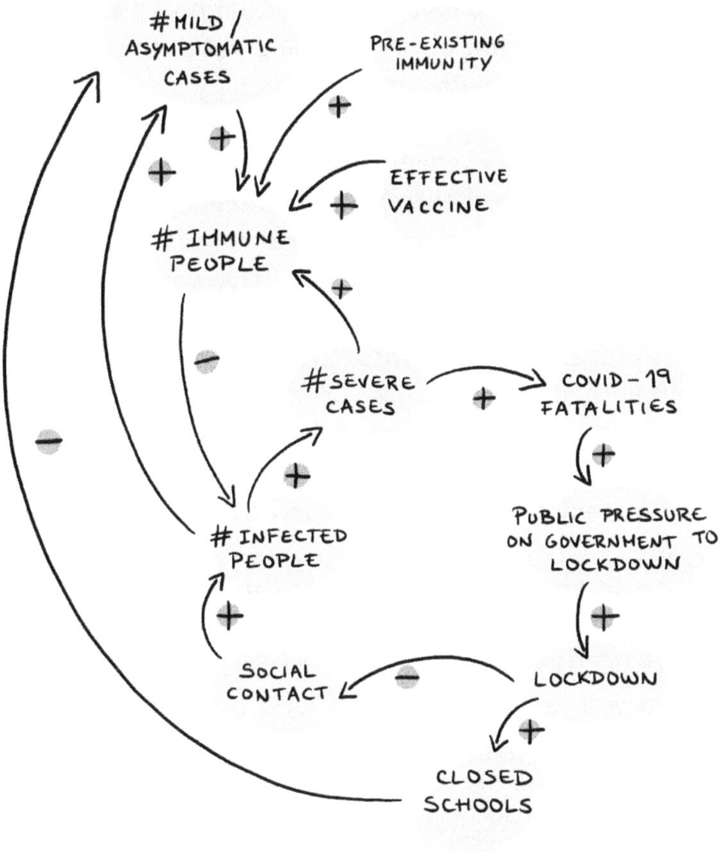

Figure 24 – Impact of closing schools on the Covid-19 cycle

But so far you are in the health management side of the disease. Lockdown affects the economy as well.

You might want to map that cycle of the causal loop with any variable you find relevant. In Figure 25, I used all-cause mortality, economic demand, companies' financial sustainability, employment, trust in government, and GDP, but you might use any other. This is the beauty of a causal loop diagram: It is not about being 100% comprehensive when mapping variables. You can always add more nodes in any system to the point of making it impossible to read. This exercise is about mapping the variables that will allow us to understand the complexity of the situation to be effective in managing it. It's not about mapping absolutely everything that affects the problem.

Following the arrows: strict lockdown reduces economic demand, which reduces spending and hurts companies' financial sustainability, which in turn generates unemployment, which reduces consumer spending and economic demand in turn.

As companies reduce their financial sustainability, this decreases the tax collection, thereby reducing the available resources for the governments to manage public health. Most governments are – as I write – focusing their public health interventions on Covid-19 only, which might increase mortality by all other causes, which can reduce the public pressure on government to lockdown as soon as people start seeing the costs.

All-cause mortality also impacts the level of trust in the government which we know is connected to economic demand. The more we trust a government, the more we spend.

When you look at the causal loop diagram of Figure 25 (remember this is just a draft for demonstration purposes), you see there is no decision without negative consequences. Public health and economy are not opposite choices; they are interrelated in many ways. They can go up and down together. All-cause mortality destroys the economy. Economic destruction lowers the public health standard and reduces life expectancy (provoking earlier deaths).

Assumptions and prejudice (in the form of ideology and personal interests) make you see only one side of the system dynamics and neglect the full chain of causality.

Technical competence might also restrict your ability to perform a good causal loop analysis. Health professionals might focus solely on the health side of it, because they don't feel competent to deal with the other parts.[145]

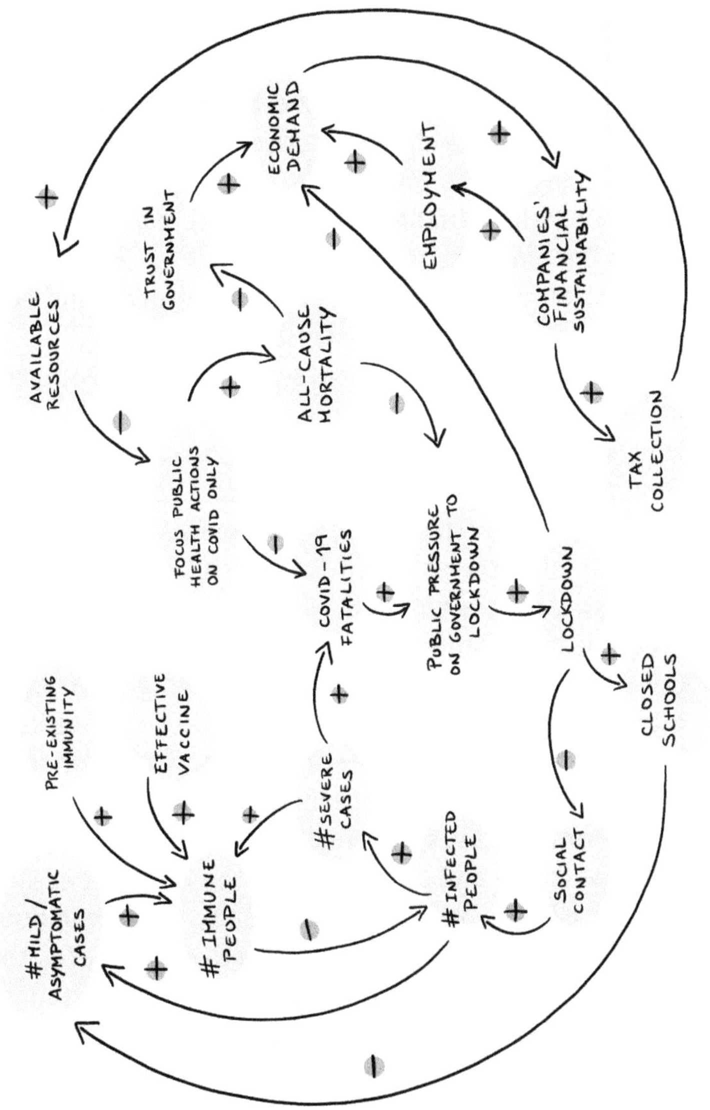

Figure 25 – Impact of Covid-19 on health and economy

If you understand the whole, you can make better decisions. By using a causal loop diagram, we can visualize in this situation:

- The positive and negative effects of a decision – in this case, we can replace the question "Do we lock down?" for "When and how will a lockdown be necessary?" or "What are the alternatives and their compared benefits?"
- The different variables that account for each loop inside the diagram
- How lockdown impacts the economic growth and economic growth impacts Covid-19 deaths
- How locking down to prevent Covid-19 death toll increases all-cause mortality
- How lockdown is a cause and effect of itself
- How governments are pressed to lockdown by public opinion and how this opinion is formed
- The role of vaccines and if it's worth betting all chips on waiting for them
- What the most important variable to measure success is. Is it good to manage public health thinking of Covid-19 fatality rate or should we consider all-cause mortality?
- How we can play with different measures to generate immunity of the different kinds: pre-existing, vaccine, asymptomatic cases, severe cases.
- What we know and don't know at the time of decision making: is there pre-existing immunity? How long does it take to develop a safe and effective vaccine? Is the immunity from asymptomatic cases strong enough? And the lines of research and data collection that we need to pursue to make even better evidence-based decisions ahead.

Every country or state is in a different situation. What might play better for the demography, geography, wealth and health status of a population, might not be possible for another one.

By mapping a complex system, we can understand that the world is not divided into pure right or wrong actions. There are many possibilities with different levels of outcomes that we might consider relevant. There are many ways to generate a desirable outcome. Often, we choose not to see them. The best combination of approaches is the one that maximizes the likelihood of success.

There are many ways to generate a desirable outcome. Often, we choose not to see them.

Formatting a solution that is better for us as a company depends on being able to understand complexity instead of ignoring it.

Benefits of systems thinking models

The benefits of using systems thinking models, powered by causal loop diagrams, for decision-making are:

1. **Comprehensive understanding of reality.**
   The more relevant causes we consider in our understanding of a situation, the better we understand it and the more evidence-based decisions we make. We only stop working on the diagram when we are satisfied with the description of reality it provides.

2. **Increased rationality.**
   Assumptions are also mapped and understood in causal loop diagrams. You may include the impact of fear, ideology, preferences, everything that we can measure, even if only qualitatively. Once mapped, these causes stop having irrational power over our decisions.

3. **Increased collaboration in the team.**
   There are no "us versus them" arguments. As we list causes and map their impact, everyone discusses nodes, impacts, evaluation criteria and establishes a common understanding of relationships between variables. This becomes a mental model collaboratively developed by the team to understand how the system works.

4. **Decisions emerge from the data.**
   Once the team establishes decision-making criteria and applies them to the causal loop, decisions that best fit the current knowledge become apparent, and all involved can see that.

5. **Flexibility of opinions.**
   Once we understand that a complex system is a delicate balance of causalities, we realize there is no magic solution for our problems. Solving part of the problem will create different problems in other parts of the system. We become more flexible in our opinions of how to proceed.

6. **Faster strategy correction.**
   As we map the expected outcomes upfront, we can compare the magnitude of the positive and negative effects and measure them as they happen. This allows for testing and revision of our models if necessary. Changing strategy is faster as soon as we detect that we were wrong in our assumptions.

7. **Remove egos from the problem.**
   No one loses face if we all collaborate in designing a system thinking approach to solving our problems. This removes egos from the situation. And we know that egos are a recurrent feature of management problems.

8. **Efficiency of resources used in solving a problem.**
   As we understand what the points of maximum leverage are (i.e. the variables that most effectively nudge the system in the right direction),[146] we save resources.

9. **Reduce problem recurrency.**
   Because we address the full cycle of causality at once, we can prevent the same problems in the future. Recurrence happens when we tackle only part of the causality cycle.

10. **Better communication among team members and with other teams' members.**
    The causal-loop diagram can become a token that promotes mutual understanding through discussion and communication.

11. **Inclusion and convergence of mental models.**
    As our knowledge of reality evolves, no circular causality diagram is ever finished. Therefore, anyone can contribute relevant ideas later in the process. We aim to include all relevant input, which allows for the convergence of mental models in one more comprehensive mental model.

12. **Eliminate groupthink.**
    Groupthink (explained in Chapter 7) happens when executive team members agree with a proposed solution without considering all relevant factors to it. A causal loop diagram eliminates groupthink by default.

13. **Eliminate silo mentality.**
    Silo mentality exists because we only see our personal interests and the ones of the people in "our group." When we know that it's impossible to satisfy only our needs and that we are both a cause and effect of

our own actions, it becomes clear that "we are in this together".

14. **Improve management quality.**
    Your management's quality is proportional to the number of variables the team considers in the management process. The level of conversations becomes richer and deeper when you can better understand the company, the market, and the world.

15. **Generate more options.**
    Because we can intervene in different nodes of the system, we are able to combine more options in the solution design.

16. **Guide research and data collection.**
    Some of the arrows might be difficult to mark as positive or inverse correlation. We might not know if some of the nodes are real, like pre-existing immunity. These are clear paths of information collection to improve decision quality.

17. **Better decision making.**
    As an outcome of all the previous benefits, we have better decision making.

18. **Increase engagement with execution.**
    Understanding the full context of decisions contributes to increased team engagement with their execution.

19. **Better company performance because of all the above.**[147]
    These are the thinking patterns of chief executive teams when making decisions and solving problems. Who wouldn't want their executive team to perform at this level?

20. **Happier life.**
    What happens when you collaborate with cordial and intelligent people, to achieve higher performance with less emotional and cognitive effort? You enter the flow state. You are happier.

We all love simplicity, even when it's poisonous

"For every complex problem, there is an answer that is clear, simple, and wrong" said the American journalist Henry Louis Mencken. I would just make this sentence sharper by using the plural. For every complex problem, there are many answers that are clear, simple, and wrong.

When you choose to deny the complexity of a problem, solutions become artificially clear and simple.

All proposed solutions based on unchecked assumptions and prejudices are clear, simple, and wrong. When you choose to deny the complexity of a problem, solutions become artificially clear and simple. And the people who oppose them are evil. We enter the "us versus them" zero-sum game. There are no winners in that game when we must continue living with each other afterward.

Every problem has several chains of causality. Only prejudice and intellectual dishonesty might make you deny part of them. Executive teams must prove their worth with decisions that can be backed up by data, results that can be objectively measured. It's the CEO's job to guarantee their executive teams get it done.

Simple actions are desirable when you address the leverage points of a system, not when you ignore the system.

According to Albert Einstein, "The definition of genius is taking the complex and making it simple." We need clear and simple actions that can be "right."

This means that they fit the data according to the best knowledge available at any given moment. It means that we have objective ways to evaluate how well we are performing. We can monitor the data and adjust decisions as we move forward. This requires understanding, instead of denying, the complexity of the systems where we live.

Simple actions are desirable when you address the leverage points of a system, not when you ignore the system. We seek those variables that nudge the system in the right direction with the least effort required.

Your company's problems, be they marketing, supply chain, sales, human resources, technology, or whatever, might be as complex as managing a pandemic. But if you increase the quality of your executive team thinking processes about the problems, you will be more effective and efficient in solving them.

And when you link this experience back to the team's purpose, processes and people, reinforcing the efficacy of your team, you are developing a chief executive team.

10

P FOR POSSIBILITIES

"One clever person can make fantastic innovations. Many people from different backgrounds and cultures can make much less, unless you create the structure that allows you to listen to them and integrate their diversity. As we did with Ricardo."

– Stefan Hilgers | Vorwerk International | Vice President

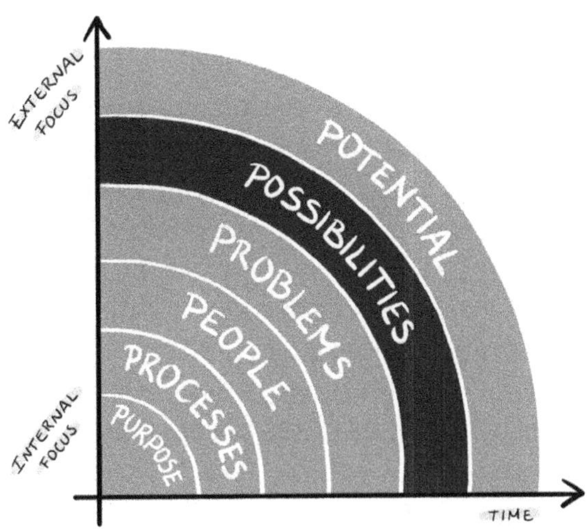

Figure 26 – P for Possibilities

Just add team learning to generate possibilities

WE FOLLOWED THE model of *The 6P's of Executive Teams®* that I shared in Chapter 5, which is the basis for my executive team development program. The P's sequence stretches from the internal to the team's external focus along time, as we see in Figure 26.

This sequence works best because defining the P for Purpose makes it easier to define the P for Processes. Defining this one makes it easier to structure the P for People, and so on. The innermost core of the team is its purpose. When there's no common purpose, there's no team. You might have quite efficient processes; you might have a good level of trust and psychological safety, but you will have no reason to work together as a team. Without a common purpose, a working group will be enough for the job.

One of the things people often ask me about is: Why should team *processes* be defined before we take care of trust and psychological safety (the *people* dimension)? Why are these two in that sequence?

The reason is quite pragmatic. Frequently, the problems that are generated by the lack of efficient and effective processes are misinterpreted by the team members and taken personally. The actions, opinions, and outputs of executives are partially determined by their company's role and processes to reach the goals. If not perceived from the outside, this complexity might lead to interpreting the behavior of that team member personally. We avoid many difficulties in personal relationships by clearing the team processes, including role accountability, before that stage. Dealing with the P for People becomes easier after that.

The first four P's come to fruition in the fifth P: P for Possibilities. This is the last of the P's that still has some inner focus on the team's functioning. The P for Potential will be completely outwardly focused.

1. You already defined the Purpose of your team.
2. You designed the most effective and efficient Processes to govern it.
3. You established the best possible level of trust to integrate cognitive diversity among its People.
4. You increased your understanding and effectiveness of your actions on the company by seeing it as a complex system with specific Problems.

At this level, your team masters challenges in the current business context.

But the business context is volatile, complex, and hostile. You need to step ahead of the game, foresee the next moves, anticipate market needs, and generate new business possibilities. To generate new Possibilities, you need to add learning to the first four P's.

To generate new Possibilities, you need to add learning to the first four P's.

What you learned about learning is wrong

The word "learning" introduces many concepts. We often first think of school learning. To us, that means absorbing predefined information outlined by the curriculum. In school, we learn a predefined body of knowledge, group of concepts, number of operations, and processes that we need to assimilate through memorization and repetition.

The structure of school learning assumes that someone knows and teaches someone else who doesn't know. Learning is, therefore, seen as unidirectional. It's top-down; the teacher teaches the pupil. Similarly, the parents teach the child. Someone more knowledgeable and expert teaches a newcomer who doesn't have that knowledge, experience, or expertise. Learning is the memorization of information, including operations and concepts applied in new contexts.

In school learning, we memorize meanings others derived before we came into the picture.

Learning in life is not predefined; it's emergent.

Learning in life is not predefined; it's emergent. Learning emerges from experience. It's often not formalized, and it is sometimes paradoxical or contradictory. Our life knowledge isn't based on a group of concepts or operations. Instead, our learning in life happens by making sense of things as we progress through hits and misses.

Learning is a side product of our attempts to reach goals and obtain benefits. We learn what works for us as we make our way in the world.

That's what we call the emergent property of *learning in life*.[148] Whereas in *school*, we have someone teaching, in *life*, no one knows the result of learning. When you are a student, you will ultimately have to pass the exam that measures what you've learned about one discipline. You need to memorize a set of right answers. If you give any other answers, you are wrong. When you have learned them all, learning reaches its end: knowing the "right answers", the "solutions" to the questions.

There is no limit to what one can learn in life. When you think you've got it all figured, a surprise invites you to learn again.

In life learning, there is no end and no right answer. What is right for you in your life might be quite wrong for someone else. There is no limit to what one can learn in life. When you think you've got it all figured, a surprise invites you to learn again. Often, answers are only momentarily "right".

School learning versus life learning

Life learning is the opposite of school learning. In life, we learn from anyone in any situation. We don't need to have a mentor, teacher, trainer, or coach formally giving us knowledge. We can learn even from people who don't want to teach or give us knowledge or ideas.

In life, we can learn from situations that don't involve other people at all. When we try and fail due to circumstances, random events, or unforeseen rules, we learn from only ourselves and our circumstances.

In school, we *memorize* the meaning of things; in life, we *make meaning* of things.

In life learning, events are the best teachers. They show us in an objective way that our beliefs have no foundation. Because they do it without malice (who can blame themselves for a natural disaster?), it is easier to accept the knowledge they offer than that of another human.

In school, we *memorize* the meaning of things; in life, we *make meaning* of things. We attribute meaning; we make sense of situations, and we derive meaning from our experiences. This is learning.

Learning in school assumes the implementation of a fixed body of knowledge. In life learning, we create a new body of knowledge that allows us to deal with what does not exist yet. The end of learning in life is to prepare us for a more satisfying, fulfilling, rewarding, and useful life.

In school learning, we assimilate predefined knowledge. In life learning, we create knowledge to deal with unstructured situations.

In school learning, we assimilate predefined knowledge. In life learning, we create knowledge to deal with unstructured situations (see Table 1).

Learning

School	Life
✓ Predefined	✓ Emergent
✓ Someone knows/ teaches	✓ No one knows the result
✓ Unidirectional (top-down)	✓ Multidirectional (360°)
✓ One right answer	✓ Many fitting answers
✓ We memorize the meaning of things	✓ We make meaning of things
✓ Closed learning units – finite body of knowledge	✓ No learning units – infinite body of knowledge
✓ Structured	✓ Unstructured
✓ Predictable environment	✓ Unpredictable environment

Table 1 – Contrasting school and life learning

Insight is cheap, action is value

Before going into what an executive team can do to become a learning team and drive organizational learning in its company, I need to address the most harmful assumption about learning.

Most people think of learning as a purely cognitive endeavor. The assumption is: You learn something when you can explain it.

When I was studying for my psychology degree, our psychotherapy professor repeated endlessly in our supervision group: "Without behavior, insight is cheap." When you support someone's change, your job is to help them ultimately solve problems and get out of pain. When do you reach the goals of the therapeutic process? When the person understands why they suffer but still suffer? Or when the person effectively reduces or even stops their emotional struggle?

School learning is mostly conceptual, theoretical, and purely cognitive. Learning in life requires action. You cannot say you've learned about personal relationships until you can act to make yours better. You cannot say you know how the stock exchange works until you consistently make money with it. You cannot assume you know your business sector until you successfully lead a company. You cannot be a credible nutritionist if you suffer from morbid obesity. You show what you know in who you are.

You show what you know in who you are.

Life is not an academic exam. Learning in life is either transformational or not learning at all.

Life learning requires behavior change. No one cares about the world as it exists between your ears. If your actions are still dead wrong, you learned nothing.

As David Kolb put it, "Learning is a process where knowledge is created through the transformation of experience."[149] We start from our substantial experience and apply reflective observation, abstract conceptualization, and active experimentation. These are the four stages of Kolb's learning cycle model. We need action to learn, and our actions measure how much we learned.

Life is not an academic exam. Learning in life is either transformational or not learning at all.

You don't have a learning organization if your company makes one mistake after the other and loses money. It doesn't matter how great your corporate university is, how many MBA graduates you have in your ranks, how much money you throw at research, or how many years you've been in business. Organizational learning is about more and better results, however you measure them. If you are not getting more or better results, you are not learning.

The executive team role in organizational learning

When the business landscape is stable, you can apply predefined knowledge to understand the situation and act on it. Do you remember the last time you could trust the business landscape to be predictable? Me neither.

Organizational learning is about more and better results, however you measure them.

The market constantly throws a stream of unstructured situations at us, and we must decide how we will deal with them. Applying predefined knowledge available to everybody else hardly qualifies as a competitive advantage.

As Peter Senge wrote, "In the long run, the only sustainable source of competitive edge is your organization's ability to learn faster than its competitors." [150] My question is: Who is responsible for guaranteeing that your organization learns faster than its competitors?

- The R&D team?
- The marketing team?
- The product team?
- The customer insights team?

Who designs the strategy, assembles all these teams, decides the amount of resources they get, validates their goals, approves their outcomes, uses their intelligence, or not?

The executive team is ultimately accountable for how much an organization can learn and how fast it does it. A culture of learning starts at the top of the company or not at all. For your company to become a learning organization, your executive team must be a learning team.

A culture of learning starts at the top of the company or not at all.

As I discussed in previous chapters and provided supporting management research, these behaviors at executive team level don't facilitate the development of learning processes:

- Inadequate CEO behavior modes
- Arrogance
- Authoritarian leadership
- Lack of competence
- Absence of a common explicit team purpose
- Silo mentality
- Fragmentation of the team into subgroups
- Lack of diversity
- Misuse of current diversity
- Groupthink
- Mistrust between team members
- Unclear and inefficient team processes
- Poor understanding of the complexity of human systems and how they operate
- Process and affective conflict
- Structural causes for non-collaborative behavior of executives

Removing the hurdles to developing a Chief Executive Team at the same time clears the way to implement a learning organization. The Chief Executive Team is the ultimate learning team in the company. CEOs must take the responsibility to drive learning in the organization through their executive teams. Delegating this is self-defeating.

Team learning model: the four types of learning

The Chief Executive Team is the ultimate learning team in the company. CEOs must take the responsibility to drive learning in the organization through their executive teams.

Learning starts with a question, a challenge, or a problem. Problems are great if you know how to befriend them. Let's start with a neutral definition: A problem is a difference between what you expected to get and what you are really getting as an outcome of your actions. This divergence is neither good nor bad. It is what it is: a gap. Only your expectations and your inability to change your behavior might make it negative – and your learning competence might make it positive.

Given that we are all capable of changing our behavior, when we learn, we translate any problem, challenge, issue, or question, as a neutral gap to feed the learning process. A gap is visual, measurable, and objective. It depends on clear criteria to exist. The gap you see might not exist for me because we use different criteria. Agreeing on a void and its causes is a good step forward in the learning process that any executive team must take.

A problem is a difference between what you expected to get and what you are really getting as an outcome of your actions.

When you find a gap, you can do several things. Let's analyze them with an example.

Level 0: no learning

Gabor is the CEO of a Direct Selling company focused on kitchen appliances. His company produces a kitchen robot that performs several functions that replace many other objects. Gabor identified a gap between monthly goals and sales results. He looked at the numbers and asked his Chief Marketing and Chief Commercial Officers some questions. They reassured him that the gap will be solved by itself.

Gabor might decide that there's nothing to be done differently to close the gap because it has nothing to do with the company's actions. And he might be right. Maybe it's a momentary glitch in the market that will go away by itself.

This is the first option in the learning model. You can decide *not* to learn. You can decide to adjust your initial expectations down to close the gap. You identify your expectations as unrealistic and accept the current outcome as the only real possibility in this option.

Deciding not to learn might be fine in some circumstances. After all, learning requires the investment of resources that maybe you can't afford to spend at the moment. Accepting the current level of results and maintaining the same actions might be the very best thing you can do when the gap does not depend on your intervention and is momentary. In many situations, though, this is not the case.

Rejecting learning to protect egos and the personal interests of managers at the expense of the company's growth is suicidal.

Rejecting learning to protect egos and the personal interests of managers at the expense of the company's growth is suicidal. This choice is more common than you might think. It manifests itself in actions like

- Find the culprit for the gap and punish them.
- "Kill the messenger" of bad news so that no one speaks about them.
- Deny that the current outcomes are happening or lie about them.
- Find good excuses to kick the can down the road without dealing with it right now.
- Explain that you did not really mean to reach the initial results; they were only meant to stretch the team.
- Decide to forget about your attempt to have different results and not count this attempt as part of the game.
- Decide you are right, and the market is wrong.

The blame game is a substantial part of a no-learning culture.

If you do any of this as an executive team, you are preventing the development of valuable know-how. The blame game is a substantial part of a no-learning culture. And if you think that some of the options above are cartoon-like and could not happen in real life, I have seen them all in different styles and intensity levels. All link back to a core lack of accountability in the executive team.

The decision not to learn from unexpected outcomes must be conscious and deliberate, never made by omission.

Level 1 learning: solve the current gap

Gabor and his team might analyze the current gap as a signal that something must change in how they do business. They might look at the sales model they are applying and find that the sales process, based on an individual demonstration of the kitchen robot at the client's home, does not use the right market intelligence.

Maybe the sales arguments were based on saving money, and their target buyer values healthy eating more than the cost of meals. Perhaps making the demonstration for single customers as the basis for a referral system might be too slow to generate traction, and they decide to try the virtual party system where you sell to a group at the same time.

The decision not to learn from unexpected outcomes must be conscious and deliberate, never made by omission.

Changing the market intelligence used, tweaking the sales model, going from individual to group product demonstrations are examples of level 1 learning. We address the strategies and techniques of what we do as the basis for solving the gap. We don't redesign the full process.

The first level of learning is to bridge the difference between what you want and what you get by addressing what you are doing – the strategies and techniques you apply.

Level 2 learning: prevent this type of gap

Gabor might look at the product or the distribution channels as the source of the current sales gap. If some of the product's specifications are making it less attractive to customers, changing them might revamp the company's sales results. This approach focuses on creating a new product that stays relevant for a longer time. It's not a quick fix, as it involves product engineering and manufacturing. Still, it can be more effective and efficient in the long run, preventing this type of gap from resurfacing in the future.

Gabor's team might also decide that going all in on Direct Selling may not be an adequate option to distribute their product worldwide. They might look at alternatives, such as setting up online and retail shops, partnerships with companies owning complementary products, and so on. In this case, the team is addressing how the company is doing business. We are not only a Direct Selling company; we also do other things to distribute our products.

The second level of learning bridges the gap between what you want and what you get by addressing how you are doing things: the operating principles and processes you follow.

Level 3 learning: define the types of gaps you want to deal with

Gabor and his executive team might analyze the gap as a possible early warning of something bigger going on in the market. They might perceive it as a change that is here to stay, requiring a different type of adaptation by the company.

The team might go back to the roots and ask themselves: why do we manufacture and sell this product? Their business model was based on specific assumptions and business orthodoxies:

- People want simplicity, and one device is simpler than 26 kitchen appliances;
- People want to have less work, and a programmable robot reduces their work;
- People want free time, and a robot that works alone can free up time for our customers;
- People trust other people who use the same product, so the direct selling model is the best for us;
- A commissioned workforce is the best in direct selling;
- We are in direct selling;
- We sell a product which is a robot;
- Quality is essential, and so on.

Gabor's executive team might want to redefine why the company does things. They might decide to challenge all or some business orthodoxies and assumptions. They might decide they are not in the product-selling business but driving the healthy eating revolution, with the kitchen robot being only one item in the business model. Other items could be a recipe software encyclopaedia, a customer community, a nutrition app, a service for online grocery distribution, healthy-eating classes, etc.

The third level of learning focuses on bridging the gap between what you want and what you get by addressing why you do things: the assumptions and orthodoxies you believe in and the mental models underlying your actions.

Each learning level has a direct impact on the lower levels. By changing the *why* of their business (the assumptions and orthodoxies), Chief Executive Teams will inevitably change *how* the business is done (operating principles and processes) and *what* the organization does (the strategies and techniques applied at any given moment).

Even if the sales results gap is small, a chief executive team might want to go for level 3 learning. The level of learning that you choose to have in your team has nothing to do with the actual size of the gap you are facing. It is determined by your mental model of the current situation and the degree of freedom you allow yourselves to propose changes to the current business model.

Business as usual is the application of past knowledge. Your future business depends on defining the types of gaps you should be solving.

Business as usual is the application of past knowledge. Your future business depends on defining the types of gaps you should be solving. This is the highest level of organizational learning, and your executive team must lead it. Figure 27 shows the 4-level learning model.

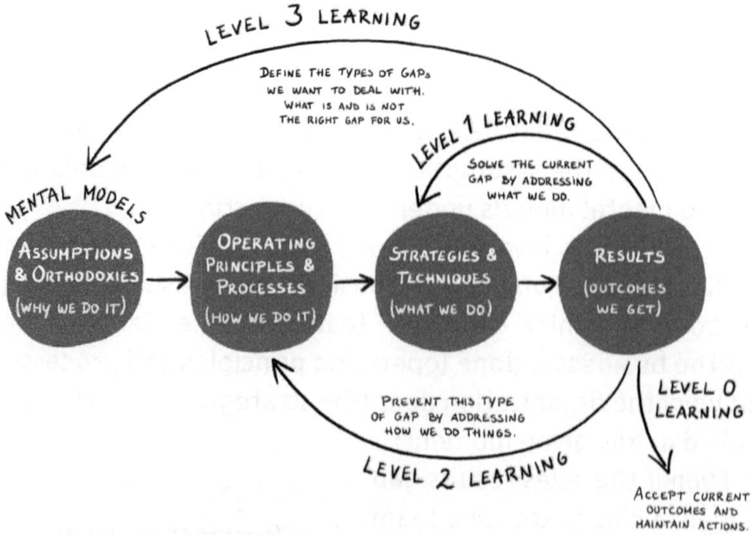

Figure 27 – The 4-level learning model

Level 0 learning = decision that there's nothing to learn from the current gap or that there's no gap at all.

Level 1 learning = decision to improve what we do while not challenging the underlying principles and processes.

Level 2 learning = decision that we need to change our principles and processes, also changing what we do.

Level 3 learning = decision that we need to be a different company by changing why, how, and what we do for our clients.

Mental model components: how the brain represents reality

It doesn't matter the business you are in; you are currently operating under mental models that define the why, the how, and the what of your business.

Kenneth Craik first laid the foundation for the concept of mental models.[151] He proposed that the mind forms models of reality and uses them to predict similar future events. By modeling reality, we aim at effectively predicting the future of the world and the result of our actions in it. This becomes the basis for the management of life and business alike.

A mental model has four components (see Figure 28):

1. **Beliefs** – the things you believe are true about your situation, assumptions about the nature of the business that go unquestioned, unexamined, and unchanged.
2. **Knowledge** – the data set, the facts, the information that you collected about the subject, its elements, and the relationship between them.
3. **Scripts** – the sequences of actions and actors who must display them to be effective in the world, rules about how things "must" be done to be who we are and do what we do.
4. **Cognitive operations** – the set of deductions, inductions, and transformations that we perform between data, knowledge, and scripts. The type of cognitive operations we perform determines if the relationship between the other components is one of reinforcement of change. We can use our acquired knowledge to change our beliefs or not. Our beliefs can limit the acquisition of knowledge to different extents, whereas our scripts might be fossilized by our beliefs and experience, or not.

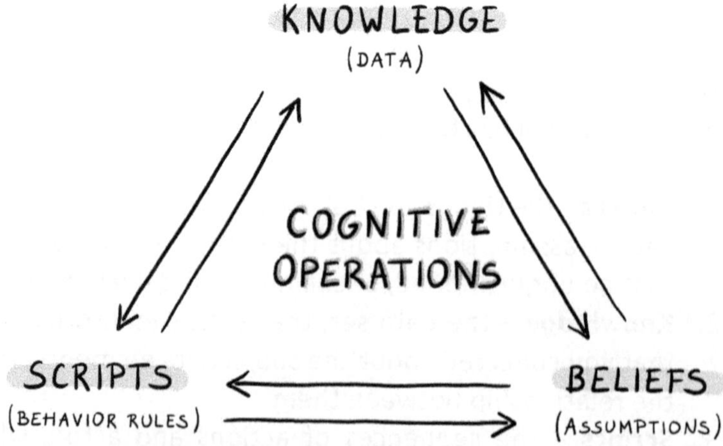

Figure 28 – Mental model components

Nothing exists for us outside of our mental models. Everything that we know is represented as aggregations of concepts in our minds. For example, the Eskimos have 47 words for snow, including a word for snow in the air versus snow shoved into the mouth of a person who simply won't stop talking.[152] The words for snow are not the reality of snow. They are the representations of it the Eskimos use, based on their knowledge, beliefs, and the scripts they acquired to deal with their reality.

Nothing exists for us outside of our mental models.

We need to understand our mental models' boundaries to improve them. The biggest fallacy of education is that it convinces us that "true" representations of reality exist. One fundamental principle of science is that we operate by increasingly accurate approximations of the "truth". Our knowledge is never exact, never finished. We can say of two ideas that one better fits the data, producing a better explanation of reality. But we can never say that any explanation fully encompasses reality. That's why the "truth" is never a goal for scientific endeavors.

Understanding our mental models, how they are developed, how they influence who we are, and how we act, is the basis of knowing ourselves. Being able to change our mental models is the beginning of freedom. If you can change your beliefs, ingrained scripts, and knowledge about something, you can decide who you are and what you do in that situation. You are no longer a victim of circumstances; you are the master of your fate. The why, the how, and the what of your life are no longer externally determined; they are internally decided. You are free.

> **Being able to change our mental models is the beginning of freedom.**

A Chief Executive Team deals with their mental models as with any other decision-making input: critically. This is what we set to achieve in the P for Possibilities.

Thinking together about our thinking process

Reviewing our mental models is difficult when we do it alone. After all, it's like looking through our glasses to see our glasses. Fortunately, there are easier ways to do it. Whereas it might be difficult for you to see how the lenses you use color your sight, someone else will find it easier to point it out.

Going through the different learning model levels I described earlier in this chapter, understanding our mental models, and better adjusting them to reality is more efficiently and effectively done as a team.

> **Most people are happy when they make up their minds about a topic because this releases them from the thinking process. They can then act without self-critique and call it freedom.**

Good leaders are concerned about the quality of everything done by their companies. Excellent leaders are worried about the quality of the thinking done in the company.

Most people are happy when they make up their minds about a topic because this releases them from the thinking process. They can then act without self-critique and call it freedom.

Most people are not demanding enough with the quality of their thinking processes. They pay little attention to how they think about something. They might understand that the efficiency and effectiveness of their actions depend on the quality of their strategies. Still, they overlook the importance of their thinking processes to the quality of their strategies.

Good leaders are concerned about the quality of everything done by their companies. Excellent leaders are worried about the quality of the thinking done in the company.

If you want to generate new possibilities, start by understanding and lifting the restrictions that your current way of thinking holds.

Collaborative learning at executive level

We learn as a team when we transform experience into gaining knowledge together. This goes beyond sharing experiences and knowledge, and having training or education to analyse case studies together.

If you want to generate new possibilities, start by understanding and lifting the restrictions that your current way of thinking holds.

All these activities are essential as knowledge management components. But if you examine them, they replicate school learning: One person "shares" their knowledge to benefit others. This is still not collaborative learning.

We learn as a team when we transform experience into gaining knowledge together.

Collaborative learning is the process by which an executive team explicitly reviews their mental models of a situation, decides the most appropriate learning level to adapt to a dynamic business environment, and designs an effective strategy to make it happen.

Collaborative learning is about co-creating knowledge to deal with unstructured situations rather than applying pre-existing knowledge to current situations.

The outcome of collaborative learning is a learning team, a team in which both the individual and the team's processes for developing know-how are always open to every member's contribution. This synergy results in a constant change of perception, understanding, and effectiveness of the team. In simple terms, a learning team is always open for transformation that brings higher levels of effectiveness.

Collaborative learning is the process by which an executive team explicitly reviews their mental models of a situation, decides the most appropriate learning level to adapt to a dynamic business environment, and designs an effective strategy to make it happen.

Collaborative learning aims at the generation of new possibilities. This allows the company to adapt to the unexpected disruptions of its market instead of becoming its victim.

A Chief Executive Team masters collaborative learning.

Ingredients of collaborative learning

Collaborative learning has different parts. Some of them happen simultaneously and some sequentially, but they don't follow in a fixed order. Instead, each Chief Executive Team blends a group of ingredients into a unique substance. When used together, these ingredients prevent affective conflict while promoting the best use of cognitive diversity through collaborative learning.

Collaborative learning is about co-creating knowledge to deal with unstructured situations rather than applying pre-existing knowledge to current situations.

1. Make time to think about thinking

A Chief Executive Team makes time to think about the thinking process. This activity is instrumental for envisioning, designing, planning, and executing strategy the main activities of an executive team. Think of it as weightlifting for the thinking muscle we call reflexivity.

Team reflexivity is defined as the "extent to which group members overtly reflect upon the group's objectives, strategies, and processes, and adapt them to current or anticipated endogenous or environmental circumstances."[153]

A Chief Executive Team masters collaborative learning.

Several studies correlate management team reflexivity to

- Increased team performance,[154]
- More effective and efficient screening of new product ideas,[155]
- Increased trust among team members who learn together,[156]
- Increased team effectiveness,[157]

- Better information sharing and learning,[158]
- Less affective conflict in the team, and
- Increased commitment to strategic decisions.[159]

In other words, investing time to streamline your thinking processes as an executive team delivers qualitative and quantitative results for the company and the team.

2. Discuss with mental models in mind

Have you ever experienced one of those arguments where one person presents contradictory opinions that do not convince the other person, who in turn does the same, and both get involved in an increasingly spirited discussion leading nowhere?

When this happens at an executive level (and it's common to see it in management meetings), we have several problems:

1. We generate a win-lose emotional state, in which whoever "loses" the argument is a "loser" and might bear a grudge until the next opportunity for payback;
2. It is very inefficient in both the time and emotional resources involved;
3. It is non-collaborative and doesn't promote finding the best decision.

How can we prevent it? By discussing with mental models in mind. Don't just put forward your ideas, viewpoints, and proposals. Also, be explicit about the assumptions, the set of data you are using, and the behavior rules you are following. Don't only deliver the consequence of your thinking process; also show its causes. Refer to Chapter 7 – *P for Processes* – for models of decision making and how they influence group dynamics.

In collaborative learning, team members don't share opinions, fixed ideas, or knowledge they have. They open the way they think about a subject for others to build on and revise.

By sharing both their mental models and how they conclude them, the team's level of understanding increases exponentially. We can better understand and correct possible flaws in each other's thought processes. This gives us the thinking power of a mastermind in the service of the company.

By doing this, you are openly admitting that you don't own the truth. What you are saying is your current opinion based on a specific mental model. Other team members can help you increase your mental model's quality by pointing out new data, better scripts, and more useful assumptions. This dialogue will not hurt your feelings. Because you are a lifelong learner, you will appreciate any input that increases your wisdom. You are on your way to become the best leader possible by learning from all sources, remember?

3. Probe the differences

Any discrepancy between mental models is a source of learning. If your assumptions, data set, or scripts for the situation are different from those of your teammates, that's good. Celebrate it as proof of cognitive diversity and a certain vaccine against groupthink. Then explore it.

Ask all questions to fully clarify the derivation of each mental model to deal with the situation. How did we decide that these are the right assumptions? What are the expected advantages of this script? What is left out of this set of knowledge? What did we include, and how did we decide to do it?

Use the four components of the mental model as a template to ask probing questions. And marvel at the cognitive diversity that exists in your team.

4. Exercise humble curiosity

The only possible attitude in collaborative learning is humble curiosity. Instead of trying to convince others, discover how they map their worlds. Be an explorer of those worlds you are invited to visit. Everybody has many good reasons to think and feel the way they do. Only when you discover them can you find bridges between their universes and yours.

You can maintain critical thinking and use it to feed your curiosity with higher quality questions and not prove others wrong. Most people at the executive level are intelligent enough to evolve their opinions by themselves. Give them time. Ask the right questions. And you might just find that you're the one evolving your vision of the world.

5. Coordinate knowledge-acquisition tasks

From my experience in supporting executive teams, a team facing unstructured information (with high uncertainty) does not have many mental models. Typically, there will be two to three representations of the situation, based on some team members' previous knowledge. All others will have more doubts than opinions. This uncertainty happens because our education system homogenizes knowledge to render efficient learning units. Schools traditionally emphasize facts versus how to learn.

As a result of mapping the alternative mental models of an executive team and probing the differences with an attitude of humble curiosity, you will be clear about the areas of most significant uncertainty.

Collect relevant information to mitigate decision-making risk. Coordinate knowledge acquisition tasks within the team.

- What do we need to do to gather the right type of data?
- How will we process it?
- How will the data we collect support decision making?
- What data will help select the best assumptions for our common mental model?

As a rule, look for black swans. For many centuries, people assumed black swans were mythical. Black swans are a symbol for impossible events. "That is as rare as a black swan" was a synonym of "impossible event" twenty centuries ago in the

Roman Empire.[160] When Europeans first arrived in Australia and saw black swans for the first time, they became a metaphor for the fragility of concepts, theories, and paradigms. All it takes to destroy our mental models' foundations is one event that disproves any of its foundational assumptions.

For faster and better learning, actively search information that contradicts your hypothesis. Create the conditions to find black swans. It's a guaranteed way to mitigate the risk of any strategy and improve your learning curve. Coordinating knowledge acquisition tasks to make it happen, on top of the other collaborative learning ingredients, is already a good step in this direction.

6. Co-create a meaning for data

You may have gotten the impression so far that I am defending a purely rational approach for collaborative learning. Instead, I aim for the integration of reason and emotion. Beliefs, assumptions, orthodoxies, and principles have considerable amounts of emotional components.

But there is another source of information that is hybrid: intuition. Although this has been long deemed an esoteric source of guidance in decision making, researchers have linked it clearly to experience. [161,162,163]

Herbert Simon (winner of the Nobel Prize in Economics) uses the example of the chess master, who can memorize the position of three times more chess pieces on a board than the novice player. This happens only when these pieces follow the possible formations that happen in a real chess match. Once you randomly disperse the pieces in positions that will never happen in a match, the chess master's memorization ability decreases to the novice standard.

The intuition of the executive team members can be a valuable resource when well managed.

Chess masters memorize and use commonly occurring patterns of pieces in a match, not numbers of random pieces.[164] During a match, the chess master stores this information as support for the decision making and works at an unconscious level, guiding their moves. This is what we call intuition.

Intuition is the unconscious recognition of patterns that became familiar in our experience in any domain. A good leader develops a lot of patterns of team interactions through their experience. An excellent investor learns stock performance patterns. Also, a doctor defines a lot of health signals and symptoms.

The intuition of the executive team members can be a valuable resource when well managed. It should deliberately guide the learning process. The team members map and look at the data and facts. What patterns emerge? What sense emerges? How does this new sense relate to the decision you need to make?

7. Decide the learning level

Now you have enough information to assess the most acceptable learning level for the situation you are facing.

- Is there anything to learn from the current gap, or shall we decide not to learn at all?
- Shall the team go for level 3 learning and change mental models, assumptions, and orthodoxies to deal with what is/will be happening in the market?
- Will we go for level 2 learning, keep the same representation of reality, and adjust our operating principles and processes to rise to the occasion?
- Or is level 1 learning enough?
- Is it just enough to correct the strategies and techniques of what we are doing right now?

Always choose the *highest* learning level appropriate to the circumstances. During the Covid-19 pandemic, many liquor distilleries shifted their production to meet the demand for hand sanitizer instead of making whisky, gin, and brandy. They did not change their operating principles and processes, strategies, nor techniques – most of the *what* and the *how* of their business model stayed the same.

The successful alcohol makers questioned the mental model of what a high-end liquor distillery is, their business assumptions and orthodoxies, to make the most of their core competencies in a new market situation.

Strategy design is the ultimate collaborative learning exercise for an executive team.

After the pandemic, as soon as the hand sanitizer price decreases below premium gin level, you will see them resuming the identity and pride of being a liquor distillery. Meanwhile, they made a good profit, secured jobs, and contributed to global health with level 3 learning. Not bad for a day's job of pivoting strategy.

8. Design a strategy, execute, and evaluate it

Strategy design is the ultimate collaborative learning exercise for an executive team. Anticipating the market by analyzing and deciding on unstructured information is the basis for a sound business strategy. The effectiveness of a company's strategy depends on how well the executive team can make sense of the market and their capabilities to deal with it.

Collaborative learning weaves innovation into a strategy. The higher the learning level, the more disruptive your actions will be.

The role of learning in innovation

Innovation happens when an executive team collaboratively learns how to disrupt a business model by changing the underlying mental models. This is better seen as an outcome of entrepreneurship, but you can make it happen at any moment, for any purpose, in your company.

Collaborative learning weaves innovation into a strategy. The higher the learning level, the more disruptive your actions will be.

As we have seen earlier, our results, the outcomes we get today, result from *what we do*, the strategies and techniques, and the actions we perform. But the strategy and techniques are determined by

- our operating principles and processes,
- the "how we do it,"
- which is determined by *why* we do it,
- the set of basic assumptions and orthodoxies, and
- the mental models we developed in and for our businesses.

Collaborative learning at the executive level challenges those assumptions to innovate.

The used car salesman reinvented

Shall we see it with a case study? Consider this one.

Innovation happens when an executive team collaboratively learns how to disrupt a business model by changing the underlying mental models.

What is the level of trust and transparency that you attribute to used car trading? If, like me, you were indoctrinated to the image of the used car salesperson as the ultimate example of a practitioner of shady, sleazy, hard-selling techniques to take advantage of your need for a vehicle, you have a dismal low trust level.

The behaviors we attribute to used car salespeople don't happen as the result of individual personality. If you work on a margin commission, your salary depends on your ability to get the most money out of the buyer's pockets. This approach means first selling the most expensive cars. You will also have a higher incentive to sell the oldest inventory items, as depreciation constantly erodes your stock's value. Your incentives are to maximize your commission, not to fulfill the client's needs better.

Combined with the car dealer's need to buy at the lowest price possible, to maximize their margin, most of the used car business centers on making sure that profit is made for the dealer and salesperson at the buyer's expense and of the original owner of the car.

But this business is based on assumptions, scripts, and knowledge of what it is and how it must be run:

- You must own inventory.
- You must pay as low as possible for your inventory.
- The dealer's margin depends on the difference between buying and selling price.
- You need to sell each item for as high a price as possible.
- Your salesforce works on commission only.
- Commission is calculated as a percentage of margin.
- You must increase stock rotation as much as possible.
- Your client is the buyer, for margin and commission come from their money.
- People want to "touch" a car before buying it.
- You sell in physical dealerships.

This segment became very rigid over time. Variations to the same business model are quite small worldwide. Because they are based on the same assumptions.

When Michael Bor, Aaron Montgomery, and Will Boland partnered up in Richmond, Virginia, to disrupt this business's nature, they aimed at all those assumptions and scripts of how the used car business should be run.[165,166]

Their company, CarLotz founded in 2011, works with the following assumptions: [167,168]

- You don't own inventory. Cars are consigned to you by the owner.
- You don't pay for your inventory.
- The dealer's margin is fixed through a flat fee.
- You don't need to sell each item for the highest price possible to be profitable.
- Your salesforce is not working on a commission.
- Stock rotation is not a concern for you.
- Your client is the original owner, for the flat fee comes from the car sale when it happens.
- People want to buy a car most conveniently for them.
- You can sell cars in an omnichannel marketplace.

CarLotz's business model is an operationalization of their mental model – the why, how and what of the business – and unlike traditional used car dealerships, it is scalable. By focusing on the car seller as the client, CarLotz serves both individual consumers seeking to sell a used vehicle and the corporate vehicle remarketers in banking, rental, fleet management, original equipment manufacturers, and other markets.

This allowed CarLotz to build a team and culture that increases transparency, integrity, and customer service compared to the traditional business model. In October 2020, ACAM and CarLotz executed a definitive business combination agreement that would make CarLotz a public company.[169]

Sensemaking is the new power

Why aren't executive teams better at collaborative learning?

Most people in executive team roles in companies around the world belong to one of two generations. They are either Baby Boomers or Generation Xers. People from these two generations grew up with the idea that "knowledge is power". It was programmed in their minds because:

1. the general level of education in the population was low. Therefore, the people who could afford a university degree were few and used that knowledge as a competitive advantage;
2. knowledge acquired through experience had a long shelf life. You could fulfill your role by doing the same things the same way for years;
3. knowledge distribution was ineffective and inefficient, so the concentration of knowledge in hubs (universities, research centers, teams, individuals) was possible.

When professional Boomers and Xers were going up the corporate ladder, they gave their best to shine individually. They sold their capacities, knowledge, skills, and commitment to the company better than anyone else. Those were the rules of the game. To land that promotion, you needed to convince your boss that it was you strategizing, deciding, and producing all the ideas that the team implemented. Without you, nothing would happen. You were the alpha and omega of the team results. It became all about you as you went up the hierarchy.

The idea that leadership can be performed individually in a global, volatile, complex, and uncertain world is bizarre.

In this scenario, when you reach the top, guess what? People expect you, "the hero", to provide all the answers. The bad news is you can't. The good news is no one can. We have been thinking that leadership is about one person bringing forward the solution to problems, developing the strategy, and having all the answers.

The idea that leadership can be performed individually in a global, volatile, complex, and uncertain world is bizarre because individual capacities are limited by our own experience, our individual values, education, and life learning. How can anyone know all the answers when reality becomes unfathomable?

To secure that this self-serving narrative fits the data, you need to create the data. And you do it by centralizing decision making, not sharing the knowledge of the processes required to decide, and not developing an effective executive team. When we fall for the "knowledge is power" mantra, it becomes a self-fulfilling prophecy.

Long ago, it was still valid. But for twenty years, knowledge has been freely available for anyone on the internet. Knowledge is nothing anymore. Knowledge is a commodity. With the advent of the internet, knowledge was replaced by know-how. Knowing how to use the knowledge freely distributed and available for anyone on the internet has been the source of power.

Sensemaking is what we need in a chaotic and volatile situation where knowledge and know-how are not useful anymore.

We have been living the last decade in the era of "know-how is power", although many executives are still lagging. But this era is ending. We are now living in an era of Artificial Intelligence. We know. Knowing how to do things, collecting and processing information to produce applicable results, are skills that soon any machine will be able to learn.

In this new era, sensemaking is a new power. Sensemaking is the process by which a group of people creates meaning for their shared experience.[170] Sensemaking is what we need in a chaotic and volatile situation where knowledge and know-how are not useful anymore. Not only are they not differentiators anymore, but in the crisis created by the government responses to the Covid-19 pandemic, we had to throw out the window everything we knew and took for granted as business know-how. The volatility of rules and regulations was so pronounced that any decision made could not build on a previous understanding of the market.

In these circumstances, you need to gather your collective intelligence and make a new sense of what is happening as you go along. This is what collaborative learning allows. By deliberately choosing the mental models we use to address unique situations, collaborative learning fosters sensemaking.

The key to better leadership is the executive team.

When you get to the CEO position, you need to be in the Achievement behavior mode, as defined in Chapter 2 – *It's happening on your shift*. This is required to develop the collective intelligence of your team through collaborative learning. You need a highly effective team to deliver on that.

But by now, your executive team members are still fighting the good fight to get to the top position themselves. They are doing their best to shine individually. That's the rule of the game, remember? Why should they collaborate with the very people – their executive team colleagues – who they have to fight with for budget, resources, people, exposure, attention, and impact in the company? Why should they do that?

The key to better leadership is the executive team. But to make it fulfill its purpose, first, you need to change the mode and motto that brought you here. You need to embrace that sensemaking is the new power, and only a Chief Executive Team can make it happen.

11

P FOR POTENTIAL

"The EMBRACO Vision of the Future Project was a key factor in the company being selected as one of the best companies to work for in the Exame survey of 2003. Ricardo J. Vargas's work in designing and implementing this project generated a high level of awareness and capacity for managing change and leadership based on company values."

– Paulo Neumann | EMBRACO | Corporate Management Advisor

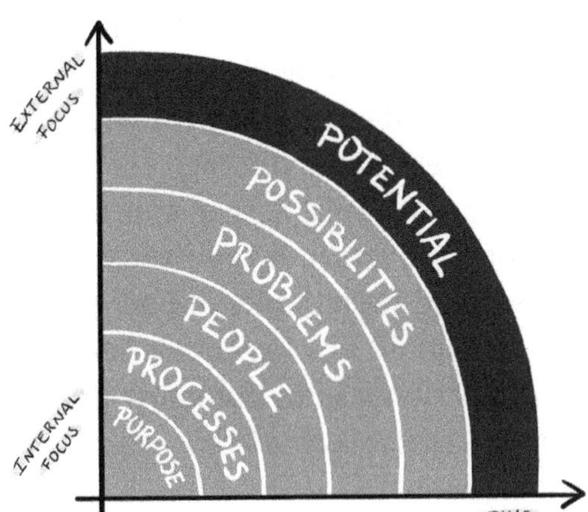

Figure 29 – P for Potential

Actualizing the future potential of your company

IN THE EXECUTIVE team's development process, we started from the innermost core of the team, its Purpose. We progressed outwards by defining its Processes, developing trust among its People, adopting better mental tools to solve Problems, and generate new Possibilities. Lastly, we focus on Potential (see Figure 29).

Potential [puh-ten-shuhl], is an adjective, meaning (1) possible, as opposed to actual; (2) capable of being or becoming.[171] Potential is unrealized, possible, dormant, conceivable, latent, and undeveloped. It is definitely about the future. How can we actualize, realize, develop, and make it present in our company?

Along the 6P's development process, the rest of the organization was always in our minds. *Team purpose* is a collaborative transformational intention of the company by the executive team. The *outcome* of actualizing the team's purpose is to transform the company eventually.

Streamlining the team's *processes* is about generating better and faster decisions to benefit the company's strategy. By increasing trust in the team's *people*, we expect to include more information and better process it, for the benefit of decision making in the company. Becoming better at solving complex systems' *problems* as a team, aims at having more effective strategy design and execution. The new *possibilities* that the team designs intend to support the company in making the most of business opportunities.

The company, as an entity, is a constant factor in the context of our work. We improve the executive team's performance dimensions and monitor its impact on the company's management KPIs. The 6P's of Executive Teams® focus on the executive team's bottlenecks to company growth. By solving them, we maximize the return of the executive team's functioning on the company.

When we get to P for Potential, we need to look *outward*. This dimension refers to how much impact we can make as an executive team, both inside and outside the company. Taking a broader perspective, how can we turn a company into an outstandingly effective and efficient team, aligned in designing and executing a strategy to *dominate its market*?

What is a company?

A company is a vehicle to achieve something. Therefore it always starts with a strategic intent to make that something happen. Often this takes the form of a company Vision or a company Mission. Together these establish the idea of what the company owners want to achieve.

The 6P's of Executive Teams® focus on the executive team's bottlenecks to company growth.

Consider this: Amazon states that its company Vision is "To be Earth's most customer-centric company, where customers can find and discover anything they might want to buy online, and endeavors to offer its customers the lowest possible prices". Do you wonder about its intention?

When Heineken communicates that it wants "To win in all markets with Heineken and with a full brand portfolio in markets where we choose"[172], we understand the company's priorities.

When the company has a well-crafted strategic intent, everyone can have clarity on who we are (Mission), where we are going to (Vision), and how we choose to get there (long-term strategic targets). This information is not an "oh, by-the-way" aside. The company's strategic intent should never be just a nice copy for office posters. When well crafted, it also sets clear indications of the required leadership to make it happen.

The company's strategic intent should never be just a nice copy for office posters.

Often, executive teams miss the opportunity to use the company's Mission, Vision, and Values as leadership tools. They focus on goals and KPIs, which are great operational management tools, but underuse their power to bind together the whole company as a team to collaborate in achieving a Vision and realizing a Mission.

The Vision and Mission are the focus of the P for Potential.

It all starts with a dream – company Vision and Mission

Company Vision is an outstanding, ambitious result we want to achieve in some years; company Mission is our reason and purpose for existence. Mission, Vision, and the long-term strategic targets combine into strategic intent, which defines what the company is trying to achieve. A well-managed company usually has a clearly defined strategic intent.

As we've seen before, strategic intent is a future picture of the company: what we will be and achieve in x years' time. Not only does it not exist yet, but it is at odds with the current reality. There is a sharp contrast between the company's dream and the reality of what it is today. And it *should* be like that. If there were no contrast, this would mean either that there's no ambition or no more market for us to grow. Neither ever happened, so we assume that there will be a gap between strategic intent and the results currently produced by your employees' behavior.

There is a sharp contrast between the company's dream and the reality of what it is today. And it *should* be like that.

The gap between what the company is and what we want it to become justifies the existence of leadership. If your company had no gap between intention and results, you, your executive team, your middle managers would be nonessential.

What the company is today is determined by the behaviors of its employees. Company results are limited by the current level of abilities and engagement of your people.

- You cannot have better processes and systems than the ones designed and operated by your employees.
- You cannot have more agility, grit, or energy than the ones your people put in their jobs.
- Your results are delivered by people.

Capital is critical because it might grant you access to better skills portfolios. But you will always be dependent on the portion of available skills on the market that you can secure for yourself – that's your gap.

The gap between what the company is and what we want it to become justifies the existence of leadership.

The gap between current and future reality can only be closed by the results your teams produce day after day, compounded over time. It's your people's incremental effort that will get the company to gradually become what it intends to be (see Figure 30).

The gap between current and future reality can only be closed by the results your teams produce day after day, compounded over time.

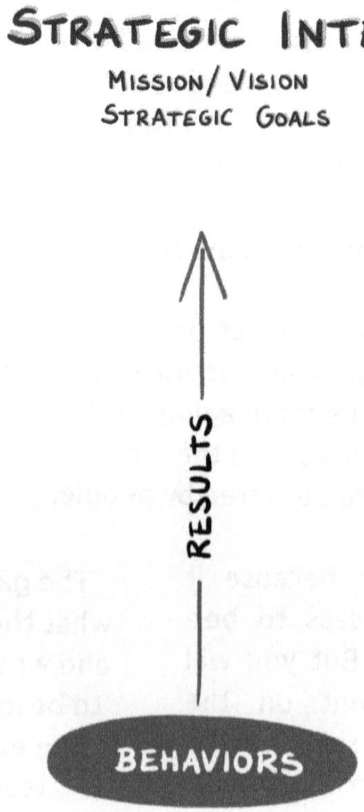

Figure 30 – Results bridge the gap between behaviors and strategic intent

For the desired results (strategic intent) to happen, your employees must act differently. You can't reach tomorrow's results with yesterday's actions. Better, faster, more efficient ways of doing jobs generate more ambitious results. And these new ways of working require new knowledge, thinking processes, and attitudes to become achievable.

You can't reach tomorrow's results with yesterday's actions.

A personal and collective transformation is necessary to create tomorrow's company. The job of making it happen is called *leadership*.

A personal and collective transformation is necessary to create tomorrow's company. The job of making it happen is called *leadership*.

Leadership is not a role or position in the hierarchy. We hear a lot of people saying, "The leader of company X", "the leader of organization Y", when referring to the person who has the role of managing that company, organization, or association. Your title as the top manager of whatever organization or team does not automatically make you a leader.

According to Mary Parker Follet, management "is the art of getting things done through the efforts of other people"[173]. Management is about maximizing the output of resources used, including people's time and effort.

Peter Drucker distinguished management from leadership: "Management is doing things right; leadership is doing the right things."[174] His definition points management in the direction of efficiency and leadership in the direction of effectiveness. Leadership is less concerned with planning and control than management, and more with transformation. But I find his definition lacks the required *clarity* to act on it.

Leadership requires the envisioning, design, and management of a *system* that transforms a company and its people to create an outstanding result." This definition focuses on my work with my executive team clients during P for Potential development phase.

Leadership requires the envisioning, design, and management of a *system* that transforms a company and its people to create an outstanding result.

The starting point of the system is its strategic intent; it creates ambition and generates tension to achieve it. When people speak of visionary leadership, they mean the Chief Executive Team could inspire them to pursue the dream company envisioned and make it happen.

Then comes the organization

A proper strategic plan translates a strategic intent into manageable chunks of work and is the basis of defining the company's business processes, supporting technology, and organization. In this sequence, only after designing your strategy, can you know what type of tangible processes, technology, and organizational structure design you need. Together they make the tangible dimension of companies, as you can see in Figure 31.

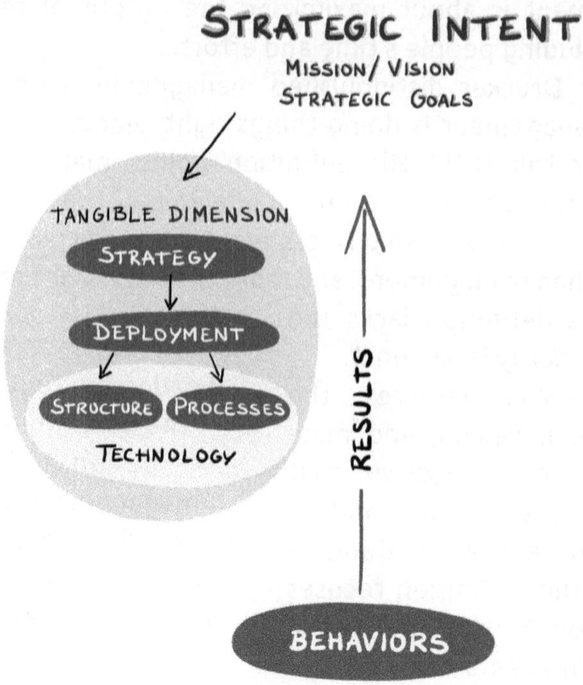

Figure 31 – The tangible dimension of companies

I witness many instances when executives make one of two mistakes in strategy formulation:

1. Designing a strategy for the *current organization they inherited* – this reduces the possibilities for *innovation* by subordinating it to a *legacy* mindset. ("This is the possible strategy for the current organization.")
2. Not reevaluating the current organizational design/structure *once a strategy is defined* – this reduces the effectiveness and efficiency of execution by subordinating it to *organizational constraints*. ("This strategy is a stretch for the current organization.")

Limiting the company strategy to what your organization can currently execute, or assuming that your current organization cannot deliver on the designed strategy, are both bad options. The first one lacks ambition; the latter lacks feasibility.

To create a company breakthrough, you need a strategic intent defined freely from the limits of your current organization. Whatever you call it – "innovative", "blue ocean", "disruptive", your new strategy requires you to break free from mindset constraints. Having gone through the P for Problems and the P for Possibilities, your executive team now has the conceptual tools to think systemically. In P for Potential, they have the freedom to think innovatively about the whole organization.

Together, strategy, processes, structure, and technology represent the organization's tangible dimension because it usually is materialized in physical evidence: documents, artifacts, machinery, buildings, organization of space, and so on. When you enter a company, you can see, feel, and read the tangible dimension.

Defining the tangible dimension is where most executive teams stop. They define the strategic intent; they ensure they have the right strategy, processes, technology, and structure.

They communicate it down the hierarchy, expect everyone else to do their job, and control the results.

Why does culture eat strategy for breakfast?

Many believe Peter Drucker originated the quote, "Culture eats strategy for breakfast"[175]. Regardless of the uncertainty about his authorship, a lot of people seem to agree with its meaning. But what is culture, and how does it eat strategy?

There are many useful definitions of culture.

- Geert Hofstede defined culture as "The collective programming of the mind which distinguishes the members of one human group from another."[176]
- Edgar Schein defined it as "The basic tacit assumptions about how the world is and ought to be that a group of people share and that determines their perceptions, thoughts, feelings, and their overt behavior."[177]
- I define it as "A system of organized behavior patterns that the members of a group use to give meaning to who they are and what they do."[178]

The definition of company culture is not a matter of corporate or employee branding. It is never a choice between different semantic options to best fit the current fashion. It results from successive choices between behavior patterns along time, leading us to conclude what works for us and doesn't. Culture is a convention that determines the accepted repertoire of solutions and behavior for a group of people. It tells us what is right and wrong, according to our experience of the past.

Culture is a convention that determines the accepted repertoire of solutions and behavior for a group of people. It tells us what is right and wrong, according to our experience of the past.

As a company evolves in its market, management decisions impact structure, processes, technology, and culture – *at the same time*. As you go about your business and make daily decisions, you are also creating

- informal interaction patterns,
- shared operating norms,
- beliefs about business fundamentals,
- company values,
- decision-making criteria,
- rules for belonging,
- tacit agreements,
- communication codes, and so on.

Some of your management decisions work, and you will use them again. Some you discard because they are not effective. The executive team interweaves useful decisions, creating norms and rules as examples of values. Communication codes define when to use tacit (unspoken) agreements as decision-making criteria connect closely to business assumptions.

By the time you have a comprehensive set of patterns, decisions, values, codes, norms, criteria, rules, they appear quite compactly knitted together for the people of that culture. Decision making becomes much more efficient. When you follow the system of organized behavior patterns we call culture, most decisions are pre-programmed.

When you belong to a culture, you don't wonder who you are and what to do.

The organization that attempts to succeed in its market by executing a specific strategy *creates* company structure, processes, and culture (both the tangible and intangible dimensions). There is no company without culture, even when it is

When you belong to a culture, you don't wonder who you are and what to do.

not documented, or there are no organizational values posters on the wall. Any human group who passed the test of time developed a culture together.

As shown in Figure 32, you can divide organizational culture components into three main intangible layers: values, beliefs, and norms.

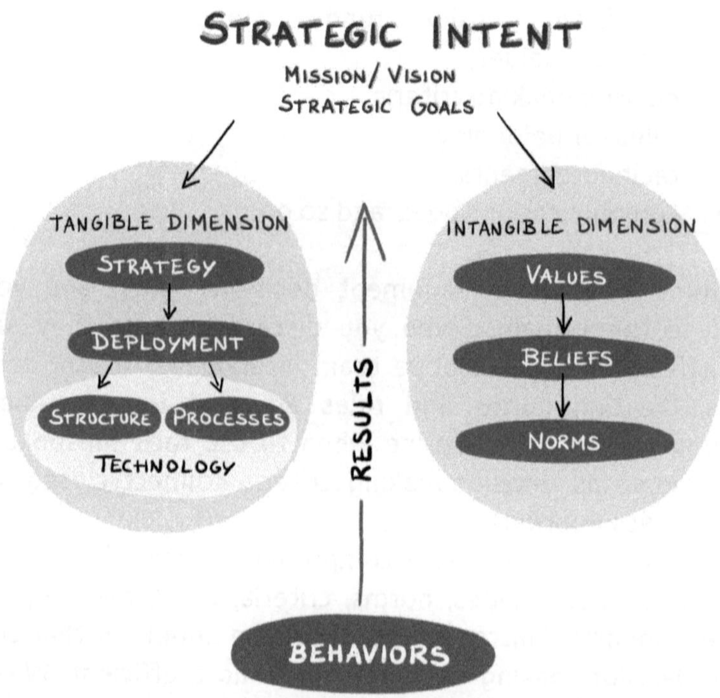

Figure 32 – The intangible dimension of companies.

Together, values, beliefs, and norms make the intangible dimension of the organization. These components are most of the times not written down; this dimension is difficult to formalize. Values and beliefs operate at an unconscious level; people are usually unaware of how they influence their behavior. And when companies write their values and norms, they do not necessarily manage their implementation by employees of all levels. You see a lot of breaches to supposed strict rules of conduct that get nothing but a verbal reprimand, if at all.

The lack of compliance is why I define culture this way: "Culture is the consolidated result of the behavior that managers have and allow in the company"[179]. Your actions create a culture in the group of people you manage by consolidating behavior patterns. The actions you allow in your employees solidify a specific culture, through verifying what is right and wrong for us to do. The unofficial rules do not need to be defined on paper. Everybody knows "how things are done around here" or says, "we know what the policy manual says, but this is what we really do."

Culture is the consolidated result of the behavior that managers have and allow in the company.

We know this quite well when the impact is negative. In 2019, the US Society for Human Resource Management published research on "The High Cost of a Toxic Workplace Culture: How Culture Impacts the Workforce - and the Bottom Line". They found many workers consider culture and managers to be closely connected. Fifty-eight percent of employees who quit a job due to workplace culture said their managers were the main reason they ultimately left. And the cost of this turnover?" It is an astounding $223 billion in the past five years."[180]

Most employees consider the only reason why a company's managers consistently behave in a certain way is because those behaviors are part of the company's desired culture. And they are right. In the absence of deliberate management by the executive team, company culture becomes whatever the middle managers make of it. And it doesn't matter what the posters on the wall, website, or yearly report say about "values and principles". That's just talk.

High-performance cultures

So far, I've explored two dimensions of the same company: tangible and intangible, assuming that there is always a level of agreement between them. But what if a new strategy goes *against* the existing culture?

- What if all our experience as a group for x years tells us that the strategy defined by top management is *wrong*?
- That it will *destroy* our sense of belonging, worth as individuals, and accumulated value over time?
- That it *conflicts* with the things we take for granted as right?
- That it will turn us into incompetent workers at the mercy of our competitors?

When *company strategy* (tangible dimension) goes against pre-existing culture (intangible dimension), *culture wins.* Because people's sense of professional worth depends on not executing it. In their mind, they make daily decisions *not* to destroy their value by boycotting the new strategy. It's an easy choice. All accumulated knowledge tells them that the new strategy is wrong.

In a study published in 1992, Kotter and Hesket[181] found a sharp difference between companies with and without performance-enhancing cultures. The revenue growth results, employment growth, stock price growth, and net income growth over 11 years were overwhelmingly in favor of having the right culture. See the results of their research on Figure 33.

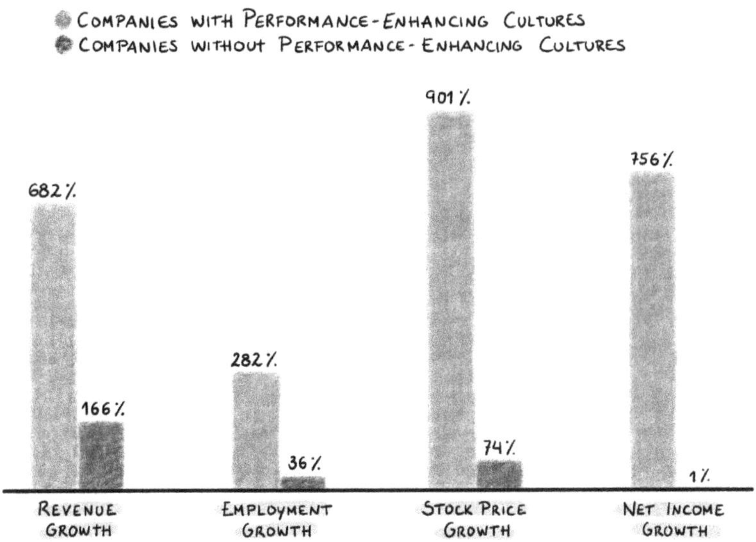

Figure 33 – Impact of performance enhancing cultures on company growth (Kotter & Hesket, 1992)

More recent studies backed up these results. Kasseem, Ajmal, and Khan found a positive relationship between organizational culture components and business excellence in general.[182] Gregor Schönborn found that "corporate responsibility with respect to external stakeholders as well as to employees, accompanied by participative leadership, are crucial cultural conditions for corporate success."[183] In 2017, John R. Graham, Campbell R. Harvey, Jillian Popadak and Shivaram Rajgopal noted that "Over half of senior executives believe that corporate culture is a *top-three driver* of firm value and 92% believe that improving their culture would increase their firm's value. Surprisingly, *only 16%* believe their culture is where it should be."[184]

The gap between the company's current and desired realities is natural, predictable, and is the basis for the management and leadership work. The more significant the gap, the bigger the potential impact your executive team might have on the company.

Developing a high-performance culture is essential. But *advertising* a new fashionable culture is not the same as *creating it*. It's not about saying that we now have stakeholder capitalism, social responsibility, or that our production system went green. All these things might be necessary, but they are instances of something else, not the core of company culture. When Kotter and Hesket measure performance-enhancing cultures and correlate them with company performance KPIs, we have a black box in between them. What creates culture's power to impact performance? How does that connection work?

Graham and colleagues mentioned (in their literature review) that empirical evidence on "whether and how corporate culture affects firm value and corporate decision making is underexplored".[185]

Walid Leithy attempted to answer this question with a study. He revealed the *direct relationship* between organizational culture and organizational performance was almost inexistent. His model "indicates that organizational culture correlates with

- work-related attitudes (job satisfaction, organizational commitment, and job involvement) and,
- work-related attitudes correlate with work behavior (turnover intention, job performance, and voluntary absenteeism).

Both work-related attitudes and work behavior correlate with organizational performance."[186]

So, the relationship between organizational culture and organizational performance happens through individual work-related attitudes and behaviors.

360° Strategic Management Model

These conclusions 100% back up the 360° Strategic Management Model[187] I present in this chapter. In 2005, I connected the relevant variables based on the available knowledge of work and organizational Psychology (what determines human behavior in general) and my professional experience as a management consultant to elaborate the 360° Strategic Management Model. But there was not much research available at the time. Sixteen years later, it's good to know that my model is current and valid.

Here is how to operationalize the missing link of how culture impacts strategy or how it "eats strategy for breakfast".

People need to have specific knowledge and know-how to

- execute the tasks of their job role in the organizational structure,
- perform their part of the processes,
- use the relevant technology, and
- understand how strategy translates into their daily life.

No one can be a better salesperson than their product knowledge, sales, or relational skills allow. We put all these things inside the box called competencies. There is a set of competencies to perform each job role successfully.

On the other hand, to align their behavior with desired company values, beliefs, and norms, people need to display adequate attitudes. These determine the required levels of accountability, initiative, self-efficacy, client orientation, quality mindset, collaboration, openness to change, job satisfaction, resilience, and results orientation,[188] among other things, that the person is expected to use on the job.

If you are a salesperson with a good level of technical competencies, but with a lack of client orientation, initiative to find new clients, and resilience to take many noes for each yes, you will not produce many deals.

The performance behavior of any individual contributor in the company will be mostly determined by the personal choices allowed by their current level of competence and attitude toward the job.

This is the **operational level** of strategy. The job of individual contributors is to make sure that the different tactics get implemented by displaying the right level of competencies and attitudes. These are the work behavior and work-related attitudes that connect company culture (intangible dimension) with results, as indicated by research (see Figure 34).

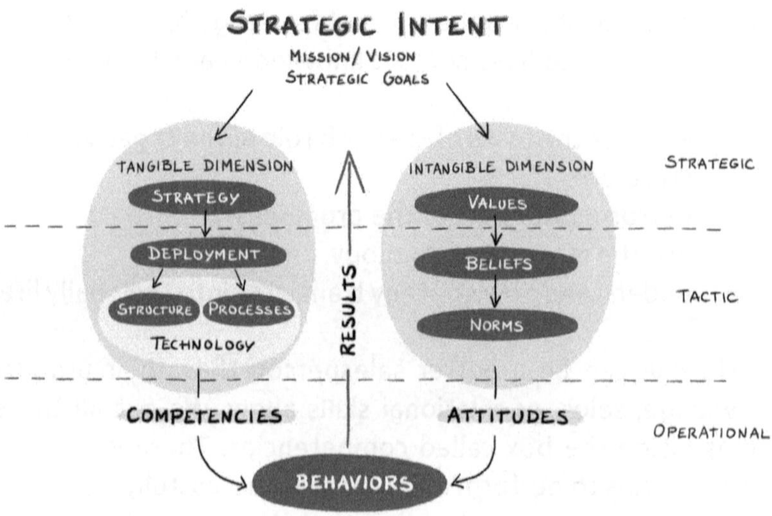

Figure 34 – 360° Strategic Management Model

Culture is a conventional organization of behavior patterns that makes it easier to align individual attitudes and behavior with the right strategy's execution. Having a set of values, beliefs, and norms accepted as the basis to decide what is good and bad behavior inside the company facilitates the right behavior. Culture can thus become a boost for leadership. And conversely, an ineffective culture can impede the goals of leadership.

If you do your job as a leader, culture boosts strategy all day.

Culture eats strategy for breakfast only if they confront each other. When they are aligned, a synergic effect supports high-performance behaviors across the company. If you do your job as a leader, culture boosts strategy all day.

Creating the context for this alignment between the tangible and intangible dimensions of the company is the **strategic level** of management (see Figure 34). This needs to be done by the executive team.

When I work with executive teams as advisor, during the P for Potential development phase, we cover the five main deliverables of the executive team:

1. To define or revise a company's strategic intent, closely articulated with the executive team's transformational purpose.
2. To design or revise the strategy to achieve it.
3. To (re)design, (re)create, and manage an organization that will execute the strategy.
4. To (re)define and manage company culture that enables the organization to execute the strategy and deliver the results.
5. To create a system to align and develop middle management leadership culture, so they can develop their direct reports' competencies and attitudes to produce the results that will get us progressively closer to the strategic intent.
6. Monitor strategy execution and culture management KPIs to make sure desired results are happening.

All of these need to be mapped, revised, and planned to guarantee that the executive team's maximum transformational potential is actualized.

Enter the middle management

The executive team can't make sure that all in the company are delivering on the expectations. That what they define at strategic level is being done at operational level. Executives can't be everywhere to ensure people do what they are expected to. It is middle management's job to bridge the current levels of competencies and attitudes of all their direct reports to the levels that will deliver the desired results.

Middle management holds the key to make sure your company becomes what its strategic intent states. Strategy execution and culture alignment are part of any manager's role. The C-suite executive team are much like generals. They decide how to fight the war and the strategy to win it, but they need the full chain of command on the ground to make it happen. When you don't have the full support and alignment of your middle managers, your chances of success become bleak.

The first-level management, the people who are managing the individual contributors, must ensure the employees working on their teams display the right attitudes and work diligently with the required competencies. The result is to produce the behaviors that generate the outcome that takes us to the strategic intent.

I dedicated a previous book[189] to the development and alignment of middle management leadership processes required to execute strategy. The bridge between strategy and culture that your company needs is developing individual contributors to deploy the necessary level of competencies and the right type of attitudes for the company to succeed. This is the **tactic level** of management, as indicated in Figure 34.

Leadership

Leadership happens when you

- define an ambitious strategic intent,
- design the strategy and create the organization to achieve it,
- make sure you have the right culture to support your strategy, and

- create the most formidable middle management team to guarantee that people develop the required competencies and attitudes to realize the company's potential.

Leadership is not a position, a personal trait, a check-list of behaviors to fulfill, or styles to follow. Leadership is making sure your company transforms itself into the desired version of itself. Transforming the frog into a prince does not happen by magic. It results from the painstaking effort, diligent work, and constant focus on the five enablers of results: clear strategic intent and strategy, well-crafted organization (structure, processes, technology), strong company culture, middle management alignment, and individual contributors' behavior.

Leadership is making sure your company transforms itself into the desired version of itself.

A Chief Executive Team is what you need to make this happen. Going through the development process I branded *The 6P's of Executive Teams®* guarantees that you have taken steps to create a formidable team to beat the market and create the legacy you defined in the P for Purpose. That is your untapped potential.

CONCLUSION

THE ROLE OF THE EXECUTIVE TEAM ADVISOR

"By the end of the first minute of a keynote speech Ricardo J. Vargas has captured the audience, which is just amazing. But even more than his great communication skills, I value the way in which he transmits the concepts of change and behavioral change. His impact is so high that people later use his metaphors and concepts as if they were their own. This is the best validation for the transmission of a concept I have ever seen."

– Catarina Horta | Novo Banco |
Human Capital Director

Hollywood type roles

WHEN I WORK with executive teams through *The 6P's of Executive Teams®* development process, sometimes my clients voice a suspicion related to my role and positioning towards the team and client company. Often, it doesn't matter what or how we communicate before the program; team members tend to attribute one of four roles to me.

Spy

Some of them think I'm a spy. As I am usually working with the executive team of the local operating company of a multinational, they believe that headquarters send me to spy on what and how they are doing. Incorrectly, they believe I will feed information back to the global Board, Operations, HR, or whoever will use it against them.

Terminator

Some people think I am a terminator. In this view, my work of developing the executive team's effectiveness is a clumsy coverup story to allow me to assess each executive team member's performance and support someone in power to eliminate low performers.

The CEO's buddy

Others think that I am a member of a secret society, a brotherhood, with the CEO. I have a secret handshake fraternity code making me a trusted friend or close associate with the CEO. Therefore, I am coming in to do the things the CEOs cannot do directly, which makes me a puppet to execute difficult or unpleasant tasks that CEOs themselves cannot do.

Magician

The fourth thing that people think about me is that I am some magician. This perception happens when the executive team is facing problems that are unavoidable and undeniable. They understand they need support and transfer the responsibility for finding a solution to someone outside the team. According to this view, a consultant, an organizational psychologist, can appear, do a magic trick, get them back on track, and solve their problems using a magic wand. They get to perform without problems again.

It's also not that easy.

I usually find a mix of these four fantasies about my role in any executive team. None of them is productive. The first three generate resistance because they are quite negative. The fourth disempowers the team from doing what they need to do.

It is good to trust someone competent and experienced in executive team development to work with your team. But it should not lead to a surrender of responsibility: "Okay, you do something because we can't." I am not a magician.

These four ideas represent a lack of awareness about the executive team dynamics and how they impact the company's functioning. When people recognize their behavior is an important variable influencing the company's performance, these Hollywood type roles don't emerge.

A Chief Executive Team is a force of transformational leadership.

Apart from this lack of awareness, I also find a limited vision of what is possible to reach with an executive team. People think in terms of business as usual, that executive teams are about managing to make sure that corporations run smoothly. Yes, they must have that as a focus, but they must also transform the company when strategy requires.

Chief Executive Teams generate a reality that goes beyond what we think is possible today. They lead the organization into adapting to changes or transformations like the ones we are living during the pandemic or – better yet – to transform and lead their markets proactively.

A Chief Executive Team is a force of transformational leadership. "Business as usual C-level working groups" display a mediocre mindset. If we think that an executive team's main responsibilities are to lead and transform an organization, business as usual is not an option.

Why do you need an external executive advisor?

Do you need an outside advisor to come and support you in the development of your executive team? The short answer is, "Yes." There are six reasons for that.

1. Expertise

An advisor stays current on the knowledge and research on leadership, organizational psychology, and executive team effectiveness. The accumulated facilitation, coaching, training, management consultancy, personal development, and public speaking skills enhance the advisor's skills. You will trust an advisor who has the experience of having done this type of work with hundreds of executive teams. You don't have this level of expertise available inside every company. It's just not possible. It comes from working with executive teams as the focus of a full-time advisory activity.

Even if you are competent in developing the executive teams you manage, as a CEO, you will stay a couple of years with each company until it reaches its full potential, and you get promoted. At best, you develop a team once every three years, not several per year. And several per year is the intensity of experience required to create a body of knowledge that allows you to become proficient in solving the different types of problems of these teams.

This experience is relevant because there are always bumps on the road to become a Chief Executive Team. If you ever bought the idea that personal or group development can be done without some form of effort, pain, or difficulty, get rid of it now. There's a huge return on investment for working with an advisor who went through the process in many different circumstances and has seen the bumps and holes on the road. An advisor's expertise makes it easier to avoid some of them, minimize others, and get out of unavoidable problems faster.

2. Positioning

The second reason is the positioning of the CEO in the systems that we call *team* and *company*. As I have discussed in previous chapters, one needs to understand how the system works and how one's position shapes our individual perspectives. The CEOs' perception is often not objective enough because it is based on the selected information they receive and biased by the cognitive biases that everyone falls into.[190] CEOs are often the last to know about their own teams' problems and difficulties, as proven by research I cited before. Their own needs and motivations also bias their perception.

Positioning is also about corporate politics. CEOs tend to become heavily involved in corporate politics because they are ambitious and want to move forward. Company politics usually have sides. People take sides in any discussion, argument, or strategy. For everything, there are pros and cons, attacks and defenses, avoidance and denial.

Managers take sides because aligning with interest groups maximizes their chances of moving up the hierarchy. Loyalty to a group is better than living in the no man's land of corporate politics. The CEO will belong to some groups, whereas some of the executive team members align themselves with other groups of interests, values, and alliances. This is normal. Chapter 4 explains the resultant additional problems to the efficiency and effectiveness of the executive team. Power struggles in the team often are a manifestation of more prominent corporate politics.

3. Default behavior mode

The third reason for needing an external advisor is the default CEO behavior mode. Chapter 2 details the five behavior modes of the CEO and their impact on the team's performance.

To develop a Chief Executive Team, you need to display *Achievement Behavior mode* consistently. When this has not been your typical behavior in the last years, it might be difficult to make the transition without an external advisor's support. You will be undertaking your own transformation on top of the executive team's changes while dealing with business challenges. It often becomes a tall order.

Suppose you were behaving a certain way through Friday of last week. On Monday, you present a new management style. You cannot just open a Monday morning management team meeting and say: "I will now ask questions, listen to what you have to say, and discuss based on your ideas. I know, until last Friday, I was telling you to shut up and execute what I say because I believed it was the right thing to do. Now I believe differently." Your team views you with amazement and suspicion. It takes the support of an external advisor to assume new leadership styles.

Everyone must move to get the executive team to greatness.

My work creates a positive context where everyone can change, where past mistakes are part of the learning process, and the whole team can progress in the right direction. You cannot develop a Chief Executive Team with a finite leadership mindset. Everyone must move to get the executive team to greatness.

4. Psychological reactance

Psychological reactance happens when we perceive that any suggestion, order, idea, or hint given to us by someone reduces our degree of freedom, and we act to restore or defend it.[191] Our reaction is usually to do the opposite of what others suggest, even when it is in our best interest to follow the suggestion.

We all have a degree of psychological reactance, although it varies individually in intensity and subject. Some have psychological reactance mostly connected with

- their close friends or family or even spouse.
- strangers.
- authority figures (police, government, bosses).
- everyone.

Psychological reactance means that in certain circumstances, we will not do something that benefits us individually or as a team just because a specific person proposed it in a way that seems like a perceived threat to our freedom.

It becomes more interesting when we understand that power tends to trigger psychological reactance. The more I perceive that someone has power over me, the more I will be tempted to think their suggestions are meant to benefit them, thereby reducing my degree of freedom. This resistance can happen with the hierarchical power of the CEO.

This reactance might surface as stubbornness and defiant behavior, although not explicit. You will see people passively resisting, delaying, blocking, and finding excuses. But deep down, it's just because they don't want to do what you ask them to, even if it's the right thing and they would benefit from it.

When people have a high degree of psychological reactance, they prefer to suffer the consequence of not having a benefit than to accept that they were actually told to do something and obeyed. Seeing themselves as someone less independent, less free than their own image of themselves, is not acceptable for some of us.

Your executive team members will all have a varying degree of psychological reactance. This factor makes an intervention done by any company employee more difficult, especially the CEO, than if done by an outsider.

In general, power is a trigger for psychological reactance; specific leadership styles can also increase it. Someone perceived as more autocratic will generate more psychological reactance than someone perceived as more laissez-faire. The behavior modes of the CEO I described in Chapter 2 are connected with more and less psychological reactance. We would expect that the *command mode* would increase psychological reactance. *Involvement* and *avoidance modes* would decrease it, and we would have less psychological reactance in *achievement mode*.

5. Speed

A client with whom I have been working for over 12 years, developing several of her executive teams, once told me at the end of a workshop: "Ricardo, it's not that we would not get there without you. But with your support, we get there three times faster, and that makes a huge difference."

When you land in the CEO position and must show results by the end of the quarter, speed matters. It's good to have someone taking care of the team's effectiveness and efficiency while figuring out what to do with the business. You might be quite good at mechanics and enjoy doing it as a hobby, but I am sure you don't regularly maintain your car. You might love cooking, but you don't cook every meal. It's not as efficient as having an expert focused on doing it as part of their daily activity.

6. Neutrality

Any internal person can't be and doesn't need to be neutral. You must decide on goals, strategies, and options. Neutrality is essential for the work I do of developing team effectiveness and efficiency.

Having a trusted advisor for your executive team creates peace of mind.

As the CEO position does not allow for neutrality, the facilitation process run by them becomes risky. The same applies to any other executive team member or colleague, even if international. As an organization employee, you need to be free to exercise your options in any process. Therefore, you need someone neutral running that process.

Having a trusted advisor for your executive team creates peace of mind. You need that.

The usual objections

If data, best practices, and expert advice show that there is value gained from developing a Chief Executive Team, why don't all the companies go in this direction? Here's what I hear: "I worry about loss of accountability, loss of efficiency, loss of control, loss of credibility, or fear this process might weaken my CEO leadership." These are the usual objections I get when I propose the idea and method of developing true executive teams instead of executive working groups.

Leadership is about results, not ego.

Let's start with the last one: "Creating a highly effective executive team might weaken CEO leadership". Explain how if you do something that improves company results this weakens your position as a CEO instead of reinforcing it. If someone thinks this, it means that they fall for the "leader must know it all and do it all" belief, the "knowledge is power" mantra.

"Loss of credibility" is connected to this. Leadership is about results, not ego. We should care more about the results we produce for our internal and external communities than about our image as leaders.

As for the other objections, we have been implementing teams in organizations for decades. Consider the self-managed teams in manufacturing, from Japan to the world since the 1950's. Companies use R&D teams, process teams, project teams, service teams, and Agile teams doing all sorts of agility work all over the company. We don't speak of loss of accountability, efficiency, or control in those cases. Why would these things happen only at the executive team level?

These objections cover up only one real cause underlying them all: *fear*. People experience fear of the new, fear of doing something different, fear of learning, fear of laughing about ourselves, about our illusions of grandeur and control, fear that we are insufficient for the role we perform, and fear of vulnerability.

Enabling our self-development starts with the acceptance of our imperfections. Whatever we don't acknowledge, we don't improve. We should fear the feeling of being insufficient, not the process of becoming abundant.

The 6P's of Executive Teams® in action

I presented on these pages an overview of the full methodology I created to develop Chief Executive Teams, along with many examples of doing it. After reading this book, you might have an outline of what you believe your team should undertake. You might even think you understand the 6 Ps well enough to get a start. But that is not the only option available. In my company, every program based on *The 6P's of Executive Teams®* is a custom project designed to meet your unique Chief Executive Team's needs and challenges.

We should fear the feeling of being insufficient, not the process of becoming abundant.

Based on my extensive experience in helping companies achieve success, we have six types of solutions for you: individually, with your executive team, and with peer CEOs (see Table 2). Adding to these, I use the Chief Executive Team assessment to inform them, and I am also a professional speaker on leadership and transformation. You can read more details about these on my website: www.chief-executive.team.

INDIVIDUALLY	WITH YOUR EXECUTIVE TEAM	WITH PEER CEOs
CHIEF EXECUTIVE COACHING	THEMATIC WORKSHOPS	CET WORKSHOP
CEO INTENSIVE PROGRAM	6P'S INTENSIVE	CET MASTERMIND

Table 2 – Chief Executive Team services

1. The Chief Executive Team Assessment

Based on our proprietary methodology, *The 6P's of Executive Teams®*, the Chief Executive Team Assessment is the right diagnostic tool to feed your senior leadership team's development program with accurate insights of where the team is and how to develop it. The tool assesses how well-structured the team is by addressing all dimensions of management team effectiveness proven by research.

All executive teams are different and at different stages of development. Each requires a unique diagnosis and development methods. This assessment is the first step of a journey that impacts the whole organization through the aligned effort of all members of your Chief Executive Team.

Based on this assessment, we can choose, fine-tune, and precisely implement the tools that will get your executive team from good to great.

2. The 6P's of Executive Teams® intensive program

The transformational program that creates a Chief Executive Team is a deep dive into *The 6P's of Executive Teams®* in a sequential format.

The 6P's Intensive is an on-site multi-day facilitation with the senior leaders of your organization. During this collaborative and transformative process, your team members will prepare and lead the company on its next breakthrough by improving its effectiveness and efficiency.

We choose which dimensions to work on, what to do more of, less of, or avoid altogether, based on your team's performance on the assessment. The number and length of workshops vary according to each team's needs. This methodology improves what already works and fixes what does not.

Some of the things we usually do in the program to create a Chief Executive Team:

- Create a compelling vision, a purpose, and a why for the team and the company
- Increase trust, psychological safety and maximize the potential of cognitive diversity.
- Improve collaboration, communication, coordination, alignment, effectiveness, and efficiency
- Use productive conflict as fuel and reduce negative conflict
- Design and implement new solutions for old problems
- Generate new possibilities for business challenges and opportunities
- Strategize business mindset and transformational values and improve the execution of the whole organization through a newly defined leadership culture
- Improve executive team performance with evidence-based approaches
- Revise and upgrade team processes for increased performance
- Design and execute leadership processes that create the culture you desire in your organization
- Participation in mentoring in mastermind programs that will give you peer support to increase the performance of your company with your executive team
- Maximize engagement of middle management levels and individual contributors, thereby boosting your company's performance
- Improve financial human capital and innovation KPIs, among others

- Maximize results in any dimension of the balanced scorecard as desired

3. Strategic workshops

Sometimes you don't need a full intervention with your team. You might already have a great team and need to fine-tune some aspects of its functioning. I can partner with you to help you diagnose exactly what you need and design it from scratch adapted to your team's needs.

Over 25 years, I have been facilitating strategic workshops with executive teams on varied topics such as:

- Strategic visioning
- Strategy roadmaps
- Board meeting facilitation
- Culture alignment
- Ideation/innovation
- Customer centricity
- Change management
- C-Level leadership
- Effective strategy implementation
- Transformational leadership
- Self-leadership
- Any topic within The 6P's of Executive Teams®

4. Chief Executive Team Masterminds

Mastermind groups offer a combination of brainstorming, education, peer accountability, and support in a group setting to sharpen your business and personal skills. A mastermind group helps you and your mastermind group members achieve success. You will act as catalysts for growth, devil's advocates, and supportive colleagues to each other.

By getting the perspective, knowledge, experience, and resources of others in the group, not only can you greatly expand your own view of the world, but you can also advance your goals and projects quicker.

I facilitate the only mastermind groups in the world focused on improving executive teams' effectiveness and efficiency. The CET Mastermind is an exclusive tool to transform your company and your executive team by transforming yourself.

Some benefits of the CET Mastermind:

- Solutions and ideas that you would not have found by yourself
- Tap into the experience and skills of others, including the facilitator
- Increased commitment to your goals as you openly share them with your peers
- Increased confidence in your decisions and actions
- An instant and valuable network to support your personal and business growth
- A sense of shared mission with other CEOs
- Design things to be the way you want them to be, not as you've heard they "should" be
- A boost to your attitude, resilience, and positivity

You should join a mastermind group if you:

- Have an interest in improving the results of your company, getting them from good to great or revamping them.
- Lead an executive team that leads a company, a bold project, a special endeavor that requires unique strategies to overcome challenges and achieve great results.
- Are responsible for the results of an entire organization and lead a team that must produce them
- Are ready to create the best year of your professional life.
- Believe you can benefit from a supportive team of mastermind partners and an experienced facilitator.

- Are ready to share and support others, learn and overcome the natural fear of change that happens when we aim for a bold vision.

5. Chief Executive Team Workshop

A well-executed workshop with a group of peer CEOs can give you the right balance between understanding the unique 6P's of Executive Teams methodology and other leaders' experience in making it happen with their teams. This experience opens opportunities and insights on how to go about it with your team.

This workshop aims at the full understanding of *The 6P's of Executive Teams®* in two days. The workshop's focus is guided by the group, creating a participative process where everyone contributes and is more committed to success outcomes. Workshop participants are more motivated and active and have more fun while reaching the goals we set at the beginning of the event.

Join me for a premium event with other leaders of Chief Executive Teams, diving deep into the changes that can empower you to maximize your team's potential and sustain its long-term effectiveness.

6. Chief Executive Coaching

I will support you in understanding and implementing the Chief Executive Team methodologies with your team. Take it step-by-step and adjust to the circumstances you face.

This approach should be your preferred follow-up to a CET Workshop or *6P's Intensive. It is ideal* when confidential issues are impacting the team performance or serious problems that you don't feel comfortable sharing with peers in a CET Mastermind.

I follow a result-focused executive coaching model. Through a short-term interactive process, I support you to improve your leadership skills, problem-solving, and strategy definition, promoting self-knowledge, and acquiring new behaviors. The coaching intervention focuses on finding solutions to achieve individual and organizational goals. A substantial part of it is to support CEOs in implementing *The 6P's of Executive Teams®* with their teams. I can also coach executive team members to become even more effective as team players as part of the team development process.

My credentials include being a Psychological Coaching Expert, by the Portuguese Psychologists Association, and a PCC® – Professional Certified Coach – by the International Coach Federation, with over 4,000 hours of experience coaching top executives worldwide. I draw from my experience of more than 25 years as a successful entrepreneur, CEO, business author, organizational and clinical psychologist, consultant, speaker, facilitator, former martial arts athlete, to create unique development experiences for my clients.

7. CEO Intensive Program

Sometimes it is not possible to bring an outside expert to work directly with the Executive Team. Sometimes it is just better to support the CEO in applying the CET Development Process with their teams. Therefore, you need a one-on-one advisor focused on your needs during a short period, in general one or two days. Then you take it from there.

The CEO Intensive program aims to boost or revamp your team's efficiency and effectiveness through an intensive collaboration between you and me. I bring all tools from 25 years of experience in coaching, leadership training, facilitation, consulting, speaking, systems change, and research in Work and Organizational Psychology to craft a unique development path for your Executive Team.

Starting from where your team is today, your leadership preferences, and your transformational vision, we will define together the areas of highest leverage to impact your company's results through your executive team's work.

As a research practitioner, I favor evidence-based, no-nonsense approaches to reach results ASAP. I adapt my methods to your goals, context, contents, and requirements. Together with the Chief Executive Team Assessment, this might be what you are looking for to transform your leadership.

8. Public Speaking

A keynote speech is the best way to guarantee that an important message is quickly taken in by many people facing a common challenge. I achieved the globally recognized Certified Speaking Professional (CSP®) designation, attributed by the Global Speakers Federation to speakers with a proven successful track record, professional ethics, and outstanding platform skills.

I regularly deliver high impact speeches worldwide, on real and virtual stages, generating insights in areas like Chief Executive Teams, Leadership, Self-Leadership, Change Management, Business Culture, Motivation, Teamwork, and Innovation.

Unlike most professional speakers, who specialize in one topic, I use the depth of my know-how about the human mind and human organizations to design tailormade speeches to achieve the results you want in your event.

Mind like water

My personal agenda is not to have one.

In the American TV series *Longstreet* (1971), Bruce Lee played martial arts expert Li Tsung. Teaching his pupil, he says, "Don't get set into one form. Adapt it and build your own and let it grow. Be like water. Empty your mind. Be formless, shapeless like water. Now you put water in a cup; it becomes the cup. You put water into a bottle; it becomes the bottle. You put it in a teapot; it becomes the teapot."[192]

As a former martial artist and a Bruce Lee fan, this sentence represents my agenda when working with an executive team. My personal agenda is not to have one. I have only two goals in a process like this.

1. I want to produce results for my client. My client is the company that will benefit from having a more effective and efficient executive team, as measured by many different KPIs. The company must feel the impact of what we are doing when we progress in the executive team restructuring.
2. I enter the system to reinforce CEO leadership. I am there to make the CEO shine. I work as much below the line as possible (almost invisibly). My job is to support the team in doing the right things and reaching the results so that they think that they did it alone. They think they could have done it without me. When I reinforce the team's effectiveness and the CEO's leadership without the team feeling I had any determining role in it, there's a job well done.

Those are the only two goals I have when I do this. I don't have a specific situation or result that a team has to be in after several months. No two executive teams are alike. These factors make them unique:

- the business sector
- the company culture
- the complexity of operations
- the financial health of the company
- the market requirements
- the diversity of the members in terms of gender, experience, tenure, cultural origin.

The human capital readiness to implement the strategy is different and plays different roles in the executive team's effectiveness.

The uniqueness of the Chief Executive Team Development Programs is their ability to simultaneously cover both the fundamentals of a management team's effectiveness and allow for complete adaptation to the needs of each team. As no two teams are alike, I use facilitation, coaching, speaking, training, and consulting as tools in all the programs I described above.

The 6P's of Executive Teams® is like a jazz improv structure. Without structure, there's chaos, not improvisation. My work is about the model, not the specific methods. It's about the *process*, not the outcome. I aim for the team to reach their best possible capabilities in each of the 6 Ps.

My mind is like water. I am there to help you fulfill your desired shape.

My mind is like water. I am there to help you fulfill your desired shape.

Closure

I started this book with a personal story about how I came into consultancy. And if you forgot it already, it was about a failure of mine as a wannabe family therapist. Had that not happened, I would probably be using my skills in the area where all my colleagues are. I would be just another therapist focused on individual behavior. But because I had that shock in my life, I can now use my skills to make a difference in thousands of people at a time.

Chief Executive Teams are special groups that multiply their impact thousandfold, therefore multiplying my impact as advisor.

I went from improving the world one person at a time to improving the world one company at a time.

I went from improving the world one person at a time to improving the world one company at a time.

You can reach me at www.chief-executive.team

ABOUT THE AUTHOR

Imagine...

...there's someone with a flawless track record of over 25 years of international consultancy, training, coaching and public speaking projects;

...he managed hundreds of change management and leadership development projects in 3 continents;

...some of his clients were awarded by projects he led;

...for over 10 years he was one of the top 5 consultants of the biggest European training company;

...that he is *the only person in the world* with the 3 globally recognized professional certifications: Certified Management Consultant, Professional Certified Coach, and Certified Speaking Professional (CMC®, PCC®, CSP®);

...he is a #1 International Bestselling Author, with 5 business books published, and has been a published author since age 15;

...he has international management and entrepreneurship experience;

...he trained over 90 international management consultants;

...he was awarded Consultant of the Year in Portugal;

...he has a degree in Psychology, an accredited expertise in Work and Organizational Psychology, an advanced expertise in Psychological Coaching and a Masters in Systemic Family Therapy;

...he is an expert in leadership, change management and company culture, using methodologies that range from therapy to systems thinking;

...he follows an evidence-based practice and contributes to science as a researcher in leadership;

...you can work with him as Personal Advisor to develop your Executive Team.

Meet Ricardo J. Vargas.

Reach him at
www.chief-executive.team
https://www.linkedin.com/in/ricardojbvargas/

May I Ask a Favor?

A great deal of a book's success is determined by the number and nature of the reviews it receives online. Online reviews help other readers discover books to help them along their journeys.

If you have found value in this book, please consider leaving an honest review at one of the online bookstores. If you purchased the book, place a review at the site where you purchased it. If this book was given to you, place your review at any of the major online retailers.

I greatly appreciate your honest feedback and reviews.

Ricardo J. Vargas

LIST OF ILLUSTRATIONS

LIST OF TABLES

BIBLIOGRAPHY

1. Bellis, M. (2017, April 4). Biography of Gordon Moore. ThoughtCo. https://www.thoughtco.com/biography-of-gordon-moore-1992167
2. Raskino, M. (2019). *2019 CEO survey: The year of challenged growth.* Gartner. https://www.gartner.com/en/newsroom/press-releases/2019-05-08-gartner-survey-reveals-that-ceo-priorities-are-slowly
3. Mitchell, C., Maselli, I., Ray, R. L., & Van Ark, B. (2020, January 6). *C-Suite challenge™ 2020: Risks, opportunities, and hot-button issues.* The Conference Board. https://www.conference-board.org/research/csuitechallenge/C-Suite-Challenge-2020
4. Moritz, B. E., Ryan, T., Davies, M., Ellis, K., Oldfield, R., Steffen, I., Kayser, H., Hyde, S., Mallon, H., Chao, R., & Cobourn, B. (2019). *22nd Annual global CEO survey: CEOs' curbed confidence spells caution.* PwC. https://www.pwc.com/gx/en/ceo-survey/2019/report/pwc-22nd-annual-global-ceo-survey.pdf
5. Moritz, B. E., Ryan, T., Davies, M., Ellis, K., Oldfield, R., Steffen, I., Kayser, H., Hyde, S., Mallon, H., Chao, R., & Cobourn, B. (2020). *23rd Annual global CEO survey: Navigating the rising tide of uncertainty.* PwC. https://www.pwc.com/gx/en/ceo-survey/2020/reports/pwc-23rd-global-ceo-survey.pdf
6. Kissel, N. H., & Foley, P. (2019, January 23). The 3 Challenges Every New CEO Faces. *Harvard Business Review.* https://hbr.org/2019/01/the-3-challenges-every-new-ceo-faces
7. Simons, T., Pelled, L. H. & Smith, K. A. (1999). Making use of difference: diversity, debate, and decision comprehensiveness in top management teams. *Academy of Management Journal, 42*(6), 662-673.
8. Barrick, M., Bradley, B., & Colbert, A. E. (2007). The moderating role of top management team interdependence: Implications for real teams and working groups. *Academy of Management Journal, 50*(3), 544-557.
9. Tanikawa, T., & Jung, Y. (2019). CEO power and top management team tenure diversity: Implications for firm performance. *Journal of Leadership & Organizational Studies, 26*(2), 256-272.
10. Opstrup, N., & Villadsen, A. R. (2014). The right mix? Gender diversity in top management teams and financial performance. *Public Administration Review, 75*(2), 291-301. https://doi.org/10.1111/puar.12310
11. Roh, H., Chun, K, Ryou, Y., & Son, J. (2019). Opening the black box: A meta-analytic examination of the effects of top management team diversity on emergent team processes and multilevel contextual influence. *Group & Organization Management, 44*(1) 112-164.

12. Gompers, P., Gornall, W. Kaplan, S. N., & Strebulaev, I. A. (2020). How Do Venture Capitalists Make Decisions? *Journal of Financial Economics, 135*(1), 169-190. https://doi.org/10.1016/j.jfineco.2019.06.011

13. García-Granero, A., Fernandez-Mesa, A., Jansen, J. J. P., & Vega-Jurado, J. (2018). Top management team diversity and ambidexterity: The contingent role of shared responsibility and CEO cognitive trust. *Long Range Planning, 51*(6), 881-893. https://doi.org/10.1016/j.lrp.2017.11.001

14. Li, Peng-Yu., & Huang, Kuo-Feng. (2019). The antecedents of innovation performance: The moderating role of top management team diversity. *Baltic Journal of Management, 14*(2), 291-311. https://doi.org/10.1108/BJM-07-2017-0202

15. Boone, C., Lokshin, B., Guenter, H., & Belderbos, R. (2018). Top management team nationality diversity, corporate entrepreneurship, and innovation in multinational firms. *Strategic Management Journal, 40*(2), 277–302. https://doi.org/10.1002/smj.2976

16. Van Doorn, S., Heyden, M. L.M., & Volberda, H. W. (2016). Enhancing entrepreneurial orientation in dynamic environments: The interplay between top management team advice-seeking and absorptive capacity. *Long Range Planning, 50*(2), 134-144. https://doi.org/10.1016/j.lrp.2016.06.003

17. Hayes, M., Chumney, F., Wright, C., & Buckingham, M. (2019). *The Global Study of Engagement: Technical Report.* ADP Research Institute. https://www.adp.com/-/media/adp/ResourceHub/pdf/ADPRI/ADPRI0102_2018_Engagement_Study_Technical_Report_RELEASE%20READY.ashx

18. Kruse, K. (2016, October 25). How the engagement-profit chain leads to a 5x higher stockprice. *Leadx.* https://leadx.org/articles/how-the-engagement-profit-chain-leads-to-a-5x-higher-stockprice/

19. Harter, J. K., Schmidt, F. L., Agrawal, S., Blue, A., Plowman, S. K., Josh, P., & Asplund, J. (2020). *The relationship between engagement at work and organizational outcomes: 2020 Q^{12} meta-analysis (10th Ed.).* Gallup. https://www.gallup.com/workplace/321725/gallup-q12-meta-analysis-report.aspx

20. Witters, D., & Liu, D. (2013, May 7). *In U.S., poor health tied to big losses for all job types: Subpar health leads to elevated absenteeism across all 14 occupations examined.* Gallup. https://news.gallup.com/poll/162344/poor-health-tied-big-losses-job-types.aspx

21. Aon Hewitt (2015). *Aon Hewitt's Model of Employee Engagement.* https://www.aonhewitt.co.nz/getattachment/77046028-9992-4d77-868a-32fbf622fec6/file.aspx?disposition=inline

22. Glint (2016). *Glint Study Reveals New Hires With Poor Onboarding Experiences Are Eight Times More Likely To Be Disengaged At Work* [Press release]. https://www.glintinc.com/press/glint-study-reveals-new-hires-poor-onboarding-experiences-eight-times-likely-disengaged-work/

23. Mölders, S., Brosi, P., Spörrle, M., & Welpe, I. M. (2019). The effect of top management trustworthiness on turnover intentions via negative emotions: The moderating role of gender. *Journal of Business Ethics, 156*, 957-969. https://doi.org/10.1007/s10551-017-3600-9
24. Mahajan, A., Bishop, J. W., Scott, D. (2012). Does trust in top management mediate top management communication, employee involvement and organizational commitment relationships? *Journal of Managerial Issues, 24*(2), 173-190. https://www.jstor.org/stable/43488132
25. Ou, A. Y., Seo, J., Choi, D., & Hom, P. W. (2017). When can humble top executives retain middle managers? The moderating role of top management team faultlines. *Academy of Management Journal, 60*(5), 1915–1931. https://doi.org/10.5465/amj.2015.1072
26. Ou, A. Y., Tsui, A. S., Kinicki, A. J., Waldman, D., Xiao, Z., & Song, J. L. (2014). Humble chief executive officers' connections to top management team integration and middle managers' responses. *Administrative Science Quarterly, 59*(1), 34-72
27. Green, M. (2019, October 9). *Oprah Winfrey Opens Up About the Moments That Changed Her Life.* People. https://people.com/movies/oprah-winfrey-moments-that-changed-my-life/
28. The Nobel Prize. (2020, November 15). *Muhammad Yunus Biographical.* https://www.nobelprize.org/prizes/peace/2006/yunus/biographical/
29. Fabiano, J. (2019, July 17). *Life and career biography of Tesla and SpaceX CEO Elon Musk.* Ladders. https://www.theladders.com/career-advice/elon-musk-life-and-career
30. Green, M. (2019, October 14). The Triumphant Life of Tyler Perry, *People*, 38-43. https://tylerperry.com/wp-content/uploads/2019/10/TylerPerry_People.pdf
31. Stettner, M. (2018, July 13). *15 CEOs Who Started on the Ground Floor.* Kiplinger. https://www.kiplinger.com/slideshow/business/T012-S001-15-ceos-who-started-on-the-ground-floor/index.html
32. Stettner, M. (2018, July 13). *15 CEOs Who Started on the Ground Floor.* Kiplinger. https://www.kiplinger.com/slideshow/business/T012-S001-15-ceos-who-started-on-the-ground-floor/index.html
33. McGregor, J. (2019, May 15). *More CEOs were forced out for ethical lapses in 2018 than poor financial performance.* The Washington Post. https://www.washingtonpost.com/business/2019/05/15/more-ceos-were-forced-out-ethical-lapses-than-poor-financial-performance/
34. PwC's Strategy&. (2017, May 17). *Global study on CEO trends indicates a significant uptick in CEOs forced out of office for ethical lapses.* https://www.strategyand.pwc.com/cn/en/press-releases/2016-ceo-success-study-cne.html
35. Karlsson, P., Turner, M., & Gassmann, P. (2019, May 15). *Succeeding the long-serving legend in the corner office.* Strategy and Business. https://www.strategy-business.com/article/Succeeding-the-long-serving-legend-in-the-corner-office?gko=90171

36. Kim, J. (2019, September 23). *Former Nissan CEO Carlos Ghosn settles SEC charges over $140 million in undisclosed compensation.* CNBC. https://www.cnbc.com/2019/09/23/ex-nissan-ceo-ghosn-settles-sec-charges-over-undisclosed-compensation.html#close

37. U.S. Securities and Exchange Comission. (2019, September 23). *SEC Charges Nissan, Former CEO, and Former Director with Fraudulently Concealing from Investors More than $140 Million of Compensation and Retirement Benefits* [Press Release]. https://www.sec.gov/news/press-release/2019-183

38. Joseph, E. (2019, September 16). *Purdue Pharma files for bankruptcy as part of a $10 billion agreement to settle opioid lawsuits.* CNN. https://edition.cnn.com/2019/09/16/us/purdue-pharma-bankruptcy-filing/index.html

39. O'Kane, S. (2019, September 24). *Volkswagen's current CEO and chairman are being charged with Dieselgate crimes.* The Verge. https://www.theverge.com/2019/9/24/20881534/volkswagen-dieselgate-charged-crimes-herbert-diess-martin-winterkorn-investors-emissions

40. Hotten, R. (2015, December 10). *Volkswagen: The scandal explained.* BBC News. https://www.bbc.com/news/business-34324772

41. Hartmans, A., & Leskin, P. (2020, August, 11). *The rise and fall of Elizabeth Holmes, the Theranos founder whose federal fraud trial is delayed until 2021.* Business Insider. https://www.businessinsider.com/theranos-founder-ceo-elizabeth-holmes-life-story-bio-2018-4

42. Lammers, J., Stapel, D. A., & Galinsky, A. D. (2010). Power Increases Hypocrisy: Moralizing in Reasoning, Immorality in Behavior. *Psychological Science, 21*(5), 737-744. http://www.jstor.org/stable/41062277

43. Mark Hurd. (2020, November 15). In *Wikipedia.* https://en.wikipedia.org/wiki/Mark_Hurd.

44. Blodget, H. (2011, December 30). *Well, There's No Longer Any Mystery Why HP Fired Mark Hurd.* Business Insider. https://www.businessinsider.com/mark-hurd-jodie-fisher-hp-2011-12.

45. Forer, B. R. (1949). The fallacy of personal validation: A classroom demonstration of gullibility. *Journal of Abnormal and Social Psychology, 44,* 118-123. https://doi.org/10.1037/h0059240

46. Dickson, D. H., & Kelly, I. W. (1985). The 'Barnum Effect' in Personality Assessment: A Review of the Literature. *Psychological Reports, 57*(2), 367-382. https://doi.org/10.2466/pr0.1985.57.2.367

47. Furnham, A., & Schofield, S. (1987). Accepting personality test feedback: A review of the Barnum effect. *Current Psychological Research & Reviews, 6*(2), 162–178. https://doi.org/10.1007/BF02686623

48. Thiriart, P. (1991). Acceptance of personality test results. *Skeptical Inquirer, 15*(2), 161-165.

49. Gladwell, M. (2005). *Blink: The Power of Thinking Without Thinking.* Little, Brown and Company.

50. Fisk, P. (2019, February). *Why do purpose-driven companies do better? Purpose-driven companies are more ambitious, they attract the best*

talent [Image] [Video] [Article]. LinkedIn. https://www.linkedin.com/pulse/why-do-purpose-driven-companies-better-peter-fisk/

51. Bartlett, C. A., & Ghoshal, S. (1994, November–December). Changing the role of Top Management: Beyond Strategy to Purpose. *Harvard Business Review.* https://hbr.org/1994/11/beyond-strategy-to-purpose
52. Sinar, E., Ray, R. L., Wellins, R. S., Neal, S., Canwell, A. L., Abel, A. L., Popiela, A., Dettmann, J., Rolland, L., Collins, L., & Cotton, T. (2018). *Global leadership forecast 2018: 25 research insights to fuel your people strategy.* DDI, The Conference Board and EY. https://www.ddiworld.com/research/global-leadership-forecast-2018
53. Kotter, J., & Heskett, J. (2011). *Corporate Culture and Performance.* The Free Press.
54. Schuyler, S., & Brennan, A. (2016). *Putting Purpose to Work: A study of purpose in the workplace.* PwC. https://www.pwc.com/us/en/about-us/corporate-responsibility/assets/pwc-putting-purpose-to-work-purpose-survey-report.pdf
55. Gartenberg, C. M., Prat, A., & Serafeim, G. (2016). Corporate Purpose and Financial Performance. *Organization Science, 30*(1), 1-18. http://dx.doi.org/10.2139/ssrn.2840005
56. Cone/Porter Novelli. (2018). *Purpose study: How to build deeper bonds, amplify your message and expand your consumer base.* https://www.conecomm.com/2018-purpose-study-pdf
57. Sirkis, C. (2020). *Are medical company taglines becoming redundant?* Cadensee. https://www.cadensee.com/articles/are-medical-company-taglines-becoming-redundant/
58. Efficiency movement. (2020, August 28). In *Wikipedia.* https://en.wikipedia.org/wiki/Efficiency_movement
59. Taylor, F. (1911). The Principles of Scientific Management. Harper & Brothers.
60. Kaplan, D., Toren, B., Fleit, C., Remick, T., & Stephenson, C. (2019). *Where Have All the Long-Tenured CEOs Gone?* Korn Ferry. https://www.kornferry.com/insights/articles/where-have-all-the-long-tenured-ceos-gone
61. Karlsson, P., Turner, M., & Gassmann, P. (2019, May 15). Succeeding the long-serving legend in the corner office. *Strategy & Business,* (95). https://www.strategy-business.com/article/Succeeding-the-long-serving-legend-in-the-corner-office?gko=90171
62. Dictionary.com. (n.d.). Synergy. In *Dictionary.com* from https://www.dictionary.com/browse/synergy?s=t
63. Burgin, M., & Meissner, G. (2017). 1 + 1 = 3: Synergy Arithmetic in Economics. *Applied Mathematics, 8*(2). https://m.scirp.org/papers/73964
64. Pasternack, B, A., Williams, T. D. & Anderson, P. F. (2001, January 1). Beyond the cult of the CEO: Building institutional leadership. *Strategy and Business, 22.* https://www.strategy-business.com/article/10841?gko=dc73e

65. Bang, H., & Midelfart, T. N. (2017). What characterizes effective management teams? A research-based approach. *Consulting Psychology Journal Practice and Research, 69*(4), 334–359.

66. Workflow. (2020, September 3). In *Wikipedia.* https://en.wikipedia.org/wiki/Workflow

67. Ancona, D. G., & Nadler, D. A. (1989). *Teamwork at the top: Creating high performing executive teams.* Working Paper 3029-89, Massachusetts Institute of Technology, Sloan School of Management. https://dspace.mit.edu/bitstream/handle/1721.1/2254/SWP-3029-20741472.pdf

68. White, M. (2019). Role clarity within teams and organizations [White paper]. https://doi.org/10.13140/RG.2.2.27986.61124

69. Peralta, C. F., Lopes, P. N., Gilson, L. L., Lourenço, P. R., & Pais, L. (2015). Innovation processes and team effectiveness: The role of goal clarity and commitment, and team affective tone. *Journal of Occupational and Organizational Psychology, 88,* 80-107. https://doi.org/10.1111/joop.12079

70. Scott, M. B., & Lyman, S. (1968). Accounts. *American Sociological Review, 33,* 46-62.

71. Lerner, J. S., & Tetlock, P. E. (1999). Accounting for The Effects of Accountability. *Psychological Bulletin, 125*(2), 255-275.

72. Bang, H., Fuglesang, S. L., Ovesen, M. R., & Eilertsen, D. E. (2010). Effectiveness in top management group meetings: The role of goal clarity, focused communication, and learning behavior. *Scandinavian Journal of Psychology, 51,* 253-261. https://doi.org/10.1111/j.1467-9450.2009.00769.x

73. Hutchison, L. (2016, May 31). Effective team role clarity starts at the top. *Russell Investments.* https://russellinvestments.com/us/blog/effective-team-role-clarity-starts-at-the-top

74. Dewar, C., Hirt, M., & Keller, S. (2019). The mindsets and practices of excellent CEOs. *Mckinsey & Company.* https://www.mckinsey.com/business-functions/strategy-and-corporate-finance/our-insights/the-mindsets-and-practices-of-excellent-ceos

75. See, K. E., Morrison, E. W., Rothman, N. B., & Soll, J. B. (2011, October 7). The decision-making flaw in powerful people. *Strategy and Business, 116*(2). https://www.strategy-business.com/article/re00162?gko=8f533

76. Carmeli, A. & Schaubroeck, J. (2006). Top management team behavioral integration, decision quality, and organizational decline. *The Leadership Quarterly, 17*(5), 441-453. https://doi.org/10.1016/j.leaqua.2006.06.001

77. Radin, J. & McDowell, T. (2012). Making decisions that matter: How improving executive decision-making can lead to better business outcomes. *Deloitte.* https://www2.deloitte.com/content/dam/Deloitte/us/Documents/process-and-operations/us-cons-making-decisions-that-matter-050212.pdf

78. Burns, R. (2000). *Making meetings happen: A simple and effective guide to implementing*. Allen & Unwin.
79. Barker, A. (2002). *How to manage meetings*. Kogan Page.
80. Cameron, E. (2005). *Facilitation made easy: Practical tips to improve meetings and workshops* (3rd ed.). Kogan Page.
81. Henkel, S. (2007). *Successful meetings: How to plan, prepare, and execute top-notch business meetings*. Atlantic Publishing Group.
82. Harvard Business School (2006). *Running meetings: Expert solution to everyday challenges*.
83. Streibel, B. (2007). *Plan and conduct effective meetings: 24 Steps to Generate Meaningful Results*. McGraw-Hill.
84. Sudhakar, G. P. (2017). The role of conflicts in top management teams. *International Journal of Business Intelligence & Innovations*, (4), 608-616.
85. Communication Theory (n.d.). *Groupthink*. https://www.communicationtheory.org/groupthink/
86. Amason, A. C. (1996). Distinguishing the effects of functional and dysfunctional conflict on strategic decision making: resolving a paradox for top management teams. *Academy of Management Journal, 39*(1), 123-148.
87. Simons, T. & Peterson, R. S. (2000). Task conflict and relationship conflict in top management teams: The pivotal role of intragroup trust. *Journal of Applied Psychology, 85*(1), 102-111. https://doi.org/10.1037/0021-9010.85.1.102
88. Kolb, J. A. (2013). Conflict management principles for groups and teams. Industrial and Commercial Training, 45(2), 79-86. https://doi.org/10.1108/00197851311309516
89. Independent Evaluation Office of the International Monetary Fund. (2011). IMF performance in the run-up to the financial and economic crisis: IMF surveillance in 2004–07. https://www.oecd.org/derec/imf/48154717.pdf
90. Teitel, A. S. (2018, January 25). Challenger explosion: How groupthink and other causes led to the tragedy. *History*. https://www.history.com/news/how-the-challenger-disaster-changed-nasa
91. Edmondson, A. C., Roberto, M. A., Watkins, M. D. (2003). A dynamic model of top management team effectiveness: Managing unstructured task streams. *The Leadership Quarterly, 14*, 297-325.
92. Dodd, B. (2010, August 7). *44 Leadership quotes from Tony Dungy*. Brian Dodd on Leadership. https://briandoddonleadership.com/2010/08/07/44-leadership-quotes-from-tony-dungy/
93. Hambrick, D. C. (1995). Fragmentation and the other problems CEOs have with their top management teams. *California Management Review, 37*(3), 110-127.
94. McLeod, S. (2018, October 24). *Theories of Selective Attention*. Simply Psychology. https://www.simplypsychology.org/attention-models.html
95. Dayan, P., Kakade, S. & Montague, P. (2000). Learning and selective attention. *Nat Neurosci*, 3, 1218–1223. https://doi.org/10.1038/81504

96. Brown, B. (2013). *The Power of Vulnerability: Teachings on Authenticity, Connection, and Courage.* Sounds True.
97. Mayer, R. C., Davis, J. H., & Schoorman, F. D. (1995). An Integrative Model of Organizational Trust. *The Academy of Management Review, 20*(3), 709-734. https://doi.org/10.2307/258792
98. Johnson-George, C., & Swap, W. (1982). Measurement of specific interpersonal trust: Construction and validation of a scale to assess trust in a specific other. *Journal of Personality and Social Psychology, 43*, 1306-1317.
99. Hofstede, G. (1980). *Culture's Consequences: International Differences in Work-Related Values.* Sage Publications.
100. Hofstede, G., Hofstede, G. J., & Minkov, M. (2010). *Cultures and Organizations: Software of the mind* (3rd ed.). McGraw Hill Professional.
101. Roeckelein, J. E. (Ed.). (2006). Elsevier's Dictionary of Psychological Theories. Elsevier.
102. Haleblian, J. & Finkelstein, S. (1993). Top management team size, CEO dominance, and firm performance: the moderating roles of environmental turbulence and discretion. *Academy of Management Journal, 36*(4), 844-863.
103. Costa, A. C. Roe, R. A., & Taillieu, T. (2001). Trust within teams: The relation with performance effectiveness. *European Journal of Work and Organizational Psychology, 10*(3), 225–244. https://doi.org/10.1080/13594320143000654
104. García-Granero, A., Fernandez-Mesa, A., Jansen, J, J.P., & Vega-Jurado, J. (2018). Top management team diversity and ambidexterity: The contingent role of shared responsibility and CEO cognitive trust. *Long Range Planning, 51*, 881-893. https://doi.org/10.1016/j.lrp.2017.11.001
105. Milliken, F. J., & Martins, L. L. (1996). Searching for common threads: Understanding the multiple effects of diversity in organizational groups. *The Academy of Management Review, 21*(2), 402-433. https://doi.org/10.2307/258667
106. Simons, T., Pelled, L. H. & Smith, K. A. (1999). Making use of difference: diversity, debate, and decision comprehensiveness in top management teams. *Academy of Management Journal, 42*(6), 662-673.
107. Barta, T., Kleiner, M., & Neumann, T. (2012, April 1). Is there a payoff from top-team diversity? *McKinsey Quarterly.* https://www.mckinsey.com/business-functions/organization/our-insights/is-there-a-payoff-from-top-team-diversity
108. Gompers, P. & Kovvali, S. (2018, July-August). The Other Diversity Dividend. *Harvard Business Review.* https://hbr.org/2018/07/the-other-diversity-dividend
109. Aggarwal, I., Woolley, A. W., Chabris, C. F., & Malone, T. W. (2019). The impact of cognitive style diversity on implicit learning in teams. *Frontiers in Psychology, 10*(112). https://doi.org/10.3389/fpsyg.2019.00112

110. Tajfel, H., Billig, M. G., Bundy, R. P. & Flament, C. (1971). Social categorization and intergroup behaviour. *European Journal of Social Psychology, 1*(2). https://doi.org/10.1002/ejsp.2420010202

111. Hsieh, C-T., Hurst, E., Jones, C. I., & Klenow, P. J. (2019). The allocation of talent and U.S. economic growth. *The Econometric Society, 87*(5), 1439–1474. https://doi.org/10.3982/ECTA11427

112. Catalyst. (2004). *The bottom line: Connecting corporate performance and gender diversity.* https://www.catalyst.org/wp-content/uploads/2019/01/The_Bottom_Line_Connecting_Corporate_Performance_and_Gender_Diversity.pdf

113. Desvaux, G., Devillard, S., Zelicourt, A., Kossoff, C., Labaye, E., & Sancier-Sultan, S. (2017, October 4). Women Matter: Ten years of insights on gender diversity. *McKinsey and Company.* https://www.mckinsey.com/featured-insights/gender-equality/women-matter-ten-years-of-insights-on-gender-diversity

114. Paskoff, S. M. (2020, January 16). Cognitive diversity: What it is and why your team needs it. *ELI, Inc.* https://www.eliinc.com/cognitive-diversity-what-it-is/

115. Chamorro-Premuzic, T. (2018, September 3). The case for boosting cognitive diversity in organizations. *Leadership Strategy.* https://www.forbes.com/sites/tomaspremuzic/2018/09/03/the-case-for-boosting-cognitive-diversity-in-organizations/#107cce982b69

116. Aggarwal, I., & Molinaro, M. S. (2013). Cognitive versatility: a new lens for understanding team composition and diversity. *Proceedings of Academy of Management Proceedings, 1.* https://doi.org/10.5465/ambpp.2013.17297abstract

117. Rosen, R. M., & Adair, F. (2007, September). CEOs misperceive top teams' performance. Assessing Performance. *Harvard Business Review.* https://hbr.org/2007/09/ceos-misperceive-top-teams-performance

118. Ferenchick E., & Rosenthal D. (2017). Identified patient in family systems theory. In J. Lebow, A. Chambers, & D. Breunlin (Eds.), *Encyclopedia of Couple and Family Therapy.* Springer, Cham. https://doi.org/10.1007/978-3-319-15877-8_282-1

119. Cottrell, D., & Boston, P. (2002). Practitioner review: The effectiveness of systemic family therapy for children and adolescents. *Journal of Child Psychology and Psychiatry, 43*(5), 573-86.

120. Carr, A. (2002). Evidence-based practice in family therapy and systemic consultation II. *Journal of Family Therapy, 22*(3), 273-295. https://doi.org/10.1111/1467-6427.00152

121. Henggeler, S. W., Clingempeel, W. G., Brondino, M. J., & Pickrel, S. G. (2002). Four-year follow-up of multisystemic therapy with substance-abusing and substance-dependent juvenile offenders. *Journal of the American Academy of Child & Adolescent Psychiatry, 41*(7), 868-74. https://doi.org/10.1097/00004583-200207000-00021

122. Senge, P. M. (2006). *The fifth discipline: The art and practice of the learning oganization* (2nd ed.). Random House Business.

123. McComas, K. (2004). When even the 'best-laid' plans go wrong. *EMBO Reports, 5*, S61–S65. https://doi.org/10.1038/sj.embor.7400257
124. Structural fix. (2020, April 7). In *Wikipedia*. https://en.wikipedia.org/wiki/Structural_fix
125. Iyengar SS, Lepper MR. (2001). When choice is demotivating: can one desire too much of a good thing? *Journal of Personality and Social Psychology, 79*(6), 995-1006. https://doi.org/10.1037//0022-3514.79.6.995
126. Darst, J. R., Newburger, J. W., Resch, S., Rathod, R. H., & Lock, J. E. (2010). Deciding without data. *Congenital heart disease, 5*(4), 339–342. https://doi.org/10.1111/j.1747-0803.2010.00433.x
127. Rosenberg, B. D., & Siegel, J. T. (2018). A 50-year review of psychological reactance theory: Do not read this article. *Motivation Science, 4*(4), 281–300. https://doi.org/10.1037/mot0000091
128. Dictionary.com. (n.d.). Homeostasis. In *Dictionary.com dictionary*. https://www.dictionary.com/browse/homeostasis?s=ts
129. Self-organization. (2020, October 22). In *Wikipedia*. https://en.wikipedia.org/wiki/Self-organization
130. American Psychological Association. (n.d.). Circular-causality. In *APA dictionary of psychology*. Retrieved January 18, 2020, from https://dictionary.apa.org/circular-causality
131. Bartoletti, M., Cimoli, T., Pinna, G. M., & Zunino, R. (2015). Models of circular causality. In R. Natarajan, G. Barua, & M. R. Patra (Eds.), *Distributed Computing and Internet Technology* (Vol. 8956, pp. 1–20). Springer, Cham. https://doi.org/10.1007/978-3-319-14977-6_1
132. Witherington, D. C. (2011). Taking emergence seriously: The centrality of circular causality for dynamic systems approaches to development. *Human Development, 54,* 66–92. https://doi.org/10.1159/000326814
133. Merritt, J. (2018). What are mental models? *The Systems Thinker*. https://thesystemsthinker.com/what-are-mental-models/
134. Weinberg, G. (2016, July 6). Mental models I find repeatedly useful. *Gabriel Weinberg*. https://medium.com/@yegg/mental-models-i-find-repeatedly-useful-936f1cc405d
135. Kahneman, D. (2011). *Thinking, fast and slow*. Farrar, Straus and Giroux.
136. Dobelli, R. (2014). *The art of thinking clearly: Better thinking, better decisions*. Hodder & Stoughton.
137. Ariely, D. (2008). Predictably irrational: The hidden forces that shape our decisions. HarperCollins Publishers.
138. Yurtseven, M. K., & Buchanan, W. W. (2015). Decision making via systems thinking in management. *Journal of Transdisciplinary studies, 8*(2). https://doi.org/10.21533/epiphany.v8i2.162
139. Cognitive bias. (2020, October 22). In *Wikipedia*. https://en.wikipedia.org/wiki/Cognitive_bias
140. Giuffrida, A., & Tondo, L. (2020, March 8). Leaked coronavirus plan to quarantine 16m sparks chaos in Italy. *The Guardian*. https://www.theguardian.com/world/2020/mar/08/leaked-coronavirus-plan-to-quarantine-16m-sparks-chaos-in-italy

141. Causal loop diagram. (2019, November 3). In *Wikipedia*. https://en.wikipedia.org/wiki/Causal_loop_diagram

142. Lannon, C. (2018). Causal loop construction: The basics. *The Systems Thinker*. https://thesystemsthinker.com/causal-loop-construction-the-basics/

143. Boardman, J., & Sauser, B. (2013). *Systemic thinking: Building maps for worlds of systems*. John Wiley & Sons.

144. Littlejohns, L, B., Baum, F., Lawless, A., & Freeman, T. (2018). The value of a causal loop diagram in exploring the complex interplay of factors that influence health promotion in a multisectoral health system in Australia. *Health Research Policy Systems, 16*, Article 126. https://doi.org/10.1186/s12961-018-0394-x

145. Bradley, D. T., Mansouri, F. K., & Garcia, L. M. T. (2020). A systems approach to preventing and responding to COVID-19. *E Clinical Medicine, 21*, https://doi.org/10.1016/j.eclinm.2020.100325

146. Meadows, D. (1999). Leverage points: Places to intervene in a system. *The Sustainability Institute*. http://donellameadows.org/wp-content/userfiles/Leverage_Points.pdf

147. Skarzauskiene, A. (2010). Managing complexity: Systems thinking as a catalyst of the organization performance. *Measuring Business Excellence, 14*(4), 49-64. https://doi.org/10.1108/13683041011093758

148. Lifelong learning. (2020, December 1). In *Wikipedia*. https://en.wikipedia.org/wiki/Lifelong_learning

149. Kolb, D. A. (1984). *Experiential learning: Experience as the source of learning and development*. Prentice Hall.

150. Senge, P. M. (1990). *The fifth discipline: The art & practice of the learning organization*. Currency.

151. Craik, K. J. W. (1943). *The Nature of Explanation*. Cambridge University Press.

152. Studio Writer. (2012, October 8). The 47 Eskimo words of snow, with meanings explained. www.studioknow.com/2012/10/eskimo-words-for-snow.

153. West, M. A. (1996). Reflexivity and work group effectiveness: a conceptual integration. In M. A. West (Ed.), *The handbook of work group psychology* (pp. 555-579). John Wiley & Sons, Ltd.

154. Maccurtain, S., Flood, P. C., Ramamoorty, N., West, M., & Dawson, J. (2009). The top team, trust, reflexivity, knowledge sharing and innovation. *Academy of Management Annual Meeting Proceedings*, (1), 1-6. https://doi.org/10.5465/AMBPP.2009.44243015

155. Hammedi, W., van Riel, A. C. R., & Sasovova, Z. (2011). Antecedents and consequences of reflexivity in new product idea screening. *Journal of Product Innovation Management, 28*(5), 662-679. https://doi.org/10.1111/j.1540-5885.2011.00831.x

156. Rong, P., Li, C., & Xie, J. (2019). Learning, trust, and creativity in top management teams: Team reflexivity as a moderator. *Social Behavior and Personality, 47*(5). https://doi.org/10.2224/sbp.8096

157. Hoegl, M. & Parboteeah, K. P. (2006). Team reflexivity in innovative projects. *R&D Management, 36*(2). https://doi.org/10.1111/j.1467-9310.2006.00420.x

158. De Dreu, C. K. W. (2007). Cooperative outcome interdependence, task reflexivity, and team effectiveness: A motivated information processing perspective. *Journal of Applied Psychology*, 92(3), 628-638. https://doi.org/10.1037/0021-9010.92.3.628

159. GE, Y. H., & Yang, W. Z. (2011). A review on the top management team reflexivity influencing strategic decision outcomes. *African Journal of Business Management*, *5*(35), 13442-13448.

160. Taleb, N. N. (2007). *The black sawn: The impact of the highly improbable.* Random House.

161. Hogarth, R. M. (2010). Intuition: A challenge for psychological research on decision making. *Psychological Inquiry, 21(*4), 338–353. https://doi.org/10.1080/1047840X.2010.520260

162. Isenman, L. (2013). Understanding unconscious intelligence and intuition. *Perspectives in Biology and Medicine, 56*(1), 148-66.

163. Patterson, R. E., & Eggleston, R. G. (2017). Intuitive cognition. *Journal of Cognitive Engineering and Decision Making, 11*(1), 5-22. https://doi.org/10.1177/1555343416686476

164. Simon, H. A. (1987). Making management decisions: The role of intuition and emotion. *The Academy of Management Executive, 1*(1), 57-64.

165. Grid, R. (2013, January 1). There is a better way: The Carlotz story. Grid. https://richmondgrid.com/there-is-a-better-way-the-carlotz-story/

166. Quick, E. (2020, October 29). Car resale startup CarLotz goes public with plans to expand. Richmond Inno. https://www.bizjournals.com/richmond/inno/stories/news/2020/10/29/carlotz-goes-public.html

167. Carlotzs. (2020). CarLotz: Used car & consignment dealer. https://www.carlotz.com/

168. Biediger, S. (2019, February 5). New business models for car shopping take their place among Northwest SA dealerships. *San Antonio Report.* https://sanantonioreport.org/new-business-models-for-car-buying-selling-take-off-in-northwest-sa/?

169. Business Wire. (2020, October, 22). CarLotz, Inc., One of the largest privately-held used vehicle retail disruptors with the industry's only consignment-to-retail sales platform, to become a public company. *Business Wire.* https://www.businesswire.com/news/home/20201022005624/en/CarLotz-Inc.-One-of-the-Largest-Privately-Held-Used-Vehicle-Retail-Disruptors-with-the-Industry%E2%80%99s-Only-Consignment-to-Retail-Sales-Platform-to-Become-a-Public-Company

170. Sensemaking. (2020, May 9). In *Wikipedia.* https://en.wikipedia.org/wiki/Sensemaking#Reference-Weick,_K.,_Sutcliffe,_K._M.,_&_Obstfeld,_D._2005

171. Dictionary.com. (n.d.). Potential. In *Dictionary.com dictionary.* From https://www.dictionary.com/browse/potential?s=t

172. Heineken. (2012). *Brewing a better future: Summary Sustainability Report 2012.* https://ceowatermandate.org/files/endorsing/Heineken_2012.pdf
173. Graham. P. (Ed). (1995). *Mary Parker Follett Prophet of Management: A celebration of writings from the 1920s.* Harvard Business School Press.
174. Drucker, F. P. (2008). *The essential Drucker: The best of sixty years of Peter Drucker's essential writings on management.* Harper Collins.
175. The Management Centre. (2020). *Culture eats strategy for breakfast: Transforming results by changing beliefs and behaviours.* https://www.managementcentre.co.uk/management-consultancy/culture-eats-strategy-for-breakfast/
176. Hofstede, G. (1980). *Culture's consequences: International differences in work-related values* (Abridged Edition). Sage Publications.
177. Schein, E. H. (1992). *Organizational Culture and Leadership* (2nd ed.). Jossey-Bass.
178. Vargas, R. (2005). *Os Meios Justificam os Fins: Gestão baseada em valores.* Pearson Prentice Hall.
179. Vargas, R. (2005). *Os Meios Justificam os Fins: Gestão baseada em valores.* Pearson Prentice Hall.
180. Mirza, B. (2019, September 25). Toxic workplace cultures hurt workers and company profits. *The Society for Human Resource Management (SHRM).* https://www.shrm.org/resourcesandtools/hr-topics/employee-relations/pages/toxic-workplace-culture-report.aspx
181. Kotter, J. P. (2011, February 10). Does corporate culture drive financial performance? *Forbes.* https://www.forbes.com/sites/johnkotter/2011/02/10/does-corporate-culture-drive-financial-performance/?sh=640e43297e9e
182. Kassem, R., Ajmal, M. M., & Khan, M. (2017). The relationship between organizational culture and business excellence: Case study from United Arab Emirates. *International Journal of Information Systems in the Sercive Sector, 8*(3). https://doi.org/10.4018/978-1-5225-1913-3.ch035
183. Schönborn, G. (2010). Value performance: On the relation between corporate culture and corporate success. *Journal of Psychology, 218*(4), 234-242. https://doi.org/10.1027/0044-3409/a000033
184. Graham, J. R., Harvey, C. R., Popadak, J., Rajgopal, S. (2017). *Corporate culture: Evidence from the field.* (National Bureau of Economic Research Working Paper No. 23255). https://doi.org/10.3386/w23255
185. Graham, J. R., Harvey, C. R., Popadak, J., Rajgopal, S. (2017). *Corporate culture: Evidence from the field.* (National Bureau of Economic Research Working Paper No. 23255). https://doi.org/10.3386/w23255
186. Leithy, W. E. (2017). Organizational culture and organizational performance. *International Journal of Economics & Management Sciences, 6*(4). https://doi.org/10.4172/2162-6359.1000442
187. Vargas, R. (2005). *Os Meios Justificam os Fins: Gestão baseada em valores.* Pearson Prentice Hall.
188. Vargas, R. (2004). *A arte de tornar-se inútil: Desenvolvendo líderes para vencer desafios.* Prentice Hall.

189. Vargas, R. (2004). *A arte de tornar-se inútil: Desenvolvendo líderes para vencer desafios*. Prentice Hall.

190. File: Cognitive bias codex en.svg. (2020, September 7). In *Wikipedia*. https://commons.wikimedia.org/wiki/File:Cognitive_bias_codex_en.svg

191. Rosenberg, B. D., & Siegel, J. T. (2018). A 50-year review of psychological reactance theory: Do not read this article. *Motivation Science, 4*(4), 281-300. https://doi.org/10.1037/mot0000091

192. Terry Lee McBride. *Bruce Lee Be As Water My Friend* [Video]. YouTube. https://www.youtube.com/watch?v=cJMwBwFj5nQ

Milton Keynes UK
Ingram Content Group UK Ltd.
UKHW020426281223
435071UK00013B/1288